The Human and Economic Implications of Twenty-First Century Immigration Policy

Susan Pozo
Editor

2018

W.E. Upjohn Institute for Employment Research
Kalamazoo, Michi

T0002732

Library of Congress Cataloging-in-Publication Data

Names: Pozo, Susan, editor.
Title: The human and economic implications of twenty-first century immigration
  policy / Susan Pozo, editor.
Description: Kalamazoo, Michigan : W.E. Upjohn Institute for Employment Research,
  2018. | Includes bibliographical references and index. |
  Identifiers: LCCN 2018027404 (print) | LCCN 2018036484 (ebook) | ISBN
  9780880996570 (ebook) | ISBN 0880996579 (ebook) | ISBN 9780880996556
  (pbk. : alk. paper) | ISBN 0880996552 (pbk. : alk. paper) | ISBN 9780880996563
  (hardcover : alk. paper) | ISBN 0880996560 (hardcover : alk. paper)
Subjects: LCSH: United States—Emigration and immigration—Economic aspects.
  | United States—Emigration and immigration—Government policy. |
  Immigrants—United States—Economic conditions.
Classification: LCC JV6471 (ebook) | LCC JV6471 .H86 2018 (print) | DDC
  325.73—dc23
LC record available at https://lccn.loc.gov/2018027404

The facts presented in this study and the observations and viewpoints expressed are the sole responsibility of the authors. They do not necessarily represent positions of the W.E. Upjohn Institute for Employment Research.

Cover design by Carol A.S. Derks.
Index prepared by Diane Worden.
Printed in the United States of America.
Printed on recycled paper.

I would like to dedicate this volume to immigrants, in honor of your many achievements and in sympathy for the sacrifices that come from leaving your home to offer your talents in a new country.

Contents

Acknowledgments

The chapters in this volume were presented during the 49th annual Werner Sichel Economics Lecture Series, hosted by Western Michigan University. The series was made possible through the financial support of the W.E. Upjohn Institute for Employment Research, the College of Arts and Sciences and the Economics Department of Western Michigan University. I am very grateful to a number of individuals for helping with the production of this volume. Allison Hewitt Colosky, Rich Wyrwa, Brad Hershbein, and the authors were instrumental in making the process run smoothly.

–Susan Pozo

1
Immigration Policy Today

Susan Pozo
Western Michigan University

This volume collects the lectures of distinguished immigration scholars delivered at Western Michigan University (WMU) during the 2016–2017 academic year, with cosponsorship from the W.E. Upjohn Institute for Employment Research. This was not the first time that the Upjohn Institute partnered with the WMU economics department to host social scientists in Kalamazoo to reflect on immigration policy. Healthy debate concerning the proposed and eventual enactment of the Immigration Reform and Control Act (IRCA) of 1986 took place on the WMU campus 30 years earlier. That legislation was charged with accomplishing two major goals. First, IRCA aimed to provide a solution for the many unauthorized immigrants residing and working in the United States at the time. The vast majority of the long-term undocumented were made eligible for legal permanent residency status. In offering this solution to the approximately 3 million undocumented immigrants, the United States rectified what many considered an inconsistency in its treatment of this population. IRCA's second goal was to impose sanctions on firms that knowingly hired undocumented immigrants in an attempt to stop the pull of undocumented immigration originating from U.S. employer demand for this labor. In sum, the overall attitude at the time was that we had a problem, partially owing to our own policies and behavior. We would be wise to make peace with the long-term undocumented within our borders while modifying the system so that we do not face this problem moving forward.

The tone of the debate raging across the United States today is far from what it was back in the 1980s. Today's cacophony of pronouncements concerning immigration is often uncivil and indisputably divisive. Policy is advanced without foundation in fact or theory, positions are rationalized on the basis of a single anecdote, and scholarly discourse is pushed aside. The chapters in this volume serve to provide counterbalance to the current chaotic debate by presenting the findings of prominent immigration scholars who use data and theory to help unravel facts about immigration, to assess the impact of immigration on a host of economic and social variables, and to analyze cumulative results stemming from past policies that addressed perceived immigration problems. These scholars offer blueprints for how one might best approach, evaluate, and reset the discourse on this difficult topic.

The book begins with a broad overview of the economic impacts of immigration on the U.S. economy by Pia Orrenius and Stephanie Gullo. This chapter sets the stage by providing a comprehensive overview of the demographic make-up of the United States, while outlining economic trends and fiscal impacts of immigration. Of note is the idea that because of their locational flexibility, immigrants move to where the jobs exist, raising productivity and economic growth by improving the allocation of resources in the economy. Immigrants do not hunker down in areas of decline and instead offer their labor and talents in areas of greatest need, boosting the economy's productivity.

In addition to providing up-to-date information on immigration and immigrants, the topics covered in Chapter 2 dovetail nicely with many of the subsequent chapters. They dive into generational differences, which are proving to be center stage for understanding how immigrants affect the economy. The authors note that in order to accurately assess the fiscal impacts of immigration, one needs to consider and clearly specify a host of assumptions while employing modeling to account for differential impacts by generation. Earnings (and tax revenues) tend to be low for the initial generation of immigrants, contributing toward fiscal deficits. The initial generation also tends to push up government expenditures on services, particularly schooling for children. However, the picture improves for the children of immigrants and subsequent generations. As assimilation takes place, revenues and spending patterns shift with subsequent generations, generating fiscal surpluses. Tracking and understanding these subtle generational impacts is important for inducing productive discussion of immigration and its impacts on the economy.

Brian Duncan and Stephen J. Trejo continue with this line of inquiry in Chapter 3. Are more recent immigrant groups slower to integrate? Is the intergenerational pace of assimilation different today relative to the past? In examining these questions, Duncan and Trejo focus on the educational attainment of different immigrant groups. And while they find that there is perhaps some truth to the idea that more recent immigrant flows are slower to assimilate, they also find that ethnic attrition, the idea that subsequent generations shed their ethnic identity, clouds the issue. If we lose track of the second generation through ethnic attrition, are we mismeasuring assimilation; in particular, are we underestimating the speed at which immigrants fully integrate into the economy?

One of the main concerns expressed by individuals skeptical of liberal immigration policies is that immigrants, particularly poor immigrants, will compete with natives for resources. The two resources that generally come up as being at risk for depletion should there be a surge in immigration are jobs and welfare. By competing with natives for jobs, the fear is that immigrant flows will worsen the income levels of native households either by undercutting wages or by directly substituting for natives in the job market—in the first case, lessening natives' job earnings, and in the second case, their job opportunities. However, economists have, by and large, shown that immigrants (at the lower end of the skills distribution) do not compete with natives for jobs. If anyone loses in the job market to immigration, it is the earlier waves of immigrants. The previous immigrant group more closely resembles the newer cohort, bearing the highest risk of being displaced.

The second area of competition for resources that is often mentioned concerns public assistance. Naturally, one would imagine that newer immigrants, with less-secure job prospects, lower seniority, less education, and a limited stock of savings and wealth, might be more prone to suffering from economic shocks and accessing public assistance. But economists have found that immigrants have relatively low welfare participation rates. This may be due in part to policy and legal statutes that prevent recent immigrants from accessing many public assistance programs, but there are other reasons for expecting that participation by immigrants in the welfare system is more sparse.

Giovanni Peri addresses the issue of resource competition in Chapter 4. With the backing of empirical evidence, Peri appeals to the idea that immigrants are very mobile. They tend to move to areas that offer jobs over staying put and using public assistance. The reluctance to use public assistance might be motivated by a fear of losing rights and the ability to stay in the United States should its usage be detected. However, there are other reasons for low welfare participation, according to

Peri. Low-skilled Mexican and Central American immigrants are a self-selected group, coming to the United States primarily to work. If there are no jobs, they move on to find work elsewhere. Peri does not see much competition between natives and immigrants in terms of using public assistance. However, he does point to another area of potential competition between immigrants and natives for resources—public schooling. Immigrants may compete with natives for educational resources, potentially crowding out natives. Peri offers solutions through policy, particularly aimed at stemming school segregation. Native-flight, resulting in segregation of immigrants in schools with declining resources, bodes poorly for the second generation and ultimately does not serve anyone well, reducing the potential of the U.S. economy in the long run.

While Peri and others in this volume offer ideas for how to implement new policies, in Chapter 5 Catalina Amuedo-Dorantes and Esther Arenas-Arroyo discuss how policies are impacting immigrant communities today. They focus on undocumented immigration and distinguishing border enforcement from interior immigration enforcement. Much of the literature has zeroed in on border enforcement, but the news that dominates the headlines today is the dramatic increase in resources that have been applied to interior enforcement. The authors analyze how interior enforcement has affected a host of variables that are not on the radar, showing, for example, how American citizen children's schooling has responded to interior enforcement, and examining the impact of enforcement on the fertility of immigrants. It is important to analyze both intended and unintended consequences of stepped-up immigration enforcement if we are to generate a complete and frank discussion of the effectiveness and implications of current immigration policy.

To understand why immigration policy is such a contentious topic, it is useful to have access to a framework to theoretically measure how different policies affect the various stakeholders in an economy. This is what Alfonso Cebreros, Daniel Chiquiar, Monica Roa, and Martín Tobal accomplish in Chapter 6. Their insight is to recognize the many parallels that can be found with respect to immigration and international trade policy impacts. In age-old standard trade models, we observe that specialization in production with subsequent trade across national borders results in winners and losers. However, generally the gains from the winners exceed the losses of the losers. Those standard models show that, with redistribution of the gain (many find that difficult to stomach), everyone would be better off in comparison to a no-trade situation. The trade models that have been developed also help us explain the political economy of tariffs and other restrictions on trade. In the same way, Cebreros and coauthors show that parallel arguments can be made by adopting trade models to explore immigration, understand resistance to immigration, and trace the impacts of policies regarding immigration.

Motivated by the European refugee crisis and in an attempt to overcome resistance to refugee inflows, the authors of Chapter 7, Jesús Fernández-Huertas Moraga and Hillel Rapoport, propose combining physical and financial solidarity in asylum policy to allocate and spread refugees across countries. A tradable refugee-admission quota system—paired with a matching system that considers preferences and skills of asylees and of countries assigned the task of taking them in—might make settlement more palatable for countries. Despite differences in context and in the operationalization of the mechanisms to settle refugees and satisfy the needs of employers for immigrants at various skill levels, employment-based visas and the refugee tradable quotas scheme could potentially result in less haggling about who is gaining and who is losing, perhaps lessening the opposition to immigration and refugee settlement.

In this age of increasingly restrictive immigration policies, it is important to continue to challenge preconceived, often biased assumptions about immigrants using sound, empirical, and theoretical research methods. The contributors to this volume assist with this task by providing data and new perspectives, and by offering policy tools crafted to solve perceived shortcomings of the system.

Recently, I attended a lecture and reading by Ha Jin, a distinguished novelist and poet. Jin was born in China, is a U.S. immigrant, and is currently professor and director of the creative writing program at Boston University. He spoke of the displacement and loneliness that comes with being an emigrant. "Once you leave, you can never come back. The space you left becomes filled in." What Ha Jin did not speak of was the companion idea that once immigrants settle, they occupy a space that becomes changed forever too. Much of the immigration rhetoric we hear today seems to idealize the world before the latest wave of immigration took place. Whether the world was better then or better now is certainly an area we can debate, appeal to data, consult models, and compare information. But the bottom line is that, given the dramatic reductions in transportation and information costs, immigrants and immigration are likely to stay, and it makes much more sense to debate the best ways to harness the benefits of immigration rather than to incite divisiveness and invoke nostalgia for a yesterday that we will never see again.

2

The Economic and Fiscal Effects of Immigration

Implications for Policy

Pia M. Orrenius
Stephanie Gullo
Federal Reserve Bank of Dallas

RECENT TRENDS IN IMMIGRATION AND ECONOMIC GROWTH

The United States is the world's largest economy and top migrant destination. U.S. GDP accounts for 25 percent of global output.[1] And although the United States makes up less than 5 percent of the world's population, it is home to 19 percent of the world's international migrants.[2] The U.S. foreign-born population increased rapidly between 1990 and 2010, rising from 19.8 million in 1990 to nearly 40 million in 2010, but growth since then has slowed.[3] The foreign born today number around 45 million, representing a little over 13 percent of the total population. And while it's true the United States takes in the most migrants, there are an increasing number of countries with higher migrant shares, such as Canada, at 22 percent, or Australia, at 28 percent. Even some Western European nations now have higher migrant shares than does the United States, including Germany and Sweden.

Immigration has contributed significantly to U.S. labor force growth. In fact, between 1995 and 2015, immigrants and their children accounted for more than half of labor force growth (National Academies of Science, Engineering and Math [NAS] 2016, p. 68). Given the contribution of immigration to employment growth, slowing immigration will slow future economic growth, particularly considering the quickening labor force exodus of the baby boomers.

Immigration to the United States is slowing, even as the economy continues to steadily grow. GDP growth has averaged about 2 percent since 2010, job growth 1.8 percent, and the unemployment rate has fallen to well below 5 percent, a rate most economists would consider to be below the NAIRU (nonaccelerating inflation rate of unemployment). Wages have begun to increase in real terms on average (if not in every group) and in certain regions more than others. In past decades, this relatively robust labor market would have attracted more immigration, both legal and illegal, but migration trends have remained modest by recent historical standards (see Figure 2.1).

The decline in illegal immigration, as measured by Border Patrol apprehensions along the U.S.-Mexico border, is by far the most pronounced change. Apprehensions today are around 400,000 per year, levels last observed in the 1970s, when the U.S. economy was about one-third its current size. The decline in inflows has resulted in a shrink-

Figure 2.1   Migrant Inflows as a Percent of Working-Age Population

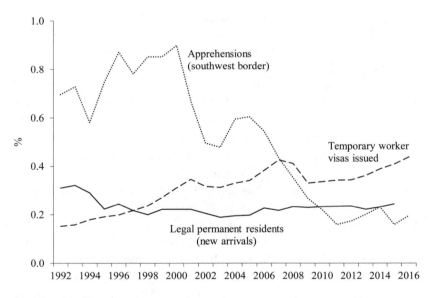

NOTE: Working-age population is 16–64.
SOURCE: U.S. Department of State, *Report of the Visa Office*, various years; U.S. Department of Homeland Security, *Yearbook of Immigration Statistics*, various years; U.S. Customs and Border Protection; U.S. Census Bureau.

ing of the unauthorized immigrant population, which peaked in 2007 at 12 million but estimates suggest was down to 11.3 million by 2016 (Krogstad, Passel, and Cohn 2017).

Inflows of legal immigrants have been more stable. New arrivals of legal permanent residents, which include family, humanitarian, and employment-based green cards, have been flat around 480,000 per year since 2010. Temporary worker visas, which declined during the Great Recession, have picked up some since 2013. Increases have been mostly in the uncapped visa programs, which include agricultural workers (H-2A) and NAFTA professionals (TN). A special provision exempting returning seasonal nonagricultural workers (H-2B) from the cap also resulted in a large increase in those visas (although that exemption was rescinded in 2016). It is very likely that the decline in illegal immigration has compelled employers to make more use of visa programs for low-skilled workers.

There is no reason to expect that the relationship between economic growth and immigration should remain constant. In fact, this relationship is likely changing along several dimensions, some of which can be addressed by public policy. Production of both goods and services is becoming less labor intensive as technology makes further inroads into the U.S. workplace. Consumption patterns are also changing. Fewer workers may be needed in the future, at least relative to economic output. However, there are also forces acting in the opposite direction, such as the aging of the U.S. labor force with the retirement of the baby boomers. The United States is currently in its most significant period of aging in history. As Figure 2.2 shows, the U.S.-born labor force, not including children of immigrants, is projected to decline by 8.2 million workers over the next two decades (2015–2035). Immigrants—first generation—and to a larger extent their children—the second generation—will make up all the growth in the labor force over this period. Hence, less immigration will mean slower labor force growth.

IMMIGRANTS IN THE U.S. LABOR MARKET

The foreign-born share of the population is a little over 13 percent, as noted above, but immigrants are overrepresented in the labor force,

Figure 2.2 Net Change in Working-Age Population (25–64), by Generation for Each Decade

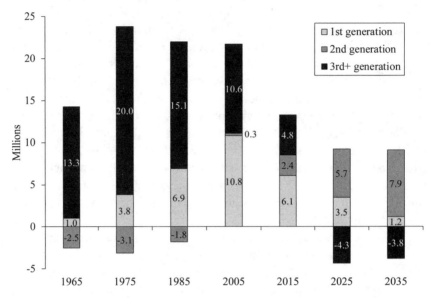

NOTE: Data for 2015 onward are projections.
SOURCE: Pew Research Center.

where they make up over 17 percent of all U.S. workers. Immigrants are more likely to work than natives primarily because they tend to be of prime working age. Nearly 60 percent of immigrants are between the ages of 25 and 54, compared with fewer than 40 percent of U.S. natives.[4] It bears noting that U.S. immigration policy, labor market regulation, and the lack of worksite enforcement of immigration laws are effective in encouraging that immigrants work or, at a minimum, requiring that they be self-sufficient. This is most obvious among male unauthorized immigrants who are not allowed to work yet have the highest labor force participation rates of any immigrant (or native) group (see Passel and Cohn [2016]).

Furthermore, immigrants are not randomly sprinkled across occupations, industries, or regions, but tend to flow into the areas where they are most in demand. The relationship between immigration and regional growth is apparent in Figure 2.3, which plots relative state growth in the

Figure 2.3 Growth in Foreign-Born Population and Employment, by State

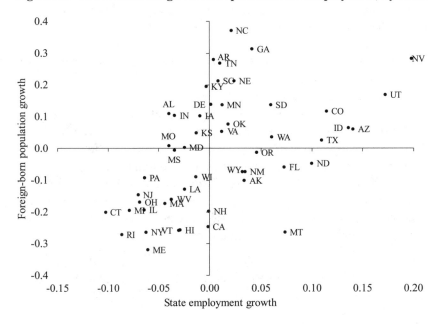

NOTE: Coordinates indicate deviation from median foreign-born population growth (vertical axis) and from median state nonfarm payroll growth (horizontal axis) from 1990 to 2016.
SOURCE: U.S. Census Bureau; 2016 American Community Survey; Bureau of Labor Statistics.

foreign-born population along the vertical axis and job growth by state along the horizontal axis, both for the 1990–2016 period. States that have experienced the fastest employment growth have had the highest relative growth in foreign-born population; these are the states in the top right quadrant and include Southern and Mountain West states. States in the lower left quadrant have had below-average job growth and immigration and include many states in the Northeast and Midwest. There are relatively few states in the top left and bottom right quadrants because growth and immigration are typically positively—not negatively—correlated.

The tendency of immigrants to flow where demand is growing is one of the most important economic benefits of immigration. Several effects follow: resources are reallocated from slowing to growing regions, which improves the allocation of workers, speeds up overall growth, and lowers the national unemployment rate. Monetary policy-makers have noted how this particular aspect of immigration increases the speed limit of the economy since growing regions are less likely to overheat, reducing the likelihood of excessive wage pressure and ensuing monetary policy action.

Immigrants also flow into occupations and industries where there is a relative need. Historically, this has been at the low and high ends of the education distribution, where U.S. workers are relatively scarce. Figure 2.4 shows that the disproportionate inflow of low-education immigrants, many of them arriving as undocumented immigrants from Mexico and Central America, has resulted in immigrants making up over half of the low-skilled labor force, those with less than a high school diploma. Immigrants are also overrepresented among workers with very high levels of education, including master's (18.8 percent),

Figure 2.4 Share of Foreign-Born Workers in the U.S. Labor Force, by Education

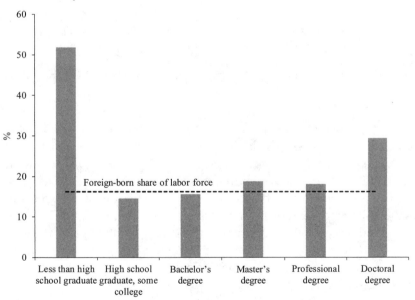

NOTE: Percent of foreign workers aged 25 and over in the U.S. labor force by education.
SOURCE: 2015 American Community Survey.

professional (18.1 percent), and PhD degrees (29.4 percent). There are relatively fewer immigrants in the categories where natives are concentrated, namely among workers with a high school diploma and some college and among those with a bachelor's degree.

It's not surprising to find immigrants at the bottom and top of the education distribution of workers. After all, nearly 30 percent of immigrants lack a high school degree or equivalent, compared with just under 10 percent of U.S. natives.[5] Immigrants are also slightly more likely to hold a graduate or professional degree, about 12 percent versus 11 percent of U.S. natives.

Unauthorized immigration has boosted the share of less-educated immigrants. Nearly half of unauthorized adults aged 25–64 lack a high school diploma (Passel and Cohn 2009). Commensurate with their relatively low educational attainment, immigrants are concentrated in low-skilled occupations such as housekeeping, farm work, food preparation, construction, and groundskeeping.

Top jobs for highly educated immigrants include STEM (science, technology, engineering, and math) and health care occupations; the high-skilled occupations with the highest share of immigrants include computer software developers, medical scientists, engineers, registered nurses, subject instructors, computer systems analysts, and dentists and physicians.

On both ends of the skill distribution, immigrants are disproportionately found in occupations and industries that have grown quickly or that U.S. natives have exited or eschewed. For example, there are stark differences when one compares the college majors of U.S.-born college-educated workers with those of immigrants. Almost half of such immigrants have a STEM major compared to 28 percent of natives (see Peri, Shih, and Sparber [2014]).

IMMIGRATION'S ECONOMIC IMPACT

The effects of immigration are similar to those of international trade. There are net economic gains from immigration (trade) that accrue to natives. The controversial aspect of immigration (trade) is not the overall benefits, but who gets them. Opening up the economy to these additional workers (goods in the case of trade) creates winners and losers among the native population, at least in the short run.

Immigration's first-order effect is to increase the labor force and, thus, economic output. As long as immigrants differ from natives, there can be additional benefits or second-order effects, such as greater efficiency and factor mobility. Immigration can also affect productivity growth. High-skilled immigration in the STEM fields is associated with innovation, which drives productivity growth.

Regarding the specifics, labor in-migration shifts out the labor supply curve, which increases total output, or gross domestic product (GDP). Most of the gain in GDP accrues to immigrant workers in the form of labor earnings, but the fall in the cost of labor also raises the return to capital. Owners of capital, who tend to be natives, get a windfall gain, whether they are business owners, landowners, or shareholders. Consumers also benefit from the lower prices and the specialization in production that may occur. The distribution of the gains is uneven, however, with owners of capital and complementary workers typically benefiting, while substitutable workers who compete directly with immigrants lose out.

Estimates of the immigration-induced increase in GDP that accrues to natives, also referred to as the "immigration surplus," are typically based on simulations or back-of-the-envelope calculations using labor's share of national income, the size of the foreign-born workforce, and the responsiveness of labor demand to changes in wages (Borjas 1995). In a standard competitive model, the immigration surplus is between 0.2 and 0.4 percent of U.S. GDP. In any case, a plausible range under standard assumptions and in a $19 trillion economy may be $40–$80 billion per year in income gains to natives from immigration.

The immigration surplus, natives' income gains from immigration, is larger when skill levels of immigrants differ from those of natives. If immigrants' skills are complementary to those of most natives, then the immigration surplus is larger than it would be if immigrants and natives were close substitutes (Borjas 1995). In fact, if immigrants and natives are exactly alike, then income per capita does not change at all in response to immigration and the immigration surplus is zero. If skilled immigrants are complementary to capital, as the literature suggests, then the immigration surplus is larger with high-skilled rather than low-skilled immigration, regardless of the skill composition of the native workforce.

High-skilled immigration has an additional benefit: there is mounting evidence that such immigration, by contributing to growth in the STEM occupations, is contributing directly to productivity growth. In the long run, increases in output per capita come from productivity growth, which is a result of technological progress. More recent work in macroeconomics has suggested that this technological progress is endogenous, stemming from investment in research and development, which generates innovations that permanently raise productivity (see Aghion and Howitt [1992] and Romer [1990]). Drinkwater et al. (2007) show that adding high-skilled immigration to an endogenous growth model substantially increases innovation, boosts the immigration surplus, and leads to a higher long-term growth rate. Jones (2002) estimates that 50 percent of total factor productivity growth between 1990 and 2010 came from the increase in the science and engineering workforce. Since immigrants made up 80 percent of that workforce growth, some economists argue that STEM immigrants accounted for as much as 40 percent of productivity growth during this time period (Peri, Shih, and Sparber 2014).

There is additional evidence that supports the correlation between high-skilled immigration and innovation. For example, Hunt and Gauthier-Lauselle (2010) find that immigrants patent new products at double the rate of U.S. natives, a difference explained by immigrants' overrepresentation in STEM occupations. They also find some evidence of positive spillovers on patenting among U.S. natives. In related work, Hunt (2011) demonstrates that these STEM immigrants are primarily entering on temporary work-based visas and student visas. Kerr and Lincoln (2010) also find that these visas play a key role by demonstrating that increases in H-1B visas (temporary skilled worker visas) significantly raise patent activity by immigrants, without reducing patenting among natives.

Immigrants also appear to be more entrepreneurial than U.S. natives. They are more likely to own a business; typically, the difference is about one or two percentage points with regard to the fraction of immigrants who are self-employed. Foreign-born business owners make up 18.2 percent of all business owners, which is greater than the immigrant share of the labor force (Fairlie and Lofstrom 2014). Immigrants are particularly overrepresented among new business owners, making up a quarter of business startups. Immigrants' entrepreneurial activities are likely a net benefit for the economy, but they may also reflect the lack of opportunities some immigrants face in the labor market. Moreover, while immigrants are more likely to start a business, immigrant-owned businesses are also more likely to fail than native-owned businesses.

Labor Market Effects

According to standard economic theory, immigrant inflows should have a negative effect on the wages and employment of existing workers, at least in the short run. Despite that clear prediction and the massive immigrant inflows that the United States has experienced since the 1970s, most empirical evidence on the wage and employment effects of immigration suggests that immigration has had either no effect or just a small adverse effect on natives' labor market outcomes (see NAS [2016]). Negative effects are not found on native workers overall, but for subgroups of workers, typically high school dropouts and prior low-skilled immigrants. There is little evidence of significant negative effects on medium- and high-skilled natives' wages.

The magnitude of the wage and employment effects on natives depends on how substitutable immigrants are for native workers. Natives whose skills are complementary to those of immigrants may see increases in their wages and employment from immigration, while natives with substitutable skills are most likely to lose. The brunt of the negative labor market impact falls on earlier immigrants, not natives, because they are most similar to new immigrants and hence compete most closely with them.

Why doesn't immigration have a more negative effect on natives? First, the number of low-skilled workers in the United States has been on the decline for several decades. There are, in a sense, fewer native workers that compete directly with low-skilled immigrants. Second, the economy—including its workers—is constantly adapting to the forces that shape economic activity. When the cost of labor falls, firms will use more labor. In other words, immigration affects the factor mix that is used by firms to produce output. Immigration can also affect the output mix; firms may begin to produce goods or services that are more labor intensive.

The decline in the cost of labor also raises the relative return to capital, as noted above, so immigration should spur investment and inflows of capital. Immigrants also tend to move to booming areas that otherwise might experience labor shortages, relieving growth bottlenecks. Natives and other immigrants may also move or change occupations or industries in response to immigration, making adverse wage and employment effects difficult to measure. And immigrants are themselves consumers and create jobs via their own effect on aggregate demand. Last but not least, certain immigrants also create jobs via their entrepreneurial activities and innovation, as discussed above.

IMMIGRATION'S FISCAL IMPACT

Apart from immigration's direct economic and labor market impacts, it has a fiscal impact—the difference between what immigrant families pay in taxes and what they consume in government-provided benefits.[6]

Immigrants, much like natives, contribute taxes in several ways: they pay taxes on earnings, including income and payroll taxes, purchases (sales taxes), housing (property taxes), motor vehicles (registration fees), and so on. Similar to natives, immigrants typically also consume at least some government-provided services, which may include public schools for their children, subsidized health care in the form of Medicaid and/or Medicare, income support programs such as the Earned Income Tax Credit, and welfare programs such as Temporary Assistance for Needy Families (TANF) or the Women and Infant Children (WIC) program, and Social Security. It bears noting that unauthorized immigrants are not eligible for most welfare programs, including TANF, and there are restrictions on the eligibility of some legal immigrants as well. Immigrants also rely on publicly provided services such as police and fire protection.

The characteristics of immigrants, such as their age, earnings, and family size, will be key to determining how much they fiscally contribute and receive. The progressivity of the tax system and the generosity of public programs will also play a role. Tax and benefit systems, as well as the characteristics of immigrants, vary greatly across states, which suggests the fiscal impacts of immigration may also be different across states.[7]

Other considerations are also key to determining fiscal effects, particularly the time horizon over which revenues and expenditures are measured. Cross-sectional or static short-run estimates look at individuals (or households) at a point in time. While this is a transparent method, it ignores the crucial role played by age and time in the United States. Dynamic or long-run estimates are much more representative of an immigrant's complete fiscal impact because tax contributions and government benefits are typically measured over an entire lifetime and will include the contributions of descendants. The downside to dynamic estimates, however, is that projecting income and benefits into the future requires making many assumptions. The 2016 National Academies of Science (NAS) report presents both static (short-run) and dynamic (long-run) estimates.[8]

Past Estimates of Immigration's Fiscal Impact

Before the 2016 NAS report, most scholars cited the fiscal estimates in the National Research Council report, *The New Americans: Economic, Demographic and Fiscal Effects of Immigration* (1997). The report finds that, over their lifetimes, low-educated immigrants, those with a high school diploma or less, impose a net fiscal cost while high-educated immigrants, those with a college degree or higher, represent a net fiscal benefit.[9] Using a similar dynamic methodology, Lee and Miller (2000) find that the initial fiscal impact of immigrants and their households is negative due to their low initial earnings and the costs of schooling their children. However, after about 16 years, the impact of a representative immigrant turns positive.

Another finding in the 1997 NRC report, which was later reinforced by updated analysis in Lee and Miller (2000), shows that immigration's fiscal impact is typically negative at the state and local level but positive at the federal government level. A key reason is that state and local governments bear the bulk of education costs, which immigrants disproportionately incur because they have more children and lower education and incomes than natives.

New Fiscal Estimates of Immigration: Static and Dynamic

The cross-sectional fiscal impact estimates from the 2016 NAS report are shown in Table 2.1, which replicates two scenarios from the 2016 report—namely, one in which immigrants are assigned the average cost of public goods (top rows), and another in which immigrants are assigned the marginal cost of public goods (bottom rows).[10] Public goods include the cost of national defense, interest on the national debt, and foreign aid, among other shared expenses.[11] The columns reflect three groups: immigrants and their minor children or 'dependents' ("first generation"), the adult children of immigrants and their dependents ("second generation"), and other U.S.-born adults and their dependents ("third generation").[12] This methodology assigns parents the education expenses of their children; in the case of immigrants, the returns to this investment in education (which mainly take the form of higher tax payments resulting from higher earnings) is thus attributed to the second generation. The rows in Table 2.1 also break the total effect into fiscal impacts at the federal versus state and local government level.

Table 2.1 Net Per Capita Fiscal Impacts of First, Second, and Third-plus Generations in 2013, by Public Goods Scenario and Level of Government

	1st generation with dependents		2nd generation with dependents		3rd generation with dependents	
	Receipts − outlays ($)	Fiscal gap (%)	Receipts − outlays ($)	Fiscal gap (%)	Receipts − outlays ($)	Fiscal gap (%)
Scenario 1: Immigrants assigned average cost of public goods						
Federal	−2,650	27.1	−3,598	27.5	−2,577	21.4
State and local	−2,372	38.6	−1,062	17.4	−1,031	17.7
Total	−5,021	31.6	−4,660	24.3	−3,608	20.2
Scenario 2: Immigrants assigned marginal cost of public goods						
Federal	963	−15.7	−4,239	30.9	−3,218	25.4
State and local	−1,746	31.7	−1,177	18.9	−1,146	19.2
Total	−782	6.7	−5,415	27.1	−4,364	23.4

SOURCE: Cross-sectional fiscal estimates based on NAS (2016, Table 8-2). Fiscal gap is defined as 1 minus receipts/outlays. Scenario 2 corresponds to scenario 5 in the NAS report.

It is notable that, with one exception, every generation, immigrant and native, at every level of government, consumes more in public benefits than it contributes in taxes. Because the nation is running a sizable deficit, the entire public represents a net cost on average. Fiscal impacts are negative in every case except immigrants in the second scenario at the federal level. In the "Total" row, the fiscal gap in funding varies from a low of 6.7 percent for the first generation to a high of 31.6 percent, also for the first generation.

The assumption about how to assign the costs of public goods makes a big difference in evaluating the fiscal impact of immigrants. Although the 2016 NAS report does not indicate a preferred or baseline specification, the marginal cost assumption is clearly the most relevant for future policy decisions because it represents the incremental effect of immigrants on public goods spending.

It is clear from Table 2.1 that the fiscal funding gap for immigrants is most acute at the state and local government level. As noted above, this is primarily due to the costs of public education; immigrant families in the United States have more children than do native families, which drives up their costs at the state and local levels relative to non-immigrants. The offset, the higher incomes and tax contributions of their children, is attributed to the second generation. Immigrants' lower incomes also mean they pay less in taxes on average than natives.

As discussed above, cross-sectional or static fiscal estimates like those presented in Table 2.1 are inherently limited by several shortcomings, including not controlling for differences in age between the foreign born and native-born populations at a point in time, and hence should be used with great caution. Long-run or lifetime estimates are preferred when, for example, evaluating fiscal impacts to formulate immigration policy. The 2016 NAS report's long-run fiscal estimates are presented in Table 2.2 and broken down for two sets of immigrants—those who arrived recently (in the last five years) and all immigrants. We again show the fiscal impact with and without assigning immigrants the cost of public goods. The top row is the weighted average of the remaining rows, which show fiscal impacts by education levels of immigrants and their dependents. Education level is a key determinant of income, so it will be an effective predictor of fiscal impact.

Table 2.2 shows that in dynamic, long-run scenarios, the present value of the net fiscal impact of immigration is typically positive and

Table 2.2 Dynamic 75-Year Per Capita Net Fiscal Impacts for Recent and All Immigrants, by Public Goods Scenario and Education Level (000s of 2012 $)

Education level	Recent immigrants[a]		All immigrants	
	No public goods	Public goods	No public goods	Public goods
Average	259	173	58	−5
Less than high school	117	−200	−196	−259
High school degree	49	−33	−47	−109
Some college	261	170	99	34
College degree	481	395	280	216
More than college degree	812	726	547	485

[a] Arrived in the past five years.
NOTE: Forecast is based on the CBO long-term budget outlook. Includes taxes and expenditures at the federal, state, and local levels for an individual and his dependents.
SOURCE: NAS (2016, Table 8-12).

can be quite large. If we assume that an additional immigrant does not increase spending on public goods, which is a reasonable assumption, a new immigrant represents a positive fiscal contribution with a net present value of $259,000. A recent immigrant has a much larger positive fiscal impact than does an immigrant who reflects the characteristics of the population of all immigrants ($58,000). The difference is because the stock of all immigrants has, on average, less education and is older than recent immigrants. The rise over time in education levels among U.S. immigrants partly reflects the rise in employment-based immigration in the post-1990 era and the more recent decline in low-skilled immigration.

Some of the estimates are astounding. A representative recent immigrant with more than a college degree contributes over $800,000 to government coffers on net over a 75-year period. In contrast, a typical recent immigrant who lacks a high school diploma represents a net cost of about $117,000 dollars. Interestingly, this net cost does not reflect disproportionate outlays as compared with similar natives. Figure 2.5 shows the difference in net fiscal 75-year impacts of immigrants versus natives by education level. Although low-skilled immigrants impose a net fiscal cost, apparent in Table 2.2, the net fiscal cost of natives of similar education is far larger. For example, the difference is on the

Figure 2.5 Immigrant-Native Difference in 75-Year Dynamic Net Fiscal Impact, by Education Level

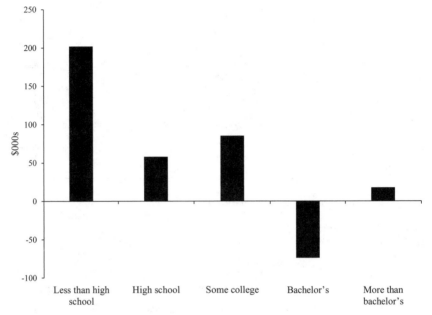

NOTE: Estimates assume no public goods are included in benefits.
SOURCE: NAS (2016, Table 8-13).

order of $200,000 less in fiscal cost of an immigrant who lacks a high school diploma versus a high school dropout native. The only education category where immigrants impose a smaller (in this case, less positive) fiscal benefit than natives is among those with bachelor's degrees.

Summary of Fiscal Impacts

New estimates of the fiscal impact of immigration reflect some of what was already known while also highlighting some important new findings. Cross-sectional estimates based on 2013 CPS data suggest that immigrants represent a net fiscal drain on average. However, so does everyone else, including natives. When immigrants are assigned the marginal cost of public goods, their fiscal impact is significantly less negative than that of natives. Immigrants' tax contributions cover 93 percent of their publicly provided benefits, while natives' contributions cover only 77 percent of theirs. The dreary overall fiscal scenario is due to large public deficits and high national debt—problems that were much less pronounced in the 1997 report. In addition, natives have grown more costly over time because they have become an older population; their health costs impose a disproportionate burden on the federal government because it pays for Medicare and subsidizes related expenses such as nursing homes. Meanwhile, immigrants are more costly than natives at the state and local levels because they have lower incomes and more minor children; this means immigrants are particularly burdensome to state and local governments, which pay for public schools.

The long-run, dynamic estimates of immigration's fiscal impact are both far more positive and arguably more relevant, at least from a policy perspective. Recent immigrants represent a large fiscal boon because they are projected to pay much more in taxes than they use in benefits over the next 75 years. Even low-skilled immigrants, those without any college education, while they impose a net long-run cost, are far less costly than similarly educated natives.

The overall results of the 2016 NAS report suggest that the rise of high-skilled immigration and more recent decline in low-skilled immigration is resolving some of the most pressing concerns around immigration's fiscal impact. Since present trends are likely to continue and possibly intensify in future immigration flows, immigration may increasingly be seen as a fiscal boon rather than a burden. Immigration may even play a part in future plans to address the nation's looming fiscal shortfalls.

IMMIGRATION POLICY

Nations use immigration policy to meet many objectives, including economic, humanitarian, political, cultural, and national security. The United States has a multifaceted immigration policy that engenders some of each of these, although it is principally a family reunification policy. Most permanent resident visas (green cards) are designated for family members of U.S. citizens, many of whom are immigrants themselves. Immediate family members of U.S. citizens include parents, spouses, and unmarried children, and they enter without limit. Other family members, employment-based immigrants, diversity immigrants, and refugees and asylum seekers are all subject to annual caps, which are typically exhausted every year.[13] After five years on a green card, permanent residents can naturalize. Once citizens, they too can sponsor their foreign-born relatives, a process that is sometimes referred to as *chain migration.*

Under this system, the United States annually issues about 1.1 million green cards. About 94 percent are to family members of U.S. citizens or permanent legal residents, people seeking humanitarian refuge, and diversity immigrants (Figure 2.6). The remaining 6 percent are to people who are immigrating for employment, most of whom are high-skilled. As can be seen in Table 2.3, no other major developed economy places such a low priority on permanent employment-based immigration.

Figure 2.6 Allocation of Permanent Resident Visas, by Category

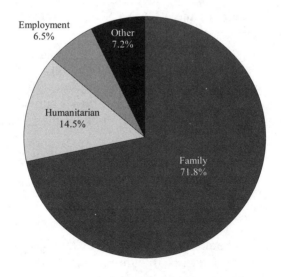

NOTE: Work includes free-movement migrants. Family includes accompanying family
   of workers. Data refer to 2015.
SOURCE: OECD (2017).

Table 2.3 Permanent Visas, by Category and Country

Country	Total number (000s)	Work (%)	Family (%)	Humanitarian (%)	Other (%)
United States	1,051	6.5	71.8	14.5	7.2
Switzerland	131	76.5	16.0	5.4	2.1
United Kingdom	379	75.9	13.0	4.8	6.3
Spain	195	72.7	20.3	0.5	6.5
Germany	686	66.2	12.0	20.9	0.9
Netherlands	147	57.6	14.3	28.1	0.0
Italy	161	48.2	30.2	18.4	3.1
France	256	44.4	40.4	6.5	8.7
Australia	226	36.6	57.2	6.1	0.1
Canada	272	28.2	58.6	13.2	0.0

NOTE: Only includes OECD countries. Work includes free-movement migrants. Family includes accompanying family of workers. Data refer to 2015.
SOURCE: OECD (2017).

Temporary Worker Programs

The United States has several temporary visa programs that help make up for the low number of hard-to-get employment-based green cards. The best known of these is the H-1B program, which brings in over 100,000 high-skilled workers in a typical year, many of them computer programmers from India and many others foreign-born STEM graduates from U.S. universities. The private sector faces a cap on H-1B visas of 85,000 each year, while there is no limit on nonprofit institutions. The number of H-1B applications outstrips supply every year.

Another important temporary job-based visa is the Trade NAFTA (TN) visa, which admits an additional 70,000-plus professionals, mostly from Canada but a growing number from Mexico. The L-1 program is for intracompany transferees (uncapped, with about 75,000 annually), and the O-1 program provides temporary visas for a small number of workers of "extraordinary ability."

The growth in temporary job-based visas has not led to any increases in the green card caps. As a result, there is a growing mismatch between the number of immigrants on temporary visas who wish to stay permanently in the United States and the number of available permanent residence visas. Although it is impossible to know how many temporary visa holders are in the green card queue, one study estimates that nearly 1.1 million people were waiting for an employment-based green card in fiscal year 2006 (Jasso et al. 2010). It is likely that many more would have applied if permanent visas were available. For those in the queue, green cards typically won't be available for many years because of the numerical limits on work-based permanent visas. Country-of-origin limits further restrict the number of visas that can go to immigrants from populous nations such as India and China.

Low-skilled workers face even longer odds. There are two temporary visa programs designed for low-skilled workers—the H-2A (for farm workers) and H-2B (other seasonal workers) programs. Both are only for work that lasts less than one year. H-2A visas are not capped and have grown considerably in recent years. H-2B visas have an annual cap of 66,000.

Illegal Immigration

Employers' usage of temporary visas has increased notably as illegal immigration has tapered off. This is encouraging in that it suggests employers will hire legal workers if that option exists and unauthorized workers are hard to find. And they are increasingly scarce. Estimates suggest the unauthorized immigrant population peaked in 2007 and has since declined from 12 to 11.3 million (Krogstad, Passel, and Cohn 2017). The Great Recession and accompanying housing bust and financial crisis may well have been the end of mass illegal immigration to the United States, at least from Mexico. Illegal immigration from Mexico never recovered from the Great Recession, and heightened enforcement is likely the reason why. Since the early 2000s, both federal and state governments have significantly tightened both border and interior enforcement and increased penalties.

In addition to more border fencing, border patrol agents, and stiffer penalties for apprehended migrants, the United States has also implemented more interior enforcement. In the wake of the 9/11 attacks, the Bush administration required that federal contractors and subcontractors participate in E-Verify, created the 287(g) program that trained state and local police to enforce federal immigration law, and launched Secure Communities, a program that checks whether immigrants in police custody are deportable. Although the Obama administration rolled back many of these programs, the Trump administration has been bringing them back, and many states have implemented their own laws in the meantime. The consequences for unauthorized immigrants are apparent not just in reduced inflows, but also in worse labor market outcomes. Research suggests that the tougher enforcement climate after 9/11 led to a decline in employment and earnings among Hispanic immigrants likely to be unauthorized (Orrenius and Zavodny 2009). Worksite enforcement and other measures likely forced some undocumented immigrants into self-employment or the shadow economy, where wages are lower and fringe benefits are rare.

IMMIGRATION POLICY REFORM

In implementing immigration reform, policymakers might consider three conclusions from this chapter: 1) there are net economic benefits to natives from immigration, so there should be immigration; 2) high-skilled and employment-based immigration is particularly beneficial, with potential to increase productivity growth and contribute positively to the fiscal balance; and 3) the United States is entering two decades in which the native labor force will shrink as the baby boomers retire. Implementing immigration reform will help offset this drag on labor force expansion and safeguard economic growth.

By following these basic principles, immigration policy could be used to advance the nation's economic and fiscal interests. The current system does not do this as well as it could because it prioritizes family reunification over work-based migration and strictly limits high-skilled immigration. The focus on family-based immigration serves the interests of earlier immigrants and only a small minority of U.S. natives. Since immigrants are already the biggest beneficiaries of immigration, it doesn't make sense to confer additional benefits on them through a system that is overwhelmingly family-based.

A good way to shift the immigration system toward employment-based immigration is to adopt an auction-based system that admits work-based immigrants and redistributes the auction revenue to natives.

In such a system, the federal government would regularly auction off permits to employers that allow them to hire highly skilled foreign workers, who would then receive visas. Visas would be portable across employers to facilitate worker mobility, and employers would be able to resell permits they no longer need (see Orrenius and Zavodny [2010] for more details). The auctions could be extended to include low-skilled and seasonal workers.

An auction-based system would have a number of advantages. Its emphasis on market forces would allocate visas to the workers most desired by employers, as measured by permit auction prices, rather than on the basis of how long someone has been standing in line or the random luck of winning a visa lottery. This emphasis on market forces is better than a point system in which bureaucrats determine how points, and hence visas, are allocated, as has historically been the case in Australia and Canada and has been recently proposed in the United States. Such systems tend to attract highly educated immigrants but not those with the best labor market prospects.

The United States also needs a legalization program to regularize the status of the more than 11 million unauthorized population. A legalization program has the benefit of boosting newly authorized immigrants' earnings, primarily because they are better able to move into higher-paying occupations instead of being trapped in just a few sectors of the economy. It also boosts tax revenues as newly authorized immigrants earn more and move out of the underground economy. The children of newly authorized immigrants are perhaps the biggest beneficiaries. Research indicates that children's educational outcomes improve when their parents obtain legal status (Bean et al. 2011). Children who are able to legalize their own status are more likely to go to college.

Of course, a major concern regarding a legalization program is whether it spurs additional unauthorized immigration. The U.S. experience suggests that increases in border enforcement are unlikely to reduce illegal immigration to publicly palatable levels. Looking to the future, minimizing unauthorized inflows will require creating a way for employers to bring in more foreign workers whose skills are aligned with employers' needs. Auctions would do this. Requiring employers to verify virtually all workers' legal status in an easy, fast, low-cost, and foolproof manner—as with the E-Verify system—is also necessary.

Notes

The views expressed here are solely those of the authors and do not reflect those of the Federal Reserve Bank of Dallas or the Federal Reserve System.

1. Source is IMF in current dollars; PPP-adjusted U.S. GDP accounts for 15.5 percent of world output.
2. The United Nations estimates the world migrant stock was 243.5 million in 2015. See http://www.pewglobal.org/interactives/migration-tables/ (accessed June 21, 2017). The UNDP estimates there are 50 million migrants worldwide with irregular status. See http://hdr.undp.org/sites/default/files/2016_human_development_report.pdf (accessed June 21, 2017).
3. We use the terms *immigrant* and *foreign-born* interchangeably in this chapter to refer to all individuals residing in the United States who were born abroad to non-U.S. parents. Immigrants thus include unauthorized immigrants, temporary and permanent resident visa holders, and naturalized citizens.
4. Authors' calculations based on 2015 American Community Survey one-year estimates.
5. 2015 American Community Survey one-year estimates.
6. The fiscal impact section is based extensively on NAS (2016) and Orrenius (2017), a version of which is also forthcoming in Spanish in *Coyuntura Demográfica*, available at http://www.somede.org/coyuntura-demografica/ (accessed March 15, 2018).
7. Chapter 9 of the 2016 NAS report presents estimates of the fiscal impact by state.
8. See Chapter 7 of the 2016 NAS report for a detailed discussion of the two methods and related assumptions.
9. Immigrants with less than a high school education were found to cost $89,000 more (based on 1996 estimates) than they contribute in taxes over their lifetimes, whereas immigrants with more than a high school education were found to contribute $105,000 more in taxes than they use in public services.
10. Tax contributions and benefits receipts are based on data from the March 2013 CPS.
11. Public goods, defined in this way, accounted for one-third of total federal spending in 2013.
12. Some immigrants' dependents are U.S.-born; in addition, some young adults who are students with very low incomes are also included as dependents.
13. Refugee admissions are capped each year, but there is no limit on green cards for refugees or asylees.

References

Aghion, Philippe, and Peter Howitt. 1992. "A Model of Growth through Creative Destruction." *Econometrica* 60(2): 323–351.

Bean, Frank D., Mark A. Leach, Susan K. Brown, James D. Bachmeier, and John R. Hipp. 2011. "The Educational Legacy of Unauthorized Migration: Comparisons across U.S.-Immigrant Groups in How Parents' Status Affects their Offspring." *International Migration Review* 45(2): 348–385.

Borjas, George J. 1995. "The Economic Benefits from Immigration." *Journal of Economic Perspectives* 9(2): 3–22.

Drinkwater, Stephen, Paul Levine, Emanuela Lotti, and Joseph Pearlman. 2007. "The Immigration Surplus Revisited in a General Equilibrium Model with Endogenous Growth." *Journal of Regional Science* 47(3): 569–601.

Fairlie, Robert W., and Magnus Lofstrom. 2014. "Immigration and Entrepreneurship." In *Handbook of the Economics of International Migration*, Barry Chiswick and Paul Miller, eds. Oxford, UK: Elsevier, pp. 877–908.

Hunt, Jennifer. 2011. "Which Immigrants are Most Innovative and Entrepreneurial? Distinctions by Entry Visa." *Journal of Labor Economics* 29(3): 417–457.

Hunt, Jennifer, and Marjolaine Gauthier-Lauselle. 2010. "How Much Does Immigration Boost Innovation?" *American Economic Journal: Macroeconomics* 2(2): 31–56.

Jasso, Guillermina, Vivek Wadhwa, Gary Gereffi, Ben Rissing, and Richard Freeman. 2010. "How Many Highly Skilled Foreign-Born Are Waiting in Line for U.S. Legal Permanent Residence?" *International Migration Review* 44(2): 477–498.

Jones, Charles I. 2002. "Sources of U.S. Economic Growth in a World of Ideas." *American Economic Review* 92(1): 220–239.

Kaushal, Neeraj. 2008. "In-State Tuition for the Undocumented: Education Effects on Mexican Young Adults." *Journal of Policy Analysis and Management* 27(4): 771–792.

Kerr, William R., and William F. Lincoln. 2010. "The Supply Side of Innovation: H-1B Visa Reforms and U.S. Ethnic Invention." *Journal of Labor Economics* 28(3): 473–508.

Krogstad, Jens Manuel, Jeffrey S. Passel, and D'Vera Cohn. 2017. "5 Facts about Illegal Immigration in the U.S." Washington, DC: Pew Hispanic Center.

Lee, Ronald, and Timothy Miller. 2000. "Immigration, Social Security, and Broader Fiscal Impacts." *American Economic Review* 90(2): 350–354.

National Academies of Sciences, Engineering and Medicine (NAS). 2016. *The Economic and Fiscal Consequences of Immigration*. Panel on the Economic and Fiscal Consequences of Immigration, Francine D. Blau and Christopher Mackie, eds. Committee on National Statistics, Division of Behavioral and Social Sciences and Education. Washington, DC: National Academy Press.

National Research Council. 1997. *The New Americans: Economic, Demographic and Fiscal Effects of Immigration*. Panel on the Demographic and Economic Impacts of Immigration, James P. Smith and Barry Edmonston, eds. Washington, DC: National Academy Press.

Organisation for Economic Co-operation and Development (OECD). 2017. *International Migration Outlook 2017*. Paris: OECD. http://dx.doi.org/10.1787/migr_outlook-2017-en (accessed January 4, 2018).

Orrenius, Pia M. 2017. "New Findings on the Fiscal Impact of Immigration in the United States." Federal Reserve Bank of Dallas Working Paper No. 1704. Dallas: Federal Reserve Bank of Dallas.

Orrenius, Pia M., and Madeline Zavodny. 2009. "The Effects of Tougher Enforcement on the Job Prospects of Recent Latin American Immigrants." *Journal of Policy Analysis and Management* 28(2): 239–257.

———. 2010. *Beside the Golden Door: U.S. Immigration Reform in a New Era of Globalization*. Washington, DC: AEI Press.

———. 2014. "The Economics of U.S. Immigration Reform." *Capitalism and Society* 9(2): Article 3.

Passel, Jeffrey S., and D'Vera Cohn. 2009. "A Portrait of Unauthorized Immigrants in the United States." Washington, DC: Pew Hispanic Center.

———. 2016. "Size of Unauthorized Immigrant Workforce Stable after the Great Recession." Washington, DC: Pew Hispanic Center. http://www.pewhispanic.org/2016/11/03/size-of-u-s-unauthorized-immigrant-workforce-stable-after-the-great-recession/ (accessed January 3, 2018).

Peri, Giovanni, and Chad Sparber. 2009. "Task Specialization, Immigration, and Wages." *American Economic Journal: Applied Economics* 1(3): 135–169.

Peri, Giovanni, Kevin Shih, and Chad Sparber. 2014. "How Highly Educated Immigrants Raise Native Wages." Washington, DC: Vox. http://voxeu.org/article/how-highly-educated-immigrants-raise-native-wages (accessed January 3, 2018).

Romer, Paul M. 1990. "Endogenous Technological Change." *Journal of Political Economy* 98(5): S71–S102.

3

Socioeconomic Integration of U.S. Immigrant Groups over the Long Term

The Second Generation and Beyond

Brian Duncan
University of Colorado Denver

Stephen J. Trejo
University of Texas at Austin

As a self-styled nation of immigrants, the United States takes great pride in its historical success as a "melting pot" able to absorb and unify people coming from diverse lands and cultures. At the same time, however, pride in our immigrant heritage always seems tempered by the nagging fear that the most recent arrivals are somehow different, that the latest wave of foreigners won't integrate into the mainstream of American society. Certainly, this fear was voiced when Irish, Italian, and other relatively unskilled immigrants arrived in large numbers at the end of the 1800s and the beginning of the 1900s (Jones 1960). Time has assuaged this particular fear. In terms of outcomes such as educational attainment, occupation, and earnings, the sizable differences by national origin that initially persisted among earlier European immigrants have largely disappeared among the modern-day descendants of these immigrants (Alba and Nee 2003; Borjas 1994; Chiswick 1977; Farley 1990; Lieberson and Waters 1988; Neidert and Farley 1985; Perlmann 2005; Perlmann and Waldinger 1997).

There is considerable skepticism, however, that the processes of assimilation and incorporation will operate similarly for the predominantly nonwhite immigrants who have entered the United States in increasing numbers over the past several decades (Gans 1992; Portes and Zhou 1993; Rumbaut 1994). Indeed, Huntington (2004) voices a particularly strong version of such skepticism with regard to Hispanic immigration. Are the descendants of present-day Hispanic and Asian immigrants following the same trajectory of intergenerational integration experienced by the descendants of earlier arrivals from Europe?

In this chapter, we shed light on this question by documenting generational patterns of educational attainment and earnings for contemporary immigrant groups. We also discuss some potentially serious measurement issues that arise when attempting to track the socioeconomic progress of the later-generation descendants of U.S. immigrants, and we summarize what recent research has to say about these measurement issues and how they might bias our assessment of the long-term integration of particular groups.

EDUCATIONAL PATTERNS IN THE FIRST AND SECOND GENERATIONS

We begin by describing patterns of educational attainment among foreign-born immigrants and their U.S.-born children. Education is a fundamental determinant of economic success, social status, health, family stability, and life opportunities (Hout 2012). In addition, information on education is available for all adults, whereas earnings data are available only for those currently working. Our primary education measure is average completed years of schooling, but similar patterns emerge for other education measures, such as the percent of individuals in the lower (less than 12 years of schooling) and upper (at least a bachelor's degree) tails of the educational distribution.

Throughout this chapter, we employ microdata from the Current Population Survey (CPS) for all months from January 2003 through December 2016. The CPS is a monthly survey of about 60,000 households that the U.S. government administers to estimate unemployment rates and other indicators of labor market activity. The sampling universe for this survey is the civilian noninstitutionalized population of the United States, which potentially generates biased estimates for groups with relatively high rates of institutionalization, such as young, African-American males (Pettit 2012). Beginning in 1980, the decennial U.S. census stopped asking respondents about the countries of birth of their parents, and the American Community Survey follows the census in this regard. In 1994, however, the CPS began collecting this information on a regular basis from all respondents. As a result, the CPS is currently the best large-scale, nationally representative U.S. data set for investigating how outcomes vary by immigrant generation.

In addition to the detailed demographic and labor force data reported for all respondents, the CPS collects earnings information each month from one-quarter of the sample, the so-called outgoing rotation groups. The data we analyze come from these outgoing rotation group samples. The CPS sampling scheme is such that surveys for the same month in adjacent years have about half of their respondents in common (e.g., about half of the respondents in any January survey are reinterviewed the following January). To obtain independent samples, we use only data from the first time a household appears in the outgoing rotation group samples (i.e., we use only data from the fourth month that a household appears in the CPS sample). By pooling together these 14 years of monthly CPS data, we substantially increase sample sizes and improve the precision of our estimates.

Using the CPS information on the countries of birth of each respondent and his or her parents, we define the following generation groups. The first generation consists of foreign-born individuals, excluding those born abroad of an American parent.[1] The second generation consists of U.S.-born individuals who have at least one foreign-born parent. Remaining persons are members of the third+ generation (i.e., the third and all higher generations), which consists of U.S.-born individuals who have two U.S.-born parents. Our analysis samples include men and women aged 25–59.

For first- and second-generation individuals overall and separately from the largest national origin groups, Table 3.1 reports average completed years of schooling and the corresponding sample sizes on which these averages are based.[2] The bottom row of the table shows average schooling levels for first- and second-generation individuals from all countries of origin (including countries not listed individually in the table). Separate calculations are presented for men and women.

For the first generation, these tables illustrate the well-known diversity of educational attainment among U.S. immigrants (Betts and Lofstrom 2000; Card 2005). Average schooling levels range from about

Table 3.1 Average Education of First- and Second-Generation Adults, Aged 25–59, by Source Country and Sex

Source country	Men, by immigrant generation				Women, by immigrant generation			
	First		Second		First		Second	
	Avg. educ.	Sample size	Avg. educ.	Sample size	Avg. educ.	Sample size	Avg. educ.	Sample size
Mexico	9.5	31,039	12.7	7,671	9.7	28,167	12.9	8,468
Puerto Rico	12.2	2,909	12.7	2,459	12.4	3,643	13.0	2,996
Cuba	13.0	2,062	14.3	821	13.2	2,051	14.6	806
Dominican Republic	11.9	1,658	13.5	363	12.0	2,599	14.1	422
Central America	9.7	8,323	13.4	938	10.3	7,940	13.9	1,054
South America	13.3	5,962	14.4	1,116	13.5	7,068	14.5	1,162
China	14.9	3,149	15.4	886	14.4	3,802	15.5	902
India	16.3	5,200	15.9	576	16.0	4700	16.0	552
Japan	15.7	560	14.4	659	14.9	1,099	14.7	645
Korea	15.4	1,898	15.0	544	14.6	2,827	15.4	530
Philippines	14.4	3,779	14.4	1,590	14.7	5,970	14.7	1,674
Vietnam	13.1	2,637	14.6	395	12.6	3,031	14.9	397
Haiti	12.8	1,056	14.1	175	12.7	1,246	14.8	235
Jamaica	13.1	1,215	14.1	286	13.5	1,756	14.8	361
Africa	14.4	4,755	14.7	604	13.6	4,238	15.0	637
Canada	15.1	1,725	14.2	3,330	14.9	2,072	14.5	3,481
Europe	14.5	10,147	14.5	12,895	14.5	11,594	14.6	13,351
All countries	12.2	99,966	13.9	38,459	12.4	106,372	14.1	40,812

NOTE: The education measure is completed years of schooling. The samples include people aged 25–59. The "first generation" consists of foreign-born individuals, excluding those born abroad of an American parent. The "second generation" consists of U.S.-born individuals who have at least one foreign-born parent. The bottom row labeled "all countries" reports outcomes for first- and second-generation individuals from all countries of origin (including countries not listed individually in the table). Sampling weights were used in the calculations.

SOURCE: 2003–2016 Current Population Survey outgoing rotation group data.

10 years for those born in Mexico and Central America to 15 years and above for those born in India, Japan, Korea, and Canada. For comparison purposes, note that average years of schooling among third+-generation non-Hispanic whites is 13.8 years for men and 14 years for women.

Additional calculations (not reported in Table 3.1) reveal that the foreign-born are greatly overrepresented among those with the lowest levels of education. Overall, 27 percent of immigrant men and 24 percent of immigrant women have completed less than 12 years of schooling, and these rates exceed 40 percent for Central American immigrants and exceed 50 percent for Mexican immigrants. In contrast, the corresponding rates of low educational attainment are below 7 percent for U.S.-born individuals overall. At the same time, however, the foreign-born are well represented among those with the highest education levels. Completion of a bachelor's degree is only slightly less common for immigrants than for the U.S.-born, whereas a substantially higher fraction of immigrants than U.S. natives have postgraduate degrees, and highly educated immigrants are heavily concentrated in science, technology, engineering, and health fields (Bound and Turner 2014). College degrees and higher levels of education are especially prevalent for immigrants from Canada, Europe, and parts of Asia (including China, India, Japan, Korea, and the Philippines). To sum up, the foreign-born are overrepresented at the bottom and, to a lesser extent, the top of the U.S. educational distribution, and they are underrepresented in the middle.

For assessing educational integration, it is particularly useful to look at the second generation, because these U.S.-born children of immigrants grew up in American schools. Table 3.1 reveals that, overall, second-generation men and women average about 14 years of schooling. Additional calculations (not reported) indicate that second-generation Americans have high school dropout rates of 6–7 percent and college completion rates of 36–39 percent (with women holding a slight educational advantage over men). These measures of educational attainment for the second generation are very similar to the corresponding measures for non-Hispanic whites in the third+ generation.[3] In this respect, the second generation as a whole has converged to the average educational attainment of the typical American.

Moreover, for the vast majority of specific national origin groups, average education levels of the second generation significantly exceed those of the typical third+-generation American. The exceptions are second-generation members of several important Hispanic groups: Mexicans, Puerto Ricans, Dominicans, and Central Americans. Note that this is not the case for *all* Hispanic groups—in particular, second-generation Cubans and South Americans exhibit relatively high levels of educational attainment. But the low schooling levels of second-generation Mexicans and Puerto Ricans and, to a lesser extent, Dominicans and Central Americans stand in sharp contrast to the much higher educational attainment of the second generations from non-Hispanic source countries.[4] As a result, Hispanics assume a central role in current discussions of immigrant integration, not just because Hispanics make up a large share of the U.S. immigrant population, but also because most indications of relative socioeconomic disadvantage among the children of U.S. immigrants vanish when Hispanics are excluded from the sample (Farley and Alba 2002; Perlmann and Waldinger 1996, 1997).

In large part, the educational deficits displayed by some second-generation Hispanic groups reflect the very low schooling levels of their immigrant parents (Perlmann 2005; Smith 2006). For example, Mexican immigrants average less than 10 years of education and under half have completed at least 12 years of schooling, so it is perhaps not surprising that their U.S.-born sons and daughters do not fully erase this enormous gap in human capital. Figures 3.1 (for men) and 3.2 (for women) provide further evidence on the relationship between the education levels of first- and second-generation individuals from the same source country. For the 17 countries/regions of origin displayed in Table 3.1, the figures plot average years of schooling for second-generation individuals aged 25–34 against those for first-generation individuals aged 50–59. These specific age groups are chosen so that the first generation more closely represents the parental cohort for the corresponding second generation. The solid regression lines in the figures highlight the central tendencies of the relationships between the average education levels of second-generation individuals from a particular source country and those of their immigrant ancestors. For reference purposes, the horizontal and vertical dashed lines indicate average years of schooling—13.8 years for men in Figure 3.1 and 14.2 years for women in Figure 3.2—for non-Hispanic whites in the third+ generation who are aged 25–34 (the same age range as the second-generation samples in the figures).

Figure 3.1 Average Education (in years) of First- and Second-Generation Men

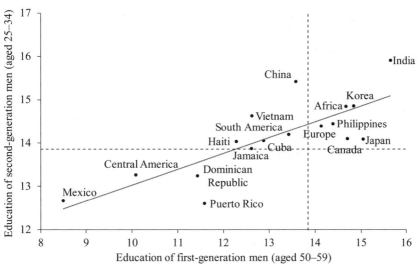

NOTE: The education measure is completed years of schooling. The first-generation samples include foreign-born men aged 50–59, excluding those born abroad of an American parent. The second-generation samples include U.S.-born men aged 25–34 who have at least one foreign-born parent. Sampling weights were used in the calculations.

SOURCE: 2003–2016 Current Population Survey outgoing rotation group data.

These figures reveal a strong relationship between the educational attainments of second-generation individuals and their immigrant predecessors. Most data points are close to the corresponding regression line, and the R-squared statistics of 0.63 for men in Figure 3.1 and 0.44 for women in Figure 3.2 indicate that much of the variation across national origin groups in the average education of the second generation is associated with differences in the human capital possessed by their immigrant ancestors.[5] Moreover, three of the Hispanic national origin groups with relatively low levels of second-generation schooling (Mexicans, Dominicans, and Central Americans) are not prominent regression outliers in these figures, which indicates that their educational deficits in the second generation are roughly what we would expect given the low schooling levels of their immigrant parents. Puerto Ricans, however, do lie well below the regression lines. Despite having education levels in

**Figure 3.2 Average Education (in years) of First- and Second-
         Generation Women**

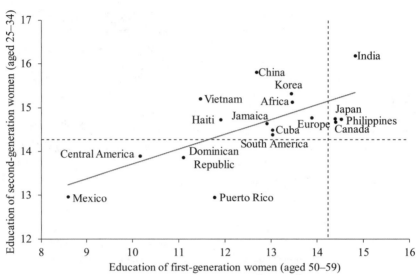

NOTE: The education measure is completed years of schooling. The first-generation
samples include foreign-born women aged 50–59, excluding those born abroad of
an American parent. The second-generation samples include U.S.-born women aged
25–34 who have at least one foreign-born parent. Sampling weights were used in the
calculations.
SOURCE: 2003–2016 Current Population Survey outgoing rotation group data.

the immigrant generation that exceed those of the other disadvantaged
Hispanic groups, by the second generation Puerto Ricans join Mexicans
at the bottom of the U.S. educational hierarchy.

Regarding the educational integration of the second generation,
the evidence presented thus far can be briefly summarized as follows.
On average, the second generation as a whole and second-generation
members from most contemporary immigrant groups meet or exceed
the schooling level of the typical American. The primary exceptions to
this pattern are several important Hispanic groups: Mexicans, Puerto
Ricans, Dominicans, and Central Americans; and the sizable educational deficits that persist into the second generation for these Hispanic
groups largely reflect the very low levels of schooling, English profi-

ciency, and other forms of human capital brought to the United States by their immigrant ancestors.

Because they start out farther behind, perhaps the lagging Hispanic groups will simply require an extra generation or so to integrate into the socioeconomic mainstream of American society. After carefully comparing the intergenerational mobility experienced by low-skill European immigrants arriving in the United States around 1900 with that experienced by modern-day Mexicans, Perlmann (2005) concludes that "Mexican economic assimilation may take more time—four or five generations rather than three or four" (p. 124), but that such assimilation is nonetheless occurring. If Perlmann is correct, then the long-term integration of Mexican Americans and other Hispanic groups may not turn out all that differently from the success stories often recounted for pervious waves of U.S. immigration.

BEYOND THE SECOND GENERATION

Given the patterns described in the preceding section, a key question becomes, How much educational progress takes place after the second generation for Mexicans and other disadvantaged Hispanic groups? To tackle this question, we must first confront the issue of how, with available data, to identify immigrant groups in the third generation and beyond. In the CPS, the only information about the national origins of third+-generation individuals comes from their subjective responses to the Hispanic origin and race questions. Using this information, Table 3.2 reports average years of schooling by immigrant generation for the various Hispanic and non-Hispanic racial/ethnic groups identified in CPS data.[6]

For Hispanics overall, Table 3.2 reveals a substantial schooling advantage of more than 2.5 years for the second generation relative to the first, but no further improvement is evident for the third+ generation. This pattern largely repeats itself for each of the Hispanic national origin groups: sizable schooling gains between the first and second generations with no signs of additional progress beyond the second generation. Puerto Ricans are a notable exception, however, with average education levels increasing by about one-half of a year between the

Table 3.2 Average Education, Aged 25–59, by Race/Ethnicity, Sex, and Immigrant Generation

Race/Ethnicity	Men, by immigrant generation			Women, by immigrant generation		
	First	Second	Third+	First	Second	Third+
Hispanic	10.3	13.0	12.8	10.6	13.2	12.9
(aggregate)	(0.02)	(0.02)	(0.02)	(0.02)	(0.02)	(0.02)
Mexican	9.5	12.7	12.7	9.6	12.9	12.8
	(0.02)	(0.03)	(0.02)	(0.02)	(0.03)	(0.02)
Puerto Rican	12.2	12.7	13.2	12.4	13.0	13.4
	(0.06)	(0.05)	(0.06)	(0.05)	(0.04)	(0.05)
Cuban	13.0	14.3	14.0	13.2	14.7	13.9
	(0.06)	(0.09)	(0.18)	(0.06)	(0.09)	(0.16)
Central/South	11.0	13.8	13.2	11.6	14.2	13.6
American	(0.04)	(0.06)	(0.13)	(0.03)	(0.06)	(0.11)
Other Hispanic	12.1	13.6	13.2	12.4	13.6	13.2
	(0.10)	(0.10)	(0.04)	(0.09)	(0.09)	(0.04)
Non-Hispanic						
White	14.4	14.4	13.8	14.2	14.6	14.0
	(0.02)	(0.02)	(0.004)	(0.02)	(0.02)	(0.003)
Black	13.5	14.0	12.9	13.3	14.5	13.3
	(0.03)	(0.07)	(0.01)	(0.03)	(0.06)	(0.009)
Asian	14.8	15.0	14.3	14.3	15.2	14.5
	(0.02)	(0.04)	(0.04)	(0.02)	(0.04)	(0.04)
Other race	14.0	14.3	13.0	14.3	14.6	13.3
	(0.16)	(0.07)	(0.02)	(0.13)	(0.07)	(0.02)
All race/ethnic	12.2	13.9	13.6	12.4	14.1	13.8
groups	(0.01)	(0.01)	(0.003)	(0.01)	(0.01)	(0.003)

NOTE: Standard errors are reported in parentheses. The education measure is completed years of schooling. The samples include people ages 25–59. The "first generation" consists of foreign-born individuals, excluding those born abroad of an American parent. The "second generation" consists of U.S.-born individuals who have at least one foreign-born parent. Remaining persons are members of the "third+ generation" (i.e., the third and all higher generations), which consists of U.S.-born individuals who have two U.S.-born parents. Sampling weights were used in the calculations.
SOURCE: 2003–2016 Current Population Survey outgoing rotation group data.

second and third+ generations. Another interesting pattern is that the gains between the first and second generations are particularly strong for the national origin groups with the least-educated immigrants (i.e., Mexicans and Central/South Americans).

Turning now to the non-Hispanic groups in Table 3.2, Asians of all three generations possess high levels of educational attainment, as do first- and second-generation whites. By the second generation, the average schooling levels of black and other race individuals exceed those of third+-generation whites. Educational attainment is dramatically lower (by a year or more, on average) for third+-generation members of the black and other race groups, a pattern that reflects the fundamental demographic heterogeneity across generations for these particular groups. First- and second-generation blacks, for example, primarily consist of immigrants from the Caribbean and Africa and their U.S.-born children. Third+-generation blacks, however, are largely the descendants of African American slaves whose families have been in the United States for many generations. The residual nature of the "other race" group also creates comparability issues across generations, especially for the third+ generation that disproportionately consists of individuals with American Indian and/or mixed-race ancestry. As a result, comparisons between the first two generations and the third+ generation for the black and other race groups are unlikely to shed much light on the intergenerational integration of immigrants. In contrast, such comparisons are more meaningful for the Hispanic and Asian groups, because these groups are more demographically homogenous across generations and because most of the third+-generation members are indeed third generation rather than from a higher generation.

The apparent lack of socioeconomic progress between second and later generations of U.S. Hispanics is surprising. Previous studies have consistently found parental education to be one of the most important determinants of an individual's educational attainment and ultimate labor market success (Haveman and Wolfe 1994; Mulligan 1997). Through this mechanism, the huge educational gain between first- and second-generation Hispanics (documented in Figures 3.1 and 3.2 and Tables 3.1 and 3.2) should produce a sizable jump in schooling between the second and third generations, because on average the third generation has parents who are much better educated than those of the second generation. Yet the improvement in schooling we expect to find between the second and third generations is largely absent (except for Puerto Ricans).

GENERATIONAL PATTERNS FOR WEEKLY EARNINGS

Until now we have used educational attainment rather than earnings to measure skills to avoid potential biases from selective labor force participation (i.e., earnings data are available only for those currently employed). Earnings, however, are perhaps the ultimate indicator of labor market success because they reflect the market's valuation of a worker's entire package of abilities and attributes, including those for which data are often lacking (e.g., family background or the quality of schooling). We now show that, in general, earnings patterns are similar to the education patterns discussed previously, particularly with respect to the apparent cessation of Hispanic progress after the second generation.

Figures 3.3 (for men) and 3.4 (for women) display weekly earnings differences associated with immigrant generation and race/ethnicity. The reported differentials are estimated from least squares regressions in which the dependent variable is the natural logarithm of weekly earnings from wage and salary work.[7] Separate regressions were run for men and women, and the samples include those aged 25–59 employed in civilian wage and salary jobs. These regressions allow intercepts to differ across racial/ethnic and immigrant generation groups, but the coefficients of the control variables are restricted to be the same for all groups. All regressions include controls for age, geographic location, and survey month/year. The controls for geographic location are dummy variables identifying the nine census divisions and whether the respondent lives outside of a metropolitan area. The controls for age are dummy variables identifying five-year age intervals. The bottom panel (Panel B) of each figure reports differentials estimated from regressions that also control for education level (i.e., dummy variables identifying the following years of schooling intervals: less than 12 years, exactly 12 years, 13–15 years, and 16 or more years). The reported differentials are all relative to the reference group consisting of non-Hispanic whites in the third+ generation.[8] Because the outcome is weekly earnings, these differentials measure the cumulative effect of differences in both hourly wages and hours worked per week.

For Hispanics overall and for Mexicans in particular, the earnings deficits in Figures 3.3 and 3.4 display a similar pattern across generations as the education data presented earlier (see Table 3.2): large gains for the second generation over the first, with little or no evidence of further gains for the third+ generation. Among men, for example, the Hispanic earnings deficit (relative to third+-generation non-Hispanic whites) drops from over 50 percent for the first generation to 21 percent for the second generation, but there is no additional decline for the third+ generation.[9] The corresponding pattern for Mexican men is quite similar. Comparing the top and bottom panels of Figure 3.3, the earnings deficits for Hispanic and Mexican men of every generation shrink by about half after controlling for education. For Hispanic and Mexican women, Figure 3.4 shows that earnings gains between the first and second generations are even larger than for men, and conditioning on education produces a greater reduction in the female earnings deficits relative to third+-generation non-Hispanic whites. Indeed, after controlling for education, earnings deficits all but disappear for U.S.-born Hispanic and Mexican women.

Broadly similar patterns emerge for Puerto Ricans, except that Puerto Rican men exhibit earnings gains between the second and third+ generations in Figure 3.3, just as they were the one group of Hispanic men to show educational gains between the second and third+ generations in Table 3.2. These educational gains for Puerto Rican men seem to drive much of their observed earnings progress, as the decline in the earnings deficit between the second and third+ generations is substantially larger without controlling for education (the relevant earnings deficit declines from 25 percent to 18 percent) than when such controls are included (the earnings deficit declines from 12 percent to 11 percent). On the whole, these results suggest that the educational disadvantage of Hispanics accounts for much of their earnings deficit, and also that Hispanic schooling gains between the first and second generations play an important role in the earnings progress between these generations.

Among the U.S.-born groups, third+-generation black men stand out with earnings deficits that remain large even after conditioning on education. Compared to non-Hispanic white men in the third+ genera-

**Figure 3.3 Weekly Earnings Differentials of Men, Aged 25–59, by Race/
Ethnicity and Immigrant Generation (relative to third+
generation, non-Hispanic whites)**

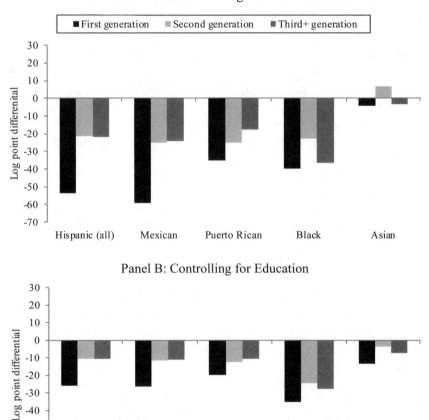

Panel A: Not Controlling for Education

Panel B: Controlling for Education

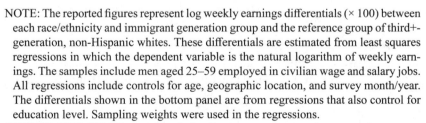

NOTE: The reported figures represent log weekly earnings differentials (× 100) between
each race/ethnicity and immigrant generation group and the reference group of third+-
generation, non-Hispanic whites. These differentials are estimated from least squares
regressions in which the dependent variable is the natural logarithm of weekly earnings. The samples include men aged 25–59 employed in civilian wage and salary jobs.
All regressions include controls for age, geographic location, and survey month/year.
The differentials shown in the bottom panel are from regressions that also control for
education level. Sampling weights were used in the regressions.
SOURCE: 2003–2016 Current Population Survey outgoing rotation group data.

Figure 3.4 Weekly Earnings Differentials of Women, Ages 25–59, by Race/Ethnicity and Immigrant Generation (relative to third+ generation, non-Hispanic whites)

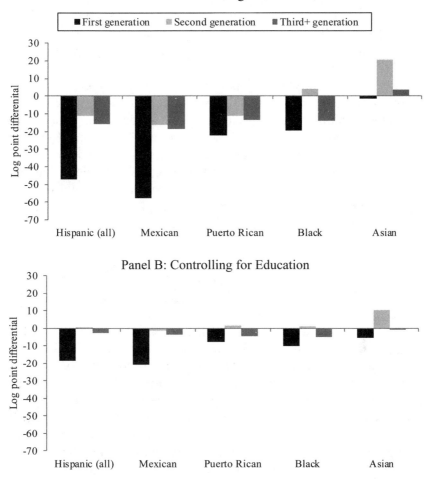

Panel A: Not Controlling for Education

Panel B: Controlling for Education

NOTE: The reported figures represent log weekly earnings differentials (× 100) between each race/ethnicity and immigrant generation group and the reference group of third+-generation, non-Hispanic whites. These differentials are estimated from least squares regressions in which the dependent variable is the natural logarithm of weekly earnings. The samples include women aged 25–59 employed in civilian wage and salary jobs. All regressions include controls for age, geographic location, and survey month/year. The differentials shown in the bottom panel are from regressions that also control for education level. Sampling weights were used in the regressions.

SOURCE: 2003–2016 Current Population Survey outgoing rotation group data.

tion with similar education, Panel B of Figure 3.3 indicates that third+-generation black men earn about 28 percent less. In contrast, the corresponding deficit is only 11 percent for Hispanic men. These findings corroborate other research that suggests that, among men, U.S. labor market opportunities are more similar to those of whites for Hispanics than for blacks (Duncan, Hotz, and Trejo 2006; Grogger and Trejo 2002; Trejo 1997). Panel B of Figure 3.4 shows that, after controlling for education, earnings of U.S.-born women do not vary much with race/ethnicity.

Contrary to the sizable gaps observed for blacks and Hispanics, earnings deficits (relative to third+-generation non-Hispanic whites) are either small or nonexistent for first- and second-generation whites (not shown in the figures) and for Asians of all generations. However, earnings comparisons for Asians become less favorable after controlling for education. As others have noted (see, for example, Sakamoto, Goyette, and Kim [2009]), the schooling advantage of Asian Americans can obscure the fact that, at least among men, they tend to earn somewhat less than whites with the same level of education.

STALLED PROGRESS FOR HISPANICS?

The education and earnings patterns presented thus far suggest that progress stalls after the second generation for Hispanics overall and for Mexicans in particular. Huntington (2004) points to several factors that could slow the pace of intergenerational integration by Hispanics today as compared to Europeans in the past. These factors include the vast scale of current immigration flows from Mexico and other Spanish-speaking countries, the substantial (though lessening) geographic concentration of these flows within the United States, and the fact that such flows have remained sizable over a much longer period of time than did the influx from any particular European country. In addition, the close proximity of Mexico to the United States facilitates return and repeat migration. These unique features of Hispanic immigration might foster the growth of ethnic enclaves in the United States where immigrants and their descendants could, if they so choose, live and work without being forced to learn English or to Americanize in other important ways.[10]

Another salient factor is that many Hispanics enter the United States as illegal immigrants. Some evidence suggests that undocumented status may hinder socioeconomic advancement not just for the illegal immigrants themselves but also for their U.S.-born children (Bean et al. 2011; Bean, Brown, and Bachmeier 2015).[11]

Moreover, today's economy provides fewer opportunities for unskilled workers to advance than did the economy that greeted earlier European immigrants (Perlmann 2005; Portes and Rumbaut 2001). Around 1900, high school completion was uncommon for native-born Americans, so while many European immigrants arrived with relatively meager educations, their skill disadvantage was smaller than that faced today by Hispanic immigrants who typically lack the additional years of high school and college that have become the norm for U.S. natives. Furthermore, recent decades have witnessed a large rise in earnings inequality among American workers, driven by substantial increases in the labor market payoffs to education and other indicators of skill (Autor and Katz 1999; Autor, Katz, and Kearney 2008; Levy and Murnane 1992). As a result, the human capital deficit possessed by most Hispanic immigrants has become even more of a liability in our modern economy that places a higher premium on knowledge and cognitive ability.

Before accepting Huntington's theoretical arguments for slower assimilation by Hispanics, however, it is important to consider several potentially serious limitations of the empirical evidence that has been presented in support of this phenomenon. First, as noted by Borjas (1993, 2006) and Smith (2003, 2006), generational comparisons in a single cross-section of data—like those reported so far—can be misleading because they do a poor job of matching immigrant parents and grandparents in the first generation with their actual descendants in later generations. If we assume that schooling is complete by the age of 25 and does not change thereafter, we can use our CPS samples to conduct an analysis of intergenerational changes in Hispanic educational attainment similar in spirit to Smith (2003).

Table 3.3 presents average schooling levels for Mexicans and Puerto Ricans similar to those displayed previously in Table 3.2, except that now separate calculations are reported for two particular age groups: 25–34 and 50–59.[12] By choosing age groups 25 years apart, we create a situation in which the older age group from a particular generation

Table 3.3 Average Education of Mexicans and Puerto Ricans, Aged 25–34 and 50–59, by Sex and Immigrant Generation

National origin and age group	Men, by immigrant generation			Women, by immigrant generation		
	First	Second	Third+	First	Second	Third+
Mexican						
25–34	9.9 (0.03)	12.7 (0.03)	12.6 (0.03)	10.2 (0.04)	13.0 (0.03)	13.0 (0.03)
50–59	8.5 (0.06)	12.5 (0.09)	12.5 (0.05)	8.6 (0.06)	12.4 (0.09)	12.4 (0.05)
Puerto Rican						
25–34	12.5 (0.10)	12.6 (0.08)	13.2 (0.09)	12.8 (0.09)	12.9 (0.07)	13.5 (0.08)
50–59	11.6 (0.11)	12.7 (0.11)	13.4 (0.16)	11.7 (0.11)	13.0 (0.12)	13.6 (0.17)

NOTE: Standard errors are reported in parentheses. The education measure is completed years of schooling. The samples include people aged 25–34 and 50–59. The "first generation" consists of foreign-born individuals, excluding those born abroad of an American parent. The "second generation" consists of U.S.-born individuals who have at least one foreign-born parent. Remaining persons are members of the "third+ generation" (i.e., the third and all higher generations), which consists of U.S.-born individuals who have two U.S.-born parents. Sampling weights were used in the calculations.
SOURCE: 2003–2016 Current Population Survey outgoing rotation group data.

potentially represents the parental cohort for the younger age group in the next generation. For example, the cohort of immigrant men aged 50–59 includes fathers of the second-generation cohort of sons aged 25–34.

If we make comparisons within age groups by reading across the rows of Table 3.3, we see the same patterns that emerged in Table 3.2: For Mexicans, huge educational improvement between the first and second generations but no progress after the second generation, whereas for Puerto Ricans' there are more modest gains between the first and second generations but also advances between the second and later generations. If, however, we instead compare age/generation groups that potentially match parents with their children (i.e., by moving northeast between the connected cells with similar shading in Table 3.3), we begin to see some educational gains for Mexicans after the second generation, especially for women. Among Mexican men, for example, average schooling rises from 12.5 years for the older second generation to 12.6 years for the younger third+ generation. The analogous educational increase between the second and third+ generations is larger for Mexican women, from 12.4 to 13.0 years. Moreover, calculating schooling progress between the first and second generations in this same way produces bigger gains than those we saw in Table 3.2: 4.2–4.4 years for Mexicans and 1.0–1.2 years for Puerto Ricans, with the larger gains for women. Despite these intergenerational advances, young third+-generation Mexicans continue to trail the average schooling of their non-Hispanic white peers by more than a year, and the corresponding deficits for Puerto Ricans are smaller but still sizable (about two-thirds of a year).

A second issue concerns measurement bias arising from "ethnic attrition." The large, nationally representative data sources typically employed to study U.S. immigrants and their descendants provide only very limited information pertaining to immigrant generations. Microdata sources such as the decennial U.S. Census, the American Community Survey, and the CPS report each respondent's country of birth, thereby distinguishing foreign-born individuals (i.e., the first generation) from the U.S.-born population. Only the CPS, however, currently collects information about the countries of birth of each respondent's parents, which allows the second generation (i.e., U.S.-born individuals who have at least one foreign-born parent) to be differentiated from higher generations of U.S.-born individuals. Furthermore, none of these surveys provide information about the countries of birth of an adult respondent's grandparents, so the third generation cannot be precisely identified.

Because of these data limitations, research on the U.S.-born descendants of immigrants often must identify the populations of interest using subjective measures of racial/ethnic identification (Duncan, Hotz, and Trejo 2006; Saenz 2005; Sakamoto, Wu, and Tzeng 2000; Snipp and Hirschman 2004; Zeng and Xie 2004). In particular, this approach is typically the only feasible option for studies that examine long-term integration by distinguishing immigrant descendants in the third and higher generations (Blau and Kahn 2007; Borjas 1994; Farley and Alba 2002; Goyette and Xie 1999; Grogger and Trejo 2002; Rong and Grant 1992; Smith 2006; Trejo 1997, 2003; Yang 2004). For example, the standard definition of third+-generation Mexicans Americans is U.S.-born individuals who have U.S.-born parents and who self-identify as Mexican in response to the Hispanic origin question.

A potential problem with this approach is that assimilation and intermarriage can cause ethnic attachments to fade across generations (Alba 1990; Alba and Islam 2009; Lee and Bean 2010; Perlmann and Waters 2007; Waters 1990), and therefore subjective measures of racial/ethnic identification might miss a significant portion of the later-generation descendants of immigrants. Moreover, if such ethnic attrition is selective on socioeconomic attainment, it can distort assessments of integration and generational progress.

Our own previous work demonstrates the salience of these issues for the specific case of Mexican Americans (Duncan and Trejo 2007, 2009, 2011). Analyzing microdata from the CPS for children living with both parents, in Duncan and Trejo (2011) we compare an objective indicator of Mexican descent (based on the countries of birth of the child, his parents, and his grandparents) with the standard subjective measure of Mexican identification (based on the response to the Hispanic origin question). We find that about 30 percent of third-generation Mexican children are *not* identified as Mexican by the Hispanic origin question in the CPS, and this ethnic attrition is highly selective. In particular, the high school dropout rate of third-generation Mexican youth (ages 16 and 17) is 25 percent higher when the sample is limited to those youth subjectively identified as Mexican. Therefore, our previous research suggests that ethnic attrition is substantial among third-generation Mexicans and could produce significant downward bias in standard measures of attainment that rely on subjective ethnic identification rather than objective indicators of Mexican descent.

Extending our earlier work in Duncan and Trejo (2017), which focused on Mexicans, we show that ethnic attrition is sizable and selective for the second- and third-generation populations of key Hispanic and Asian national origin groups. Importantly, these results indicate that ethnic attrition generates measurement biases that vary across groups in direction as well as magnitude, and that correcting for these biases is likely to raise the socioeconomic standing of the U.S.-born descendants of most Hispanic immigrants relative to their Asian counterparts. The results to date, however, shed more light on the direction rather than the ultimate magnitude of these measurement biases, and so at this point it is unknown whether correcting for selective ethnic attrition would produce a small or large improvement in the relative attainment of later-generation Hispanics.

A third but related issue is that the data limitations just described imply that, for adults, researchers typically cannot distinguish the "true" third generation from higher generations (e.g., this is why Tables 3.2 and 3.3 and Figures 3.3 and 3.4 refer to the "third+" generation). This is potentially a problem because Mexicans in generations beyond the third are disproportionately descended from ancestors who came of age in places (e.g., Texas rather than California) and times (e.g., before the Civil Rights era) where Mexicans faced discrimination that was more severe and often institutionalized (Alba 2006; Foley 1997; Montejano 1987). The more limited opportunities for advancement experienced by these families may result in lower attainment for Mexicans in the fourth and higher generations compared with their third-generation counterparts whose families experienced less hostile environments. Alba et al. (2011) and Bean, Brown, and Bachmeier (2015) provide evidence of this pattern for schooling levels, highlighting the importance of distinguishing third-generation Mexicans from higher generations.

In recent work with coauthors (Duncan et al. 2017), we exploit previously untapped information from the National Longitudinal Survey of Youth 1997 (NLSY97) that provides, among other things, the countries of birth of respondents' grandparents. For a sample of adults aged 28–34, these data allow us to minimize ethnic attrition by identifying third-generation Mexicans using ancestors' countries of birth rather than subjective ethnic identification, and they also allow us to distinguish third-generation Mexicans from higher generations. We find substantial educational progress between second- and third-generation Mexicans that is largely hidden when we instead mimic standard data sets and aggregate the third and higher generations into a "third+" generation. This analysis provides promising evidence of generational progress for a recent cohort of Mexican-American adults. Indeed, in this birth cohort, the high school graduation rate of third-generation Mexicans is only slightly below that of non-Hispanic whites from the fourth and higher generations.[13] These NLSY79 findings are consistent with recent evidence of improving high school completion rates for U.S.-educated Hispanics from 1990 to 2010, with particularly large gains during the second half of this period (Murnane 2013).

CONCLUSION

Research on the educational attainment of the descendants of U.S. immigrants reveals clear success stories as well as reasons for concern. On the one hand, most national origin groups arrive with relatively high educational attainment and/or experience enough improvement between the first and second generations such that they quickly meet or exceed, on average, the schooling level of the typical American. On the other hand, several large and important Hispanic groups (including Mexicans and Puerto Ricans) are exceptions to this pattern, and their prospects for future upward mobility are subject to much debate (Alba et al. 2011; Alba, Jimenez, and Marrow 2014; Alba, Kasinitz, and Waters 2011; Bean, Brown, and Bachmeier 2015; Haller, Portes, and Lynch 2011a,b; Park, Myers, and Jimenez 2014; Perlmann 2005, 2011; Portes 2006; Telles and Ortiz 2008).

Because of the measurement issues and data limitations that we have discussed, Mexican Americans in particular and Hispanic Americans in general probably have experienced significantly more socioeconomic progress beyond the second generation than available data indicate. Even so, because many Hispanic immigrants arrive in the United States with relatively low levels of human capital, it may take longer for their descendants to integrate fully into the American mainstream than it did for the descendants of the European immigrants who arrived near the turn of the twentieth century. Closing the remaining educational gap between Hispanics and other Americans should be a key component of any effort to hasten such integration.

Notes

1. In the discussion that follows, we will use the terms *first generation* and *immigrant* as synonymous with foreign-born individuals, in contrast to the official terminology used by the U.S. government in which immigrants are legal permanent residents, and *nonimmigrant aliens* are other foreigners such as tourists, business travelers, and recent refugee arrivals. The data analyzed here cannot make such distinctions among foreign-born individuals. In addition, individuals born in Puerto Rico and other outlying areas of the United States are included within our first-generation group. Persons born in Puerto Rico are U.S. citizens and enjoy unfettered mobility between the island and the U.S. mainland, and therefore Puerto Ricans are not, strictly speaking, a U.S. immigrant group. Nonetheless, island-born Puerto Ricans who move to the United States and their U.S.-born descendants encounter many of the same adjustment issues as conventional immigrant groups. Accordingly, the socioeconomic mobility of Puerto Ricans is often analyzed using models and methods developed to study U.S. immigrant groups (e.g., Feliciano 2001; Hirschman 2001).

2. The specific countries (e.g., Mexico) and regions (e.g., Europe) of origin identified in these tables collectively represent 88 percent of the first-generation individuals and 92 percent of the second-generation individuals in our samples. Second-generation individuals with parents born in different foreign countries have been assigned the national origins of their fathers. We follow Jaeger's (1997) recommendations for how to construct a completed years of schooling variable from the CPS information collected about postsecondary degrees obtained.

3. For third+-generation, non-Hispanic whites, the comparable measures for men are an average education level of 13.8 years, a high school dropout rate of 5.8 percent, and a college completion rate of 33.9 percent. The corresponding measures for women are 14.0 years, 4.5 percent, and 36.3 percent, respectively.

4. Similar patterns have been found by researchers employing a variety of different data sets and measures of educational attainment. See, for example, Rumbaut (2005) and Perreira, Harris, and Lee (2006).

5. Borjas (1994) and Card, DiNardo, and Estes (2000) provide detailed analyses of the transmission of human capital across immigrant generations for a large number of national origin groups over several decades. These studies confirm the strong relationships suggested by Figures 3.1 and 3.2.

6. Using answers to the questions regarding Hispanic origin and race, we assign each individual to one of five mutually exclusive and exhaustive racial/ethnic

groups: Hispanic (of any race), and non-Hispanic white, black, and Asian (including Native Hawaiian and Pacific Islander), and a residual "other race" category. Hispanics are disaggregated further by national origin group (Mexican, Puerto Rican, Cuban, Central/South American, or Other Hispanic). Starting in 2003, the CPS permits respondents to designate more than one race, similar to the 2000 and 2010 censuses and the American Community Survey (del Pinal 2004; Grieco and Cassidy 2001). The Hispanic origin question, however, still requires a single response. Our "other race" category includes any non-Hispanics who designated two or more major race groups, as well as those who identified with an "American Indian or Alaskan Native" group. Therefore, the non-Hispanic categories white, black, and Asian represent individuals who designated a single major race group. In the 2010 Census, only 2.3 percent of non-Hispanics designated more than one major race group (Humes, Jones, and Ramirez 2011). Consequently, our decision to include only those who report a single race in the white, black, and Asian race groups does not have much effect on the estimates.

7. CPS outgoing rotation group data do not report self-employment income.

8. To save space, the figures do not show the corresponding earnings differentials for Hispanic national origin groups besides Mexicans and Puerto Ricans (the two Hispanic groups with sizable third+ generations), for the "other race" group, and for first- and second-generation non-Hispanic whites.

9. For ease of exposition, we will refer to the estimated log earnings differentials as if they represented percentage earnings differences (after multiplying the log differentials by 100). Strictly speaking, however, log differentials closely approximate percentage differences only when the log differentials are on the order of 0.25 or less in absolute value. For larger differentials, the implied percentage difference can be calculated as $(e^c - 1) \times 100$, where c is the log differential and e is Euler's number (i.e., the base of natural logarithms).

10. Contrary to Huntington's thesis, however, available evidence suggests rapid linguistic assimilation for the U.S.-born descendants of contemporary immigrant groups (Alba et al. 2002). This holds even for Hispanics who live in areas with high concentrations of Spanish-speaking immigrants. In Southern California, for example, 96 percent of third-generation Mexicans prefer to speak English at home rather than Spanish, and only 17 percent of third-generation Mexicans retain the ability to speak fluent Spanish (Rumbaut, Massey, and Bean 2006).

11. In this context, Puerto Ricans constitute an interesting case study because they are U.S. citizens and automatically enjoy all of the associated legal rights, including the ability to migrate to and work in the United States. Therefore, issues pertaining to undocumented immigration cannot explain the incomplete socioeconomic integration of the U.S.-born descendants of migrants from Puerto Rico.

12. Table 3.3 focuses on Mexicans and Puerto Ricans because these are the Hispanic national origin groups with the largest U.S. populations of individuals beyond the second generation.

13. Even in this birth cohort, however, rates of attending and completing college for third-generation Mexicans are still substantially below those of non-Hispanic whites.

References

Alba, Richard D. 1990. *Ethnic Identity: The Transformation of White America.* New Haven, CT: Yale University Press.

————. 2006. "Mexican Americans and the American Dream." *Perspectives on Politics* 4(2): 289–296.

Alba, Richard D., Dalia Abdel-Hady, Tariqul Islam, and Karen Marotz. 2011. "Downward Assimilation and Mexican Americans: An Examination of Intergenerational Advance and Stagnation in Educational Attainment." In *The Next Generation: Immigrant Youth in a Comparative Perspective,* Richard Alba and Mary C. Waters, eds. New York: New York University Press, pp. 95–109.

Alba, Richard D., and Tariqul Islam. 2009. "The Case of the Disappearing Mexican Americans: An Ethnic-Identity Mystery." *Population Research and Policy Review* 28(2): 109–121.

Alba, Richard D., Tomás R. Jiménez, and Helen B. Marrow. 2014. "Mexican Americans as a Paradigm for Contemporary Intra-Group Heterogeneity." *Ethnic and Racial Studies* 37(3): 446–466.

Alba, Richard D., Philip Kasinitz, and Mary C. Waters. 2011. "The Kids Are (Mostly) Alright: Second Generation Assimilation; Comments on Haller, Portes and Lynch." *Social Forces* 89(3): 733–762.

Alba, Richard D., John Logan, Amy Lutz, and John Stults. 2002. "Only English by the Third Generation? Loss and Preservation of the Mother Tongue among the Grandchildren of Contemporary Immigrants." *Demography* 39(3): 467–484.

Alba, Richard D., and Victor Nee. 2003. *Rethinking the American Mainstream: Assimilation and Contemporary Immigration.* Cambridge, MA: Harvard University Press.

Autor, David, and Lawrence F. Katz. 1999. "Changes in the Wage Structure and Earnings Inequality." In *Handbook of Labor Economics,* Vol. 3A. Orley Ashenfelter and David Card, eds. Amsterdam: North Holland, pp. 1463–1555.

Autor, David, Lawrence F. Katz, and Melissa S. Kearney. 2008. "Trends in U.S. Wage Inequality: Revising the Revisionists." *Review of Economics and Statistics* 90(2): 300–323.

Bean, Frank D., Susan K. Brown, and James D. Bachmeier. 2015. *Parents without Papers: The Progress and Pitfalls of Mexican-American Integration.* New York: Russell Sage Foundation.

Bean, Frank D., Mark Leach, Susan K. Brown, James Bachmeier, and John Hipp. 2011. "The Educational Legacy of Unauthorized Migration: Comparisons across U.S.-Immigrant Groups in How Parents' Status Affects Their Offspring." *International Migration Review* 45(2): 348–385.

Betts, Julian R., and Magnus Lofstrom. 2000. "The Educational Attainment of Immigrants: Trends and Implications." In *Issues in the Economics of Immigration*, George J. Borjas, ed. Chicago: University of Chicago Press, pp. 51–115.

Blau, Francine D., and Lawrence M. Kahn. 2007. "Gender and Assimilation among Mexican Americans." In *Mexican Immigration to the United States*, George J. Borjas, ed. Chicago: University of Chicago Press, pp. 57–106.

Borjas, George J. 1993. "The Intergenerational Mobility of Immigrants." *Journal of Labor Economics* 11(1): 113–135.

———. 1994. "Long-Run Convergence of Ethnic Skill Differentials: The Children and Grandchildren of the Great Migration." *Industrial and Labor Relations Review* 47(4): 553–573.

———. 2006. "Making It in America: Social Mobility in the Immigrant Population." *Future of Children* 16(2): 55–71.

Bound, John, and Sarah Turner. 2014. "U.S. High-Skill Immigration." In *Diversity and Disparities: American Enters a New Century*, John Logan, ed. New York: Russell Sage Foundation.

Card, David. 2005. "Is the New Immigration Really So Bad?" *Economic Journal* 115(507): 300–323.

Card, David, John DiNardo, and Eugena Estes. 2000. "The More Things Change: Immigrants and the Children of Immigrants in the 1940s, the 1970s, and the 1990s." In *Issues in the Economics of Immigration*, George J. Borjas, ed. Chicago: University of Chicago Press, pp. 227–269.

Chiswick, Barry R. 1977. "Sons of Immigrants: Are They at an Earnings Disadvantage?" *American Economic Review* 67(1): 376–380.

del Pinal, Jorge H. 2004. *Race and Ethnicity in Census 2000*. Census 2000 Testing, Experimentation, and Evaluation Program: Topic Report No. 9. Washington, DC: U.S. Census Bureau.

Duncan, Brian, Leon Jeffrey Grogger, Ann Sofia Leon, and Stephen J. Trejo. 2017. "New Evidence of Generational Progress for Mexican Americans." Working Paper No. 24067. Cambridge, MA: National Bureau of Economic Research.

Duncan, Brian, V. Joseph Hotz, and Stephen J. Trejo. 2006. "Hispanics in the U.S. Labor Market." In *Hispanics and the Future of America*, Marta Tienda and Faith Mitchell, eds. Washington, DC: National Academies Press, pp. 228–290.

Duncan, Brian, and Stephen J. Trejo. 2007. "Ethnic Identification, Intermarriage, and Unmeasured Progress by Mexican Americans." In *Mexican*

Immigration to the United States, George J. Borjas, ed. Chicago: University of Chicago Press, pp. 227–269.

———. 2009. Ancestry versus Ethnicity: The Complexity and Selectivity of Mexican Identification in the United States." In *Research in Labor Economics*. Vol. 29, *Ethnicity and Labor Market Outcomes*, Amelie F. Constant, Konstantinos Tatsiramos, and Klaus F. Zimmerman, eds. Bingley, UK: Emerald Publishing, pp. 31–66.

———. 2011. "Intermarriage and the Intergenerational Transmission of Ethnic Identity and Human Capital for Mexican Americans." *Journal of Labor Economics* 29(2): 195–227.

———. 2017. "The Complexity of Immigrant Generations: Implications for Assessing the Socioeconomic Integration of Hispanics and Asians." *Industrial and Labor Relations Review* 70(5): 1146–1175.

Farley, Reynolds. 1990. "Blacks, Hispanics, and White Ethnic Groups: Are Blacks Uniquely Disadvantaged?" *American Economic Review* 80(2): 237–241.

Farley, Reynolds, and Richard Alba. 2002. "The New Second Generation in the United States." *International Migration Review* 36(3): 669–701.

Feliciano, Cynthia. 2001. "The Benefits of Biculturalism: Exposure to Immigrant Culture and Dropping Out of School among Asian and Latino Youths." *Social Science Quarterly* 82(4): 865–879.

Foley, Neil. 1997. *The White Scourge: Mexicans, Blacks and Poor Whites in Texas Cotton Culture*. Berkeley: University of California Press.

Gans, Herbert J. 1992. "Second-Generation Decline: Scenarios for the Economic and Ethnic Futures of the Post-1965 American Immigrants." *Ethnic and Racial Studies* 15(2): 173–192.

Goyette, Kimberly, and Yu Xie. 1999. "Educational Expectations of Asian American Youth: Determinants and Ethnic Differences." *Sociology of Education* 72(1): 22–36.

Grieco, Elizabeth M., and Rachel C. Cassidy. 2001. "Overview of Race and Hispanic Origin." Census 2000 Brief C2KBR/01-1. Washington, DC: U.S. Census Bureau.

Grogger, Jeffrey, and Stephen J. Trejo. 2002. *Falling Behind or Moving Up? The Intergenerational Progress of Mexican Americans*. San Francisco: Public Policy Institute of California.

Haller, William, Alejandro Portes, and Scott M. Lynch. 2011a. "Dreams Fulfilled, Dreams Shattered: Determinants of Segmented Assimilation in the Second Generation." *Social Forces* 89(3): 733–762.

———. 2011b. "On the Dangers of Rosy Lenses; Reply to Alba, Kasinitz, and Waters." *Social Forces* 89(3): 775–782.

Haveman, Robert, and Barbara Wolfe. 1994. *Succeeding Generations: On the Effects of Investments in Children*. New York: Russell Sage Foundation.

Hirschman, Charles. 2001 "The Educational Enrollment of Immigrant Youth: A Test of the Segmented-Assimilation Hypothesis." *Demography* 38(3): 317–336.

Hout, Michael. 2012. "Social and Economic Returns to College Education in the United States." *Annual Review of Sociology* 38: 379–400.

Humes, Karen R., Nicholas A. Jones, and Roberto R. Ramirez. 2011. "Overview of Race and Hispanic Origin: 2010." 2010 Census Brief C2010BR-02. Washington, DC: U.S. Census Bureau.

Huntington, Samuel P. 2004. *Who Are We? The Challenges to America's National Identity*. New York: Simon and Schuster.

Jaeger, David A. 1997. "Reconciling the Old and New Census Bureau Education Questions: Recommendations for Researchers." *Journal of Business and Economics Statistics* 15(3): 300–309.

Jones, Maldwyn A. 1960. *American Immigration*. Chicago: University of Chicago Press.

Lee, Jennifer, and Frank D. Bean. 2010. *The Diversity Paradox: Immigration and the Color Line in 21st Century America*. New York: Russell Sage Foundation.

Levy, Frank, and Richard J. Murnane. 1992. "U.S. Earnings Levels and Earnings Inequality: A Review of Recent Trends and Proposed Explanations." *Journal of Economic Literature* 30(3): 1333–1381.

Lieberson, Stanley, and Mary C. Waters. 1988. *From Many Strands: Ethnic and Racial Groups in Contemporary America*. New York: Russell Sage Foundation.

Montejano, David. 1987. *Anglos and Mexicans in the Making of Texas: 1836–1986*. Austin, TX: University of Texas Press.

Mulligan, Casey B. 1997. *Parental Priorities and Economic Inequality*. Chicago: University of Chicago Press.

Murnane, Richard J. 2013. "U.S. High School Graduation Rates: Patterns and Explanations." *Journal of Economic Literature* 51(2): 370–422.

Neidert, Lisa J., and Reynolds Farley. 1985. "Assimilation in the United States: An Analysis of Ethnic and Generation Differences in Status and Achievement." *American Sociological Review* 50(6): 840–850.

Park, Julie, Dowell Myers, and Tomas R. Jimenez. 2014. "Intergenerational Mobility of the Mexican-Origin Population in California and Texas Relative to a Changing Regional Mainstream." *International Migration Review* 48(2): 442–481.

Perlmann, Joel. 2005. *Italians Then, Mexicans Now: Immigrant Origins and Second-Generation Progress, 1890–2000*. New York: Russell Sage Foundation.

———. 2011. "The Mexican American Second Generation in Census 2000: Education and Earnings." In *The Next Generation: Immigrant Youth in a Comparative Perspective*, Richard Alba and Mary C. Waters, eds. New York: New York University Press, pp. 69–94.

Perlmann, Joel, and Roger Waldinger. 1996. "The Second Generation and the Children of the Native Born: Comparisons and Refinements." Working Paper No. 174. Annandale-on-Hudson, NY: Jerome Levy Economics Institute.

———. 1997. "Second Generation Decline? Children of Immigrants, Past and Present—A Reconsideration." *International Migration Review* 31(4): 893–922.

Perlmann, Joel, and Mary C. Waters. 2007. "Intermarriage and Multiple Identities." In *The New Americans: A Guide to Immigration Since 1965*, Mary C. Waters and Reed Udea, eds. Cambridge, MA: Harvard University Press, pp. 110–123.

Perreira, Krista A., Kathleen Mullan Harris, and Dohoon Lee. 2006. "Making It in America: High School Completion by Immigrant and Native Youth." *Demography* 43(3): 511–536.

Pettit, Becky. 2012. *Invisible Men: Mass Incarceration and the Myth of Black Progress*. New York: Russell Sage Foundation.

Portes, Alejandro. 2006. "Review Essay: Paths of Assimilation in the Second Generation." *Sociological Forum* 21(3): 499–504.

Portes, Alejandro, and Ruben G. Rumbaut. 2001. *Legacies: The Story of the Immigrant Second Generation*. Berkeley: University of California Press.

Portes, Alejandro, and Min Zhou. 1993. "The New Second Generation: Segmented Assimilation and Its Variants among Post-1965 Immigrant Youth." *Annals of the American Academy of Political and Social Science* 530: 74–96.

Rong, Xue Lan, and Linda Grant. 1992. "Ethnicity, Generation, and School Attainment of Asians, Hispanics, and Non-Hispanic Whites." *Sociological Quarterly* 33(4): 625–636.

Rumbaut, Ruben G. 1994. "The Crucible Within: Ethnic Identity, Self-Esteem, and Segmented Assimilation among Children of Immigrants." *International Migration Review* 28(4): 748–794.

———. 2005. "Turning Points in the Transition to Adulthood: Determinants of Educational Attainment, Incarceration, and Early Childbearing Among Children of Immigrants." *Ethnic and Racial Studies* 28(6): 1041–1286.

Rumbaut, Rugen G., Douglas S. Massey, and Frank D. Bean. 2006. "Linguistic Life Expectancies: Immigrant Language Retention in the Southern California." *Population and Development Review* 32(3): 447–460.

Saenz, Rogelio. 2005. "Latinos and the Changing Face of America." In *The*

American People: Census 2000. Reynolds Farley and John Haaga, eds. New York: Russell Sage Foundation, pp. 352–379.

Sakamoto, Arthur, Kimberly A. Goyette, and Chang Hwan Kim. 2009. "Socio-economic Attainments of Asian Americans." *Annual Review of Sociology* 35: 255–276.

Sakamoto, Arthur, Huei-Hsia Wu, and Jessie M. Tzeng. 2000. "The Declining Significance of Race among American Men during the Latter Half of the Twentieth Century." *Demography* 37(1): 41–51.

Smith, James P. 2003. "Assimilation across the Latino Generations." *American Economic Review* 93(2): 315–319.

———. 2006. "Immigrants and the Labor Market." *Journal of Labor Economics* 24(2): 203–233.

Snipp, C. Matthew, and Charles Hirschman. 2004. "Assimilation in American Society: Occupational Achievement and Earnings for Ethnic Minorities in the United States, 1970 to 1990." *Research in Social Stratification and Mobility* 22: 93–117.

Telles, Edward E., and Vilma Ortiz. 2008. *Generations of Exclusion: Mexican Americans, Assimilation, and Race*. New York: Russell Sage Foundation.

Trejo, Stephen J. 1997. "Why Do Mexican Americans Earn Low Wages?" *Journal of Political Economy* 105(6): 1235–1268.

———. 2003. "Intergenerational Progress of Mexican-Origin Workers in the U.S. Labor Market." *Journal of Human Resources* 38(3): 467–489.

Waters, Mary C. 1990. *Ethnic Options: Choosing Identities in America*. Berkeley: University of California Press.

Yang, Philip Q. 2004. "Generational Differences in Educational Attainment among Asian Americans." *Journal of Asian American Studies* 7(1): 51–71.

Zeng, Zhen, and Xie, Yu. 2004. "Asian-Americans' Earnings Disadvantage Reexamined: The Role of Place of Education." *American Journal of Sociology* 109(5): 1075–1108.

4
Immigrants and Poverty

How Do They Cope with It,
How Do They Affect Natives?

Giovanni Peri
University of California, Davis

The most important predictors of poverty status for a household are the main demographic and schooling characteristics of its members, particularly the breadwinner within it. Individuals without a high school diploma, especially if they are young and single parents, are much more likely to be in poverty relative to more educated, older, and married heads of household. A large share of the first group (about 25 percent as of 2014) is foreign-born (vis-à-vis around 13 percent of immigrants in the overall population); this implies that an important fraction of immigrants belongs to a demographic group at high risk of poverty. However, does their immigrant status affect their income, their probability of working, and their probability of being in poverty relative to similarly educated natives? And given the high risk of poverty associated with low schooling levels, are immigrant households participating in social welfare programs (Temporary Assistance for Needy Families [TANF], Medicaid, Supplemental Nutrition Assistance [SNAP], Supplemental Security Income [SSI], and others) at a higher or lower rate than similar natives? Are they more likely or less likely to work, and what share of their income is wage income?

In this chapter I first describe how immigration is related to poverty levels in the United States, mainly because some large groups of immigrants—namely, Mexican and Central Americans—are at high risk of poverty due to their education and demographic characteristics. Overall, immigration to the United States is rather balanced between the more and less educated, and a significant share of immigrants (about 33 percent in 2014) is college-educated and holds high-paying jobs. However, immigrants from Mexico and Central America constitute a large part of the group of young individuals without a high school diploma; hence, they are at high risk of poverty. I show how these immigrant households at high risk of poverty (i.e., with a less-educated head of household) differ from native households at similar levels of income in their economic and social characteristics. In particular, I show how immigrants' employment rates and their reliance on wages are much higher than natives'. There is some evidence that in recent decades these immigrants have been penalized more severely during periods of recessions and high unemployment, and their incomes have been more strongly affected by the slow growth of the median wage in the U.S. economy. I also show their participation in welfare and social assistance programs, even those for which they or their children are eligible, is significantly lower than natives'. After measuring these differences for the 2000–2014 period, I review the potential explanations for low participation in welfare programs related to eligibility, lack of information, reliance on wage income, and fear of enforcement.

Given the high participation of immigrants in the labor market, I analyze whether competition between immigrants and low-skilled natives may be a source of decline in the labor income of the less educated, indirectly affecting their poverty status. I review recent studies on this topic and conclude there is not much evidence of negative labor market effects of immigrants. Namely, the presence of immigrants does not seem to deteriorate the employment and wage prospects of less-skilled natives. This is likely because their presence attracts investment and induces adjustment in specialization, technology, and efficiency at the local level. These are all channels that can spur growth and, especially in the long run, benefit natives. Another relevant role of immigrants in local economies has been that of absorbing temporary shocks as they respond faster—and in larger numbers—to changes in employment opportunities and are more willing to move across labor markets. The presence of immigrants, even at low skill levels, is associated with booming economies and contributes to generate thick and differentiated labor markets that are attractive to firms.

The low rate of participation in welfare programs among immigrants (and their children) in general, and of undocumented immigrants in particular, and the existing evidence that they move in response to labor demand rather than to utilize welfare programs, implies that immigrants likely do not crowd out natives from welfare. However, a very important aspect in which immigration can generate concerns for lower-income natives' access to local public goods, and for their ability to assimilate, is the potential of crowding public schools. I will review several strands of research suggesting that, on one hand, large inflows of non-English-speaking low-income families into a school district may generate a significant outflow of native families and a deterioration of the average school quality in the area. On the other hand, existing research emphasizes that the assimilation and convergence of second-generation immigrants crucially depends on the level and quality of schooling. Hence, investment in schooling, such as expanding capacity and school programs in areas that receive large inflows of low-income immigrants, can be a crucial component for the economic success of these areas and of the immigrants' children in the medium and long run.

To identify the most effective policies, it is crucial to consider these different aspects and the multifaceted connections between immigration and poverty. Recognizing, for instance, that earnings have a crucial role in immigrants' income emphasizes the important connection between labor market access and immigrants' ability to stay out of poverty. Immigration policies affecting their legal status (regularization, legalization, temporary visa status) and labor policies affecting their access to some occupations (e.g., licensing) are likely to be very important as they restrict or broaden the ability of immigrants to work. Similarly, policies that support the wage income of the low skilled without penalizing their employment opportunities (e.g., minimum wage provisions) are likely to have important consequences on the immigrant households' ability to stay out of poverty.

At the same time, immigrants' limited reliance on welfare (even when eligible) generates the challenge of understanding the reasons behind this and addressing the issue by increasing accessibility and participation. Certainly, the precarious "undocumented" status of a large share of low-skilled immigrants and the fear (and uncertainty) of enforcement seems to be one of the reasons. These immigrants can be afraid and do not come out of the shadows even to claim the welfare benefits for which their (usually U.S.-born) children qualify. At the same time, such low participation implies that some policies related to scaling up these programs will be less effective for immigrants than natives. To the extent that those policies affect immigrants' health status, early childhood development, and ability to go to school, such low participation can be a hurdle for future assimilation and economic success of second-generation immigrants from low-income families. Policies that improve access to schooling for young undocumented immigrants, and policies that open the possibility of regularization (such as the DREAM Act), can have a significant antipoverty effect on the second generation. At the same time, the strain on school districts from an inflow of low English proficiency kids and the risk that native children leave or experience a reduction in the quality of their education is real and should be tackled by investing the increased economic revenue created by immigrants—and by companies that employ them—into expanding school capacity, enriching programs, and increasing the number of teachers.

This chapter begins by describing the evolution of employment, welfare participation, and wage income for immigrants at high risk of poverty during the 2000—2014 period. In the first section I point out the key features and differences between natives and immigrants and review the recent trends in their employment, wages, and welfare income relative to similar natives. I also identify, using regression analysis, the differences in employment probability and income between immigrants and natives after controlling for observables. This section also focuses on the effects of recession on immigrants and on explaining why immigrants are less likely to enroll in welfare programs relative to natives. I then discuss the existing literature on the impact of low-skilled immigrants on labor markets and the likely mechanisms connecting immigration to local economic success and their link with the income and employment opportunities of low-skilled natives. A large part of the evidence in this area is that immigrants expand local labor markets and the local economies with no negative effects, especially in the long run, on natives' labor market opportunities. After that, I analyze the impact of immigration on local schooling quality and on natives' attendance, and the role of schooling in allowing second-generation immigrants to integrate and to succeed economically. I then use the important findings from the research literature to inform important policy ideas. Which labor market and schooling policies are more relevant to improving the economic outcomes of communities with large inflow of immigrants who are at risk of poverty? Which policies can turn the challenges from these inflows into opportunities for growth and employment? The specific characteristics of immigrant families and communities should help design the appropriate policies.

IMMIGRANTS, POVERTY, EMPLOYMENT, AND WELFARE

The most basic statistics providing an assessment of the nexus between immigration and poverty is the poverty rate (percent of households below poverty line) for natives, Mexican-Central American (MCA) immigrants, and other immigrants 18 years and older. Such statistics for years 2000–2014 are shown in Figure 4.1, Panel A. Figure 4.1, Panel B shows the average real yearly wage for each of those three groups in the same period. Both charts reveal that MCA immigrants are, on average, poorer than natives and have lower wage income.[1] Other immigrants, in turn, have very similar poverty rates and higher average wage income relative to the native population.

These aggregate statistics, however, reflect more than anything else the composition of each group in terms of education. Schooling is very strongly associated with income and, as the schooling levels of MCA immigrants are significantly lower than natives (and, in particular, the share of high school dropouts among them is much larger), it is the education composition that explains the higher risk of poverty and lower mean wage of MCA immigrants. Other immigrants have higher average schooling relative to natives, and this is reflected in their higher wage income.[2]

Hence, going beyond this composition-driven difference, the comparison changes drastically if one considers wage income and poverty rates only for the groups at highest risk of poverty, represented by adults (18 or older) with no high school diploma. The percentage in poverty and the average wage income (in 1999 constant $) for that group are shown in Figure 4.2, Panels A and B, respectively. The poverty rate of MCA immigrants in this group is comparable to that of natives. In fact, it is lower than natives in the expansionary years of 2005–2008 and then after 2012. Similarly, poverty rates for other immigrants in this group are lower than for natives and are more subject to economic fluctuations. As for average yearly wage income, its value was significantly higher in this group for MCA immigrants than for natives (with other immigrants in between). Low-educated MCA immigrants earned an average wage income close to $12,000 per year in 2014, while low-educated natives earned close to $6,500. This substantial difference is

Figure 4.1 Poverty Rates and Average Wages in the Adult Population

Panel A: Poverty Rate, by Nativity, 2000–2014 (heads of household 18+)

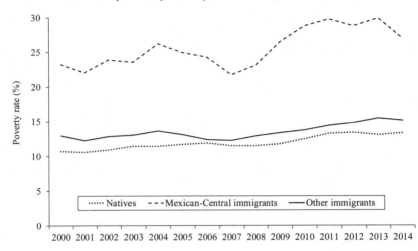

Panel B: Average Wage, by Nativity, 2000–2014 (heads of household aged 18+)

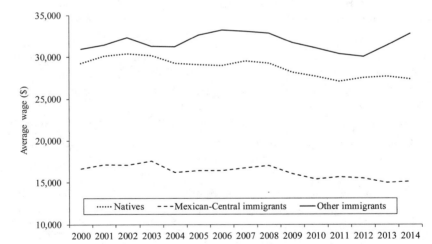

NOTE: Nativity is defined based on place of birth. Poverty rate is defined as the percentage of heads of households with family income below the federal poverty threshold. Wages are calculated for employed persons and are defined as wages and benefits earned in the previous 12 months.

SOURCE: Author's calculations using data from the ASEC sample of the CPS using heads of household aged 18 years and older.

Figure 4.2 Poverty Rates and Average Wage in the Adult Population with No High School Diploma

Panel A: Poverty Rate by Nativity, 2000–2014 (heads of household 18+)

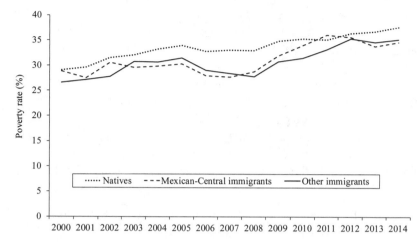

Panel B: Average Wage, by Nativity, 2000–2014 (heads of household aged 18+)

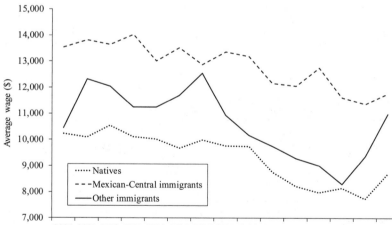

NOTE: Nativity is defined based on place of birth. Poverty rate is defined as the percentage of heads of households with family income below the federal poverty threshold. Wages are calculated for employed persons and are defined as wages and benefits earned in the previous 12 months.

SOURCE: Author's calculations using data from the ASEC sample of the CPS using heads of household aged 18 years and older with less than a high school diploma.

determined by the much larger employment rate of MCA immigrants in this group. Figure 4.3 shows the stunning difference in the employment/population ratio—for heads of households—in the group with no high school diploma between MCA immigrants, other immigrants, and natives. While this ratio was around 0.7 for MCA immigrants, with some increase in the 2004—2008 period and decline during the great recession, the ratio for natives was 0.38 in 2000 and only about 0.33 in 2014.

This extremely high employment rate of MCA immigrants among the low skilled was already noted by Duncan and Trejo (2012) and, as I will show below, persists after the inclusion of several individual controls and cannot be explained by location of immigrants or by their individual characteristics. Low-skilled MCA immigrants work at much higher rates than natives, and although they get paid somewhat less than

Figure 4.3 Employment/Population Ratio, by Nativity, 2000–2014 (heads of household aged 18+, no high school diploma)

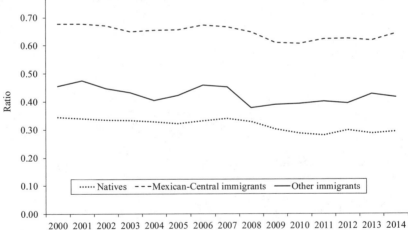

NOTE: Nativity is defined based on place of birth. Employed persons are persons at work or not at work, but with a job, in the last week. Population is the population of heads of household aged 18 years and older.

SOURCE: Author's calculations using data from the ASEC sample of the CPS using heads of household aged 18 years and older with less than a high school diploma.

natives per hour worked, their wage incomes are significantly higher because they work more hours per day and more weeks per year.

How is it, then, that in spite of this much better performance on the labor market, MCA immigrants with no diploma have roughly the same probability of being in poverty as natives with no high school diploma? The answer is their significantly lower participation in welfare programs and the significantly smaller income they draw from welfare sources. Figure 4.4 shows the share of total income from wages for households whose head has no high school diploma (and is 18 years or older). For MCA immigrants, this percentage was between 80 and 90 percent of their household income in 2000–2014. For natives, however, it was only 60–70 percent, and for other immigrants it represented about 70 percent of their household income. The remaining part of income, once

Figure 4.4 Share of Income from Wages, by Nativity, 2000–2014
(heads of household aged 18+, no high school diploma)

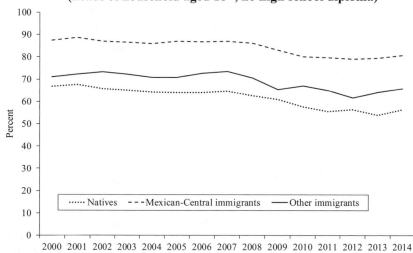

NOTE: Nativity is defined based on place of birth. Wages are defined as wages and benefits earned in the previous 12 months. Total income includes income from wages and benefits, business and farm earnings, welfare (public assistance), disability, SSI, worker's compensation, unemployment insurance, veteran's benefits, child support, and alimony.

SOURCE: Author's calculations using data from the ASEC sample of the CPS using employed heads of household aged 18 years and older with less than a high school diploma.

wages are accounted for, is essentially the sum of payments from welfare programs; namely, SNAP, SSI, TANF, Unemployment Insurance,
Disability Insurance, Veteran Compensation, and a few others. Hence,
implicitly, Figure 4.4 shows that native households with a low-skilled
head rely on public assistance for more than 30 percent of their yearly
income. To the contrary, MCA immigrant households with a similarly
educated head receive only 10–15 percent of their income from welfare
programs.

It is instructive to see whether MCA-immigrant-headed households
with low levels of education differ from "similar" native households in
other characteristics. The reason for their lower reliance on some social
security programs (several of which may be targeting children) could
be driven by the smaller household size. Figure 4.5, Panel A, shows the
share of families headed by a single parent among the less educated.
One sees a similar percentage between natives and MCA immigrants,
with the percentage of single parents increasing in MCA families in
the post-2007 period. The return of one parent to Mexico or the much
smaller inflow of two-parent families after the recession 2007–2009
may be the reason for this trend. In any case, the difference between
MCA and native households in this respect is rather small and unlikely
to explain the differential in welfare income dependence. At the same
time, MCA families tend to be larger relative to native families. Panel B
of Figure 4.5 shows that low-skilled MCA households include 1.5 children on average versus only 0.5 for the native households. This larger
family size may also be a reason for the similar poverty rates, in spite
of the much larger wage and employment rates of MCA. It certainly
makes the low participation in some welfare programs even more puz-
zling. The higher fertility rates of immigrant families in general, and
Mexicans in particular, is a well-known phenomenon that is changing
the demographic features of the United States. Children in low-skilled
families grow up in highly welfare-dependent households if they are
U.S. natives, and programs such as SNAP and Medicaid may be crucial
to providing access to food and health care. To the contrary, if they are
Mexican immigrants, they grow up in poor working families, and fluctuations of the U.S. business cycle will affect their ability to access food
and health care much more significantly.

Figure 4.6 shows the reliance on income from several welfare programs, constituting the bulk of the assistance to poor families in the

Figure 4.5 Family Structure of Households Whose Head Has No High School Diploma

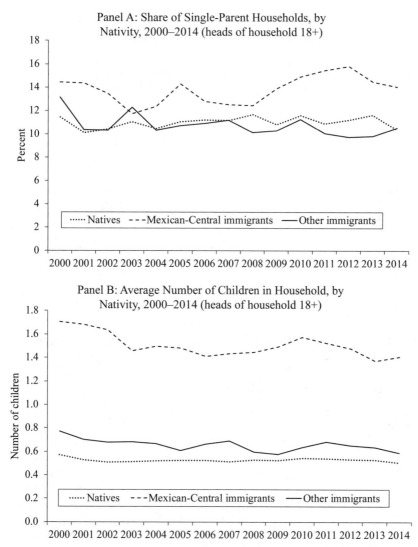

Panel A: Share of Single-Parent Households, by Nativity, 2000–2014 (heads of household 18+)

Panel B: Average Number of Children in Household, by Nativity, 2000–2014 (heads of household 18+)

NOTE: Nativity is defined based on place of birth. A "single-parent household" is defined as a household with children and only one parent living in the household. The average number of children per household by nativity is calculated as the total number of persons under 18 living in households divided by the total number of persons living in households for each nativity group.

SOURCE: Author's calculations using data from the ASEC sample of the CPS using households headed by a person with less than a high school diploma.

**Figure 4.6   Share of Total Household Income from Public
             Assistance Programs**

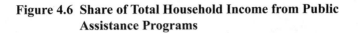

Panel A: Share of Total Income from Disability, by Nativity, 2000–2014
(heads of household aged 18+, no high school diploma)

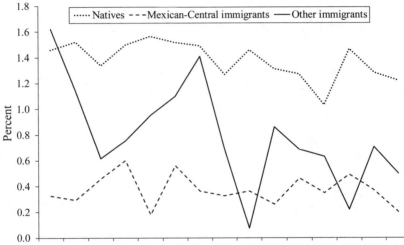

Panel B: Share of Total Income from Food Stamps, by Nativity, 2000–2014
(heads of household aged 18+, no high school diploma)

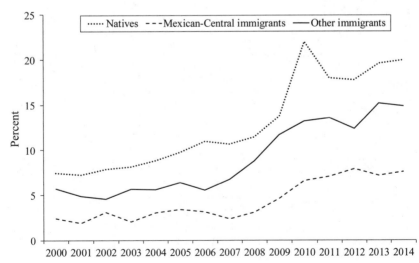

Panel C: Share of Total Income from Unemployment Insurance,
Workers' Compensation, and Veterans' Benefits, by Nativity, 2000–2014
(heads of household aged 18+, no high school diploma)

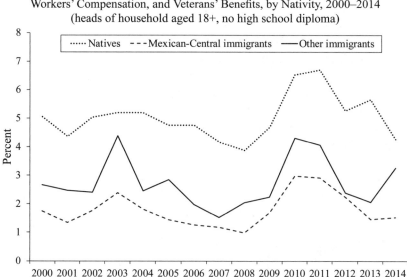

Panel D: Share of Total Income from Supplemental Security Income, by Nativity,
2000–2014 (heads of household aged 18+, no high school diploma)

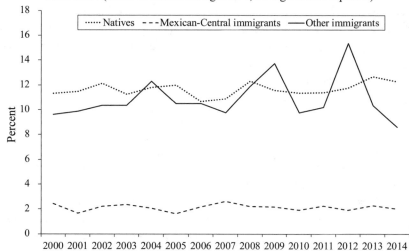

NOTE: Nativity is defined based on place of birth. Total income includes income from wages
and benefits, business and farm earnings, welfare (public assistance), disability, SSI, worker's
compensation, unemployment insurance, veterans' benefits, child support, and alimony. Total
household income is the sum of total income for each individual aged 18 years and older plus the
value of food stamps received by the household.
SOURCE: Author's calculations using data from the ASEC sample of the CPS using employed
heads of household aged 18 years and older with less than a high school diploma.

United States. It indicates the income (or income equivalent) obtained from that specific program by the household as a percentage of their total income. Natives rely on each of the considered programs, as share of income, more than MCA immigrants. Even for programs whose cash equivalent increases with the number of children (such as SNAP), in spite of the larger number of children per family, immigrant households receive less as a share of their income relative to natives.

Differences in Employment Rate and Reliance on Welfare: Regression Analysis

The summary statistics shown above describe different economic characteristics/behavior of low-skilled MCA immigrants relative to natives. MCA immigrants are more likely to work and to receive wage income, which in turn constitutes a much larger share of their total income. On the other hand, they are less likely to receive welfare income from SSI, Disability Insurance, SNAP, UI, and other welfare sources. In this section I confirm that a large portion of this difference is due neither to observable characteristics of immigrants' households, such as their age, family structure, or number of children, nor to the state where they live and its economic conditions. In fact, a large and significant fraction of higher employment rates of low-skilled immigrants and their higher reliance on wages and lower reliance on welfare income survives the inclusion of individual and state-specific controls in a regression analysis. To show this, I estimate the following regression:

$$(4.1) \quad y_{ist} = \alpha_0 T_t + \alpha_1 X_{ist} + \alpha_2 D_{st} + \beta_M (\text{MCA})_{ist} + \beta_O (\text{OTH})_{ist} + \varepsilon_{ist}$$

The variable captures alternative outcomes for individual i in state s at time t. It will alternatively be a dummy for being employed in the reference week, or the number of weeks worked in a year, or the probability of being in poverty or the logarithm of wage or the share of income from wages and from other welfare sources. The term T_t is a year fixed effect and is included in all regressions. The term X_{it} is a set of individual controls including age dummies, a dummy for being married, and dummies for the number of children in the household (omitting 0 children). The term D_{st} represents a set of state-by-year effects that absorb the local economic conditions relative to a state in a specific year. They account for the differential location of immigrants and natives and for their relative economic conditions in those states. Finally, $(MCA)_{ist}$ is a variable equal to one if individual i is a MCA-born immigrant and zero otherwise and $(OTH)_{ist}$ is a variable equal to one if the individual is a foreign born not from Mexico or Central America. The variable ε_{ist} is an idiosyncratic zero-mean error. The period considered for this regression is 2000–2014. In specifications that analyze the different sources of household income, I include only the heads of households. Alternatively, in specifications analyzing the labor market outcomes of individuals, I include the whole adult population with no high school diploma.

The estimates on the coefficients β_M and β_O capture the difference in outcome between natives (the omitted category) and each type of immigrant once I control for the covariates. By progressively including more controls relative to the individual and to the state-year economy, I can isolate differences that are associated genuinely with the nativity characteristics of people (such as different language spoken and immigration status) rather than with other observable characteristics.

Table 4.1 shows the estimates of the coefficients β_M and β_O when considering the employment rate—a dummy for being employed in the reference week (Panel A) or the number of weeks worked (Panel B) as dependent variables. Table 4.2 shows those estimates when the dependent variable is the probability of being in poverty (Panel A) and, conditional on working, the log of yearly wages (Panel B). The first column of each table reports the estimates from a specification on heads of household including only the time dummies as controls. Column (2) includes the individual controls, Column (3) adds state-by-year fixed effects, and Columns (4)–(6) show coefficients on the same specifications but include all individuals with no diploma rather than only head of households.

The findings are clear and consistent. When estimating the employment rate for household heads, Column (1) finds a higher probability of working for low-skilled MCA immigrants relative to low-skilled U.S. natives by 33 percentage points. More than half of this difference can be attributed to different characteristics and location, but a full 14 percentage point difference remains after controlling for individual variables and state-year dummies (Column [3]), and it is highly statistically significant. Similarly, after controlling for individual and state-year effects, MCA immigrants worked 6.8 extra weeks in each year relative

Table 4.1 Unskilled Immigrant-Native Differential in Employment and Weeks Worked

Specifications	Sample: Head of households, no diploma			Sample: Adults, no diploma		
	(1) Only year effects	(2) Individual controls	(3) State-year FE + Individual	(4) Only year effects	(5) Individual controls	(6) State-year FE and Individual
Panel A: Independent variable: Dummy "employed"						
MCA immigrants	0.330***	0.132***	0.137***	0.281***	0.137***	0.147***
	(0.00342)	(0.00358)	(0.00398)	(0.00234)	(0.00246)	(0.00273)
Other immigrants	0.105***	0.0722***	0.0813***	0.0633***	0.0553***	0.0621***
	(0.00522)	(0.00440)	(0.00469)	(0.00346)	(0.00304)	(0.00323)
Individual controls	No	Yes	Yes	No	Yes	Yes
State-by-year fixed effect	No	No	Yes	No	No	Yes
Observations	150,818	150,818	150,818	318,867	318,867	318,867
Panel B: Independent variable: weeks worked last year						
MCA immigrants	16.87***	6.561***	6.867***	14.32***	6.679***	7.195***
	(0.166)	(0.171)	(0.191)	(0.113)	(0.119)	(0.132)
Other immigrants	4.984***	3.246***	3.634***	3.196***	2.409***	2.639***
	(0.260)	(0.218)	(0.233)	(0.171)	(0.149)	(0.158)
Individual controls	No	Yes	Yes	No	Yes	Yes
State-by-year fixed effect	No	No	Yes	No	No	Yes
Observations	150,818	150,818	150,818	318,867	318,867	318,867

NOTE: *** significant at the 99% confidence level. Individuals age 18 and older, no high school diploma. The reported coefficients and standard errors (in parentheses) are obtained from OLS regressions as Equation (4.1) in the text. Each column/panel reports coefficients from a different regression. Columns 1–3 include only head of households with no high school diploma in the sample. Columns 4–6 include all adults with no diploma. The dependent variable is listed at the top of the panel, the explanatory variable is in the first column. The observations are pooled individuals resident in the United States, from the March CPS over the years 2000–2014. Each regression includes year fixed effects.
SOURCE: Author's calculations using CPS data.

to natives, and conditional on working, they earn a 5 percent higher yearly wage because of their longer working period per year rather than higher hourly wage. Panel A of Table 4.2 shows that, after controlling for location and individual characteristics, the low-skilled MCA immigrants were about as likely to be in poverty as U.S.-born individuals. Other immigrants (dummy OTH) show differences relative to natives in the same direction, but smaller than MCA ones for most of these variables. They are 8 percent more likely to be employed than natives, work 3.6 more weeks per year, and their wages, conditional on working, are 10 percent higher than natives. The results obtained including all adult individuals (not just household heads) are comparable in that they show similar differences in employment rates and weeks worked between MCA immigrants and natives and somewhat larger differences (in favor of MCA immigrants) in wages.

Despite the better labor market performance relative to natives, low-skilled MCA immigrants are not much less likely to be in poverty than low-skilled natives (see Table 4.2, Panel A). The reason for this is shown in Table 4.3, which shows the regression estimates for the immigrant-native differential (i.e., β_M and β_O) when the dependent variables are the share of household income from wages (Panel A), the share from SSI (Panel B), the share from SNAP (Panel C), and the share from UI, Workers' Compensation, and veterans' benefits (Panel D). As usual, the three columns include progressively more controls, starting with time dummies only, then adding individual, and then state-year controls. I only include household heads in this regression because the unit of analysis is a household. Focusing on the columns that include all controls, namely (3) and (6), one can see that for low-skilled MCA immigrant households, wages account for 13 percent more of their total income than for the similar low-skilled native household. This difference is almost completely accounted for by the higher welfare program participation of natives. Natives have 4 percent higher incomes from SSI, 4.3 percent higher income contribution of SNAP, and 1.6 percent higher income contribution from UI and Workers' Compensation. If immigrants, all else equal, used welfare at a rate similar to that of natives, their total incomes would be significantly higher and their poverty rate lower.

The regressions that I estimated cannot rule out the differences between immigrants and natives in labor market behavior and reliance

Table 4.2 Unskilled Immigrant-Native Differential in Poverty Rates and Wages

	Sample: Head of households, no diploma			Sample: Adults, no diploma		
	(1)	(2)	(3)	(4)	(5)	(6)
Specifications	Only year effects	Individual controls	State-year FE and individual	Only year effects	Individual controls	State-year FE and individual
	Panel A: Independent variable: Dummy "poverty"					
MCA immigrants	0.0106***	−0.0151***	−0.0043	0.0268***	−0.00119	0.0142***
	(0.00335)	(0.00348)	(0.00395)	(0.00218)	(0.00232)	(0.00259)
Other immigrants	−0.00864*	0.00740	0.0222***	−0.0149***	−0.00558*	0.00698**
	(0.00487)	(0.00474)	(0.00505)	(0.00305)	(0.00302)	(0.00320)
Individual controls	No	Yes	Yes	No	Yes	Yes
State-by-year fixed effect	No	No	Yes	No	No	Yes
Observations	150,818	150,818	150,818	318,867	318,867	318,867
	Panel B: Independent variable: ln(yearly wages)					
MCA immigrants	0.215***	0.0809***	0.0501***	0.341***	0.150***	0.144***
	(0.00818)	(0.00840)	(0.00986)	(0.00676)	(0.00676)	(0.00779)
Other immigrants	0.215***	0.157***	0.0990***	0.301***	0.0776***	0.0414***
	(0.0140)	(0.0137)	(0.0151)	(0.0112)	(0.0108)	(0.0118)
Individual controls	No	Yes	Yes	No	Yes	Yes
State-by-year fixed effect	No	No	Yes	No	No	Yes
Observations	94,793	94,793	94,793	146,712	146,712	146,712

NOTE: *** indicates significance at the 99% confidence level. Individuals age 18 and older, no high school diploma. The reported coefficients and standard errors (in parentheses) are obtained from OLS regressions as Equation (4.1) in the text. Each column/panel reports coefficients from a different regression. Columns 1–3 include only head of households with no high school diploma in the sample. Columns 4–6 include all adults with no diploma. The dependent variable is listed at the top of the panel, the explanatory variable is in the first column. The observations are pooled individuals residing in the United States, from the March CPS, over the years 2000–2014. Each regression includes year fixed effects.
SOURCE: Author's calculations using CPS data.

Table 4.3 Unskilled Immigrant-Native Differential in Wage and Welfare Dependence

Specifications	(1) Only year effects	(2) Individual controls	(3) State-year FE and individual	(4) Only year effects	(5) Individual controls	(6) State-year FE and individual
	Panel A: Dependent variable is wages as % of household income			Panel B: Dependent variable is SSI as % of total household income		
MCA immigrants	21.26***	13.36***	13.44***	−8.923***	−3.246***	−4.327***
	(0.279)	(0.288)	(0.338)	(0.152)	(0.151)	(0.192)
Other immigrants	6.340***	4.876***	5.289***	−0.323	0.559*	0.0799
	(0.539)	(0.517)	(0.560)	(0.340)	(0.322)	(0.351)
Individual controls	No	Yes	Yes	No	Yes	Yes
State-by-year fixed effect	No	No	Yes	No	No	Yes
Observations	120,334	120,334	120,334	120,334	120,334	120,334
	Panel C: Dependent variable is SNAP as % of total household Income			Panel D: Dependent variable is UI, WC, and Vet as % of total household income		
MCA immigrants	−7.509***	−6.169***	−4.377***	−3.088***	−1.529***	−1.656***
	(0.175)	(0.191)	(0.197)	(0.0985)	(0.0878)	(0.114)
Other immigrants	−2.855***	−2.121***	−1.774***	−2.355***	−2.372***	−2.593***
	(0.302)	(0.299)	(0.314)	(0.161)	(0.164)	(0.186)
Individual controls	No	Yes	Yes	No	Yes	Yes
State-by-year fixed effect	No	No	Yes	No	No	Yes
Observations	120,334	120,334	120,334	120,334	120,334	120,334

NOTE: *** significant at the 99% confidence level. Households whose head is 18 and older, has no high school diploma. The reported coefficients and standard errors (in parentheses) are obtained from OLS regressions as Equation (4.1) in the text. Each column/panel reports coefficients from a different regression. The dependent variable is listed at the top of the panel, the explanatory variable is in the first column. The observations are pooled individuals resident in the United States, from the March CPS, over the years 2000–2014. Each regression includes year fixed effects.
SOURCE: Author's calculations using CPS data.

on welfare are due to unobservable characteristics of immigrants possibly related to their skills and attitudes. Nevertheless, I will discuss research findings that suggest that immigration status—undocumented, especially—and their limited familiarity with these programs may play an important role in reducing their participation.

The Impact of Recessions/Expansions on Wage and Employment of Immigrants

The larger probability of working for low-skilled MCA immigrants and their stronger reliance on wage income, as well as their lower participation in welfare programs, should imply that economic recessions are more painful for that group. Relative to similarly educated natives, the income and economic well-being of MCA immigrants is more dependent on the state of the economy, and these changes affect their economic status more than that of natives. The high sensitivity of low-skilled immigrants to the business cycle could also be strengthened by the fact that many immigrants' jobs are in sectors such as manufacturing and construction, which have a strong cyclicality of employment. The recent recession (2007–2009) has been an example of an economic downturn with very large loss of jobs in those two sectors, and this made it particularly painful for MCA immigrants.

Orrenius and Zavodny (2010) focus on this issue and show clearly that the employment and wages of Mexican immigrants were much more sensitive to state-specific economic growth in the 1994–2009 period when compared with the wages of natives. While they consider all workers, they also show that among those with no high school diploma, Mexicans' employment probability responds to average GDP growth in a state with elasticity seven times larger than non-Hispanic white workers with no diploma. Namely, a drop in GDP growth by one percentage point in a U.S. state reduced the employment probability of low-skilled natives in that state by 0.14 percentage points, and such a drop was not statistically significant. To the contrary, it decreased the employment rate of low-skilled immigrants by about 1 percentage point, and the drop was significantly different from 0 in a statistical sense.

In our regression analysis, in order to capture potential differential effects of recessions on employment and income of MCA (and other) and unskilled natives, I include in regression (1) two interaction terms. I interact the dummies MCA and OTH with a dummy variable taking a value of one during recession years within our considered period. Considering only the officially sanctioned national recessions (in the NBER classification), this dummy takes a value of one in 2001 and in the triennium 2007–2009. The presence of a time effect in each regression makes the inclusion of the main effect for a "recession dummy" redundant. Table 4.4 shows the estimated coefficients on the MCA and OTH dummies and the interaction with the recession dummy, with "probability of employment" as the dependent variable, and Table 4.5 shows the coefficients of the dummies and interactions in regressions with wages as a share of household income as dependent variable (Panel A) and SNAP as a share of household income (Panel B). The interaction dummies may be a rough way of capturing the recession effect as they simply identify regression year at the national level and do not exploit the state-specific severity of the recession (as done in Orrenius and Zavodny [2010]).

The results from Table 4.4 show a negative but small additional recession effect for low-skilled MCA immigrants on the order of 1 percent, significant at a 95 percent confidence level only in one specification. This implies that recessions erode about 1 percentage point of the 13 percentage point difference in employment rate between low-skilled MCA immigrants and natives. This is not a large effect but it still suggests a somewhat stronger exposure of immigrants to recessions. Table 4.5, on the other hand, does not find any significant differential effect of recessions on reliance on wage income or reliance on SNAP of MCA immigrants. While both groups increased significantly the use of welfare, especially SNAP in recessions (as shown in Figure 4.6), the difference between the two groups does not seem to change with it.

Overall, the results in the literature and (in part) those from our simple regression analysis suggest that MCA immigrants are somewhat more exposed to the employment effects over the business cycle, and given their larger dependence on wage income, they may suffer more significant income losses in recessions.

However, there are two other margins (besides changes in employment or wages) along which MCA immigrants seem to respond to economic cycles more than natives. These adjustments should help somewhat reduce the fluctuations of their wages and employment rates. The

Table 4.4 Unskilled Immigrant-Native Differential in Employment, Recession-Year Effect

	Sample: Head of households, no diploma			Sample: Adults, no diploma		
	(1)	(2)	(3)	(4)	(5)	(6)
Specifications	Only year effects	Individual controls	State-year FE and individual	Only year effects	Individual controls	State-year FE and individual
	Dependent variable: Dummy "employed"					
MCA immigrants	0.328***	0.129***	0.139***	0.279***	0.134***	0.149***
	(0.00402)	(0.00407)	(0.00459)	(0.00275)	(0.00281)	(0.00314)
Other immigrants	0.107***	0.0709***	0.0814***	0.0633***	0.0534***	0.0634***
	(0.00615)	(0.00522)	(0.00557)	(0.00407)	(0.00357)	(0.00380)
(MCA immigrants) × (Recession years)	−0.00723	−0.0107	−0.00894	−0.00617	−0.0102**	−0.00906
	(0.00758)	(0.00702)	(0.00802)	(0.00520)	(0.00491)	(0.00557)
(Other Immigrants) × (Recession years)	−0.0134	−0.00469	−0.000279	−0.0079	−0.00426	−0.00481
	(0.0116)	(0.00959)	(0.0102)	(0.00775)	(0.00669)	(0.00710)
Individual controls	No	Yes	Yes	No	Yes	Yes
State-by-year fixed effect	No	No	Yes	No	No	Yes
Observations	150,818	150,818	150,818	318,867	318,867	318,867

NOTE: **significant at the 95% confidence level; ***significant at the 99% confidence level. Individuals age 18 and older, no high school diploma. The reported coefficients and standard errors (in parentheses) are obtained from OLS regressions as (1) in the text, including the interactions of the immigrant origin dummies with a dummy for recession years (namely 2001, and 2007–2009). Each column reports coefficients from a different regression. Columns 1–3 include only head of households with no high school diploma in the sample. Columns 4–6 include all adults with no diploma. The dependent variable is the dummy "employed," the explanatory variable is in the first column. The observations are pooled individuals resident in the United States, from the March CPS, over the years 2000–2014. Each regression includes year fixed effects.

SOURCE: Author's calculations using CPS data.

Table 4.5 Unskilled Immigrant-Native Differential in Welfare Dependence, Recession-Year Effect

Specifications:	(1) Only year effects	(2) Individual controls	(3) State-year FE + Individual	(4) Only year effects	(5) Individual controls	(6) State-year FE and Individual
	Panel A: Dependent variable is wages as % of household income			Panel B: Dependent variable is SNAP as % of total household income		
MCA immigrants	20.27***	12.28***	13.26***	−6.604***	−5.057***	−4.303***
	(0.328)	(0.333)	(0.393)	(0.210)	(0.221)	(0.235)
Other immigrants	5.992***	4.484***	5.399***	−2.573***	−1.802***	−2.051***
	(0.649)	(0.624)	(0.674)	(0.362)	(0.360)	(0.377)
MCA immigrants × Recession years	0.237	−0.119	0.664	−0.393	−0.204	−0.284
	(0.624)	(0.607)	(0.740)	(0.337)	(0.329)	(0.373)
Other immigrants × Recession years	−0.506	−0.442	−0.423	0.538	0.653	1.064
	(1.162)	(1.099)	(1.187)	(0.661)	(0.646)	(0.669)
Individual controls:	No	Yes	Yes	No	Yes	Yes
State-by-year fixed effect	No	No	Yes	No	No	Yes
Observations	120,334	120,334	120,334	120,334	120,334	120,334

NOTE: *** significant at the 99% confidence level. Households whose head is 18 and older, has no high school diploma. The reported coefficients and standard errors (in parentheses) are obtained from OLS regressions as Equation (4.1) in the text, inclusive of an interaction between the immigrant dummy and a dummy for recession years (2001 and 2007–2009). Each column/panel reports coefficients from a different regression. The dependent variable is listed at the top of the panel, the explanatory variable is listed the first column. The observations are pooled individuals resident in the United States, from the March CPS, over the years 2000–2014. Each regression includes year fixed effects.

SOURCE: Author's calculaitons using CPS data.

first is that, especially during the Great Recession of 2007–2009, low-skilled immigrants were significantly more mobile, looking for jobs across U.S. labor markets relative to low-skilled natives. Cadena and Kovak (2016) show that, among low-skilled workers, the net migration-response to local economic shocks was much larger for immigrants than for natives. They also show that such net flow of migrants across local labor markets reduced somewhat the local wage fluctuation for natives so that labor markets with a larger share of low-skilled immigrants experienced smaller fluctuations in the employment and wages of natives.

The second channel of adjustment to the business cycle is represented by the fact that during periods of recession, net immigration from Mexico declines significantly and return-migration to Mexico increases. Hence, during economic booms the supply of low-skilled Mexicans increases while during recessions it decreases. Simpson and Sparber (2013) document this mechanism as it worked during the 2000–2009 period, showing the effects of state business cycles on the location of new immigrants and their net flow. These two mechanisms should somewhat reduce the wage vulnerability of MCA immigrants in the United States and may be responsible for the small effects I find in Table 4.4. Overall, it appears the employment sensitivity of MCA immigrants to U.S. business cycles is somewhat larger than for natives. This implies, for this group, that the income consequences of recessions are proportionally larger than for natives.

Why Do Immigrants Have Low Participation Rates to Welfare Programs?

The lower participation and reliance on welfare programs of low-skilled MCA immigrants relative to natives depend, at least in part, on their ineligibility for some of these programs. First, undocumented immigrant families and families on temporary visas (such as seasonal workers or agricultural workers on H1A and H2A visas) do not qualify for any welfare support, including SNAP, SSI, UI, and Disability Insurance. Their children, however, if they are U.S. born, do usually qualify for SNAP and Medicaid. The group of undocumented can be as large as half of the group of MCA immigrants with no diploma and, hence, the behavior of undocumented MCA immigrants strongly affects the average for this group.[3] Second, even Legal Permanent Residents' eligibility for some of these programs has been restricted drastically after the welfare reforms of 1996 (the Personal Responsibility and Work Opportunity Act). This reform created a very sharp distinction between citizens and noncitizens in their access to welfare, and overall it made welfare much more connected to searching for a job. Further, it capped the maximum dollar amount that could be received by a family over their lifetime. More importantly as it relates to immigrants, the 1996 reforms reduced the role of the federal government in covering several welfare programs for noncitizens, and it pushed states to decide whether to reinstate the programs at their expense. Some less generous states have kept the eligibility of noncitizens quite limited, and this has significantly reduced foreign-born participation (see Bitler and Hoynes 2011).

The reason for restricting noncitizen access, motivating part of the 1996 reform, was a fear that welfare transfers would be a magnet for immigrants and entice them to locate in states that were particularly generous. Some studies (e.g., Borjas 1999) claimed that the location of low-skilled immigrants was significantly affected by state welfare generosity and that this constituted a burden for the state and federal government. However, the evidence on this was always mixed, and several studies showed that the generosity of welfare among U.S. states did not play much of a role in the location of immigrants (e.g., Kaushal 2005; Zavodny 1999)

While the 1996 reform limited eligibility of noncitizens—and some states have maintained those restrictions—a second important factor potentially reducing participation was the immigrants' perception. The reforms created a general understanding that noncitizen's eligibility to means-tested programs was significantly restricted and may have created a so-called chilling effect that has discouraged even eligible households from applying and claiming some of these benefits. More recently, a combination of the chilling effect from welfare policies together with toughening of the enforcement for undocumented immigrants may have discouraged some immigrants—both documented and undocumented—from participating in programs for which they or their children are eligible. An interesting study by Watson (2014) shows that the participation in Medicaid among eligible children of immigrants was negatively affected by the intensity of enforcement against undocumented immigrants (measured as number of individuals identified for deportation) in the state-year. Undocumented parents whose children are eligible for Medicaid may be less likely to participate and expose themselves by travelling to doctors, filling out forms, and interacting with public agents who can help them if they perceive a strong enforcement effort against undocumented. Not just welfare policy but immigration policies and enforcement may contribute to this chilling effect in the participation of immigrants in some welfare programs.

Another important factor in determining the participation of immigrants in these means-tested programs when eligible is immigrants' ability to navigate the details of applications and requirements. Their limited knowledge of the English language and U.S. policies may discourage families from applying; further, their awareness of the existence of these programs may also be limited. Furtado and Theodoropulos (2013) show that participation in programs such as SSI is greater when immigrants can rely on a local network of coethnic people who have already applied for those and who are likely to help them navigate the system and bridge language and cultural barriers. Immigrants are more likely to apply and receive these benefits if they are in an area with a high percentage of long-term resident conationals. This may reflect assimilation of norms, but also the existence of language and information costs in the application process that can be reduced by previous immigrants and the network of information and informal services they provide.

Importantly, the low participation in welfare programs by MCA immigrants could also be due to the motivation of these people to migrate to the United States and the selection of type of workers who migrate. Most low-skilled immigrants moved to the United States to have a job and to raise the living standards of their family through their (hard) work, attracted by wage and employment opportunities. Many of them also migrate with the idea that they may return to their home country once they have achieved a certain degree of economic success (or a target of income, as is often described in this literature; see, for example, Dustmann and Weiss [2007]). This may create a stigma of reliance on welfare transfers and a sense of not accomplishing one's immigration goals, so MCA immigrants are willing to look harder for a job and accept lower-wage jobs relative to individuals raised in the United States.

It is also important to notice that this tendency of working more and not relying on welfare income, which is typical of U.S. low-skilled immigrants, is not a feature of, for example, low-skilled European immigrants. In countries where welfare states are generous, such as Sweden, Norway, and Finland, evidence (e.g., Bratsberg, Raaum, and Red 2010; Hansen and Lofstrom 2009; Koninig 2011) shows that they rely more on welfare and have lower participation rates in the labor force relative to similar natives. The generosity of welfare programs in some European countries is substantial, and the access for refugees is complete so that those countries can become magnets for low-skilled immigrants. Thus, the motivation and selection of immigrants and the incentive structure in place in the receiving country seems important in determining the dependence on either working or welfare for low-skilled immigrants. In this respect, the United States selects working immigrants, and the job availability and limited generosity of welfare programs keeps them working, even if they are not documented.

A final consideration on low-skilled immigrants is also important. Within the group of low-skilled people, which is the one at highest risk of incarceration (and possibly drug use and alcohol abuse), the MCA immigrants are significantly less prone to incarceration and health problems, some of which are related to risky behavior such as smoking (Hispanic immigrants are 18 percent less likely to smoke than non-Hispanics) and drinking. Butcher and Piehl (2007) show that low-skilled immigrants—particularly newly arrived immigrants—have a much lower rate of incarceration relative to similar natives. Fear of deportation, higher probability of working, and possibly a selection of individuals without a history of alcohol and substance abuse among the immigrants could be the reason for the lower incidence of crime and health issues. Remarkably, despite their more limited access to health care due to their immigration status, first-generation Hispanic immigrants enjoy significantly better health than non-Hispanic whites in the United States. Relative to similarly aged whites, they are 39 percent less likely to have heart disease and 49 percent less likely to have cancer.[4] Although several studies try to identify the causes of better health among MCA immigrants—the explanations range from diet to working to incidence of risky behavior—the picture of a healthier low-skilled population among MCA immigrants relative to natives seems clear.

In summary, while a large share of MCA immigrants live in poverty because their low education only gives access to relatively low-paying jobs, they constitute a type of economically poor population that is different from natives. Relative to natives who are similar in age, education, and location in the United States, they have a much higher probability of working, they work longer hours, they are in families with more children, and they rely less on welfare cash and noncash transfers. They are also healthier and less likely to be incarcerated. Hence, it is likely that policies oriented to enhancing labor market access, education, and opportunities rather than toward welfare transfers may be more effective in improving the economic outcome of this group, especially by raising their income and decreasing their chances of being in poverty. I will discuss some of these policies later in the section titled "Policy Ideas."

INDIRECT EFFECT OF IMMIGRANTS ON NATIVE JOB OPPORTUNITIES AND INCOME

Immigrants constituted almost 26 percent of the adult population with no high school diploma in 2014—in some states this percentage was much larger—and economists have asked whether the immigrants' presence and their very high propensity to be employed comes at the expense of native workers' opportunities or wages. Do MCA immigrants in a labor market crowd out natives because of strong job competition? Or do they complement natives, allowing growth and the expansion of the economy and leaving natives' opportunities unaffected? By affecting the labor income of natives, or their employment opportunities, immigrants could affect their probability of being in poverty and their reliance on welfare income. I consider this to be a potential indirect effect of immigrants on U.S. poverty in that immigrants' labor market competition can affect natives' outcomes. I discuss the plausibility of the existence of such an effect and how large it could be.

The answer to this question depends on several factors. First, researchers find that in the United States low-skilled immigrants move to places where job opportunities are more abundant. Hence, one can observe that low-skilled immigrants and low-skilled natives' employment/wages are positively correlated across locations and over time. Basso and Peri (2015) clearly show this point by documenting that local labor markets (commuting zones) experiencing increases in immigrants' share, in any decade between 1970 and 2010, also experienced growth in low-skilled natives' wages in the same decades. In this respect, therefore, there is no negative association between the inflow of immigrants and the wages or employment of natives across areas and over time; rather, the opposite association is observed. Second, as low-skilled immigrants come to a local economy, firms expand (Olney 2013); manual production tasks (largely performed by immigrants) become less expensive, which creates complementary opportunities for other production tasks performed by natives (Peri and Sparber 2009); firm's technology adjusts (Lewis 2011) to make the most of immigrants' skills; and immigrants boost local goods and service demand (Bodvarson, Van der Berg, and Lewer 2008). Overall, native workers can benefit from these transformations in response to immigration. Third, low-skilled immigrants take jobs in niches that natives are leaving (in agricultural, personal services, and manufacturing), which generates market segmentation that reduces job competition between natives and immigrants. Fourth, locations where low-skilled immigrants go (especially large metropolitan areas) are also locations chosen by many highly skilled immigrants. Hence, the relative proportion of more- and less-educated workers, which could affect their relative wages, did not change much because of immigration in many large labor markets. In particular, considering the years since 2000 (as shown in Peri [2011]), net immigration in the United States has been more college intensive than unskilled intensive and hence has not produced dramatic shifts in the relative supply of labor—and certainly not toward a larger share of workers with no college degree. Combining these factors and mechanisms, and depending on their relative intensity, inflows of immigrants can be absorbed with negative, positive, or null changes in native's labor market opportunities. Ultimately, the impact of immigration on low-skill wages needs to be assessed empirically, and several studies have done just that.

Turning to such empirical evidence, it usually reveals small effects of the inflow of immigrants on less-educated natives' labor market performance using several approaches (either reduced-form regression analysis; quasi-experiments/difference in difference; or more structural, production-based approaches) and different levels of analysis (national or local). Card (1990, 2009), Peri and Sparber (2009), Peri and Yasenov (2015), and Card and Peri (2016) all find small and not very significant effects. A series of papers by George Borjas (Borjas 2003, 2006, 2015; Borjas and Katz 2007) indicate, instead, the existence of significant negative effects of immigration on native low-skilled wages. However, once spurious bias and measurement error are accounted for (Basso and Peri 2015; Card and Peri 2016; Peri and Sparber 2009), and once the specifications of skill complementarities are made more flexible (Ottaviano and Peri 2012), my assessment is that no significant negative effects survive. While it is hard to rule out small negative wage and employment effects for low-skilled natives, it is also difficult to dismiss small positive gains. Overall, the evidence is consistent with no effects on less-educated natives.

Some studies focus on the impact of immigration on specific groups of natives, such as young workers (Smith 2012) or previous immigrants (Card 2001), and they point out a somewhat stronger competition effect and some negative wage impact on those groups. This makes sense, as these groups can be more exposed to low-skilled immigrant competition; however, there is also significant evidence that young people adjust their occupation (Peri and Sparber 2009) and skill level (Hunt 2012) in response to immigrants, and hence the overall impact can be small.

Peri (2011) looks more directly at the connection between immigration and native poverty. In that paper I analyze—using aggregate estimates of the elasticity of substitution between high and low-skilled workers and between immigrants and natives of similar education and age—the indirect effect of inflows of immigrants during the 2000–2010 period on the poverty rates of natives in U.S. cities and states, through their wage competition. The main result of the paper is that, because of the large share of highly educated immigrants arriving in 2000–2010, and because of the relatively small competition effect on less-skilled natives, in most cases such impact was small. In fact, during the 2000–2010 period in some locations, skilled immigrants helped reduce native poverty by creating job opportunities as low-skilled workers are complementary to high-skilled ones. For instance, an inflow of immigrant engineers, business people, and scientists increases income in a location and generates higher demand for services, creating jobs that low-skilled natives provide (such as construction workers, janitors, and baby sitters). My assessment in that paper was that immigration did not constitute a relevant factor in determining poverty rate increases in U.S. cities and states in the recent decade (2000–2010). Instead, during that period the great recession produced a significant increase in poverty rates, related to the local labor market characteristics rather than to the inflow of immigrants.

So, while immigrants contribute directly to higher poverty rates in the United States—a significant percentage of them are in the group of less-educated, and this group has a significant probability of being in poverty—I do not find evidence of two other channels relating immigrants to poverty. First, within the group of less educated, they are, if anything, slightly less likely to be in poverty and much more likely to work. Second, there seems to be no evidence of an effect on natives' poverty through their labor market effects. When I included the economic role of highly skilled immigrants, they may actually reduce natives' poverty through improved labor markets; that group can largely contribute to economic growth that may benefit all workers in the long run (see Peri 2011).

Few studies analyze the impact of immigrants on other local economic variables that may also have a role in determining economic well-being of natives. Notably, Cortes (2008) shows the effect of immigrants in reducing the price of low-skill-intensive services such as gardening, landscaping, personal services, baby-sitting, house cleaning, and others. This may contribute to a positive effect on real income at the local level, as money will go farther when purchasing these services locally. However, Cortes also shows how these prices are likely to be more relevant in the consumption basket of wealthier people, and thus they will not affect the real income of poor families as much.

Much less developed is the analysis of the impact of immigrants on availability and quality of local public goods, such as health care or recreation facilities. Does the presence of immigrants strain these local services? Are local resources for low-income families crowded by immigrants? Given the low reliance on welfare income and the lower participation in welfare programs, immigrants may not be such a burden. However, I am not aware of detailed analysis of the type done for their labor market effects at the local level. One exception is the impact of low income immigrants on schooling and on school quality. As immigrants have larger families, lower incomes, and possibly lower

English proficiency, their presence may affect local schools. I focus on this aspect in the next section.

IMMIGRANTS AND SCHOOLING

Public schooling is a crucially important local public service. It is a key tool to increase opportunities of children of low-income families, and in the long run it plays a crucial role in social mobility. The quality of schooling can be very different across districts, and the location of U.S. families with children is affected in a significant way by considerations of school district quality. The role of primary and secondary public schools in providing the education and tools needed to succeed in the labor market is widely recognized by economists. Being in a district with well-functioning schools, good teachers, and good programs is likely to significantly increase the chances of children in low-socioeconomic-status households to improve their economic perspectives, find a good career, and be socially mobile. Hence, in the long run and for the intergenerational transmission of poverty, the quality of schools and possibly the quality of the peers can be a most relevant factor.

Immigrants can transform school districts in three crucial ways. First, if native families see immigrant inflows as a threat to the quality of their school districts, they may leave for other school districts (that are prevalently nonimmigrant). Alternatively, they may segregate in private schools when the inflow of MCA immigrants increases, generating a lack of integration and diversity in schools that could affect the abilities of those left behind. Segregation between immigrants and natives will increase because of natives' demand for a homogeneous schooling environment, the consequence of which can be important for the learning environment of low-income family children. If native families with higher incomes leave school districts where immigrants arrive, the socioeconomic level of peers will decline for low-income children and they will not benefit from a group of peers that may be more motivated and higher-achieving. Second, if the inflow of immigrants is not accompanied by an investment in schools and new programs, overcrowding of schools can produce a negative effect on educational attainment and deteriorate human capital accumulation. Third, if school integration and peer effects are particularly important for the assimilation and economic success of immigrant children, then this segregation will be particularly damaging to them. I will analyze each aspect in turn, reviewing the existing evidence and research.

Several reports (e.g., Orfield et al. 2016) and some sociological studies (e.g., Wells 2009) describe a high level of segregation of MCA immigrants in U.S. schools, particularly in California, as it is home to the largest number (and population share) of Hispanic immigrants and children. Orfield et al. (2016) show that the average Latino student in the United States was attending a school in which 47 percent of "other" students were Latinos. This reveals high segregation, as the average presence of Hispanics/Latinos nationally was equal to 16–17 percent. Similarly, in most western U.S. states, 40–50 percent of Latino children were in schools that are 90–100 percent Latinos, and in California Latino children attend schools that are, on average, 87 percent Latino. Typically, many of these children are second-generation MCA immigrants, and the large degree of segregation in schools is in part due to the overall geographic concentration of MCA immigrants and the fast growth of this population in the recent decades.

However, Cascio and Lewis (2012) reveal a concerning trend showing that U.S.-born non-Hispanic families leave school districts where MCA immigrants arrive and/or move their children to private schools. In their analysis of California elementary and middle schools, they show that between 1970 and 2000, for each inflow of 10 low-English proficiency Hispanic children, about 14 non-Hispanic white children left the district. The concentration of non-Hispanic white children in private schools and the overall segregation of Hispanic and non-Hispanic across school districts increased substantially. The study uses past settlement of Mexicans to predict the areas that would receive the highest inflow of new MCA immigrants and compares the outflow of children and their families from those districts relative to other adults, in response to immigration. This method isolates native flight driven by school considerations rather than by other aspects of the inflow of immigrants and finds a significant effect.

An older study by Ellen et al. (2002) analyzes the degree of segregation of immigrant students in New York City and identifies a large variation across groups. That study, mainly descriptive, emphasizes that highly segregated low-income immigrants (such as Dominicans in New

York) were attending schools in which their peers were more likely in poverty, had low English proficiency, and had teachers with lower experience and lower education. While the paper falls short of establishing causal connections, it shows a picture in which low-income immigrant children are segregated in schools whose quality and peer indicators were quite low. Given the existing literature emphasizing the important role of teacher quality (e.g., Rivkin, Hanushek, and Kain 2005) and peer academic quality (e.g., Sacerdote 2001) on students' academic achievements, one can argue that immigrants segregated in lower-quality schools will experience worse educational outcomes and possibly negatively affect their career opportunities in the long run.

There is no systematic direct evidence for the United States on the impact on school performance, and long-run schooling achievement (of natives and immigrants) proceeding from the high level of segregation described above. Researchers have not analyzed whether the higher concentration of children from low-educated immigrant families affect the outcomes of natives. Nevertheless, research relative to Norway (Hardoy and Schone 2013), Denmark (Jensen and Rasmussen 2011), Israel (Gould, Lavy, and Paserman 2009), and several other European countries (Brunello and Rocco 2013) seems aligned in finding that increased immigrant concentration in elementary and middle schools reduced students' Program for International Student Assessment scores, increased the probability of dropping out, and possibly reduced their probability of college attendance. Such findings may reveal that limited school resources are strained when immigrant children with low language proficiency levels arrive, that peer effects may matter, or that segregation along income and ethnic lines may be bad for learning, especially if the combination of crowding and segregation leave low-income children concentrated in disadvantaged schools.

The most studied issue recently has been the impact of immigrant inflow on the probability of U.S.-born individuals to attend college (Hunt 2012; Smith 2012). On one hand, as argued above, school competition may reduce the quality of schooling (if many children from non-English speaking and low socioeconomic status households produces a deterioration of the learning environment) and hence may negatively affect the probability that U.S. natives go to college. On the other hand, the presence of less-skilled immigrants may induce natives to seek careers and a job specialization that complements them rather than competes with them. This would increase the incentive to extend their education to college as that degree gives access to jobs that are not in competition with those performed by less-educated immigrants. Both studies find evidence that the inflow of less-skilled immigrants in a cohort and in a state increases the probability that natives in that cohort will attend college. Hence, the incentives induced by a labor market price mechanism may in part offset the negative direct impact through school crowding. At least for a subset of natives who have a reasonable prospect of going to college, the competition of unskilled immigrants may increase their enrollment and graduation rates from college.

POLICY IDEAS

The economic characteristics and choices of immigrants at high risk of poverty described in this chapter—in particular, their differences with respect to natives with similar skills—should provide guidance for predicting and understanding the potential impact that policies may have on their income and economic well-being. I consider an overview of different types of policies that can affect the economic success of low-skilled immigrants and their children, sometimes called second-generation immigrants. Rather than being exhaustive, I suggest some important policy ideas that can be considered as crucial when addressing issues of immigrants and poverty.

Path to Legalization and Intensity of Enforcement

Given the high propensity to work, improving access to jobs—especially better paid ones—is going to be a crucial aspect of any policy that aims to increase the socioeconomic status of first-generation low-skilled immigrants. The largest contribution on this side is probably achieved by allowing undocumented immigrants a legal status and a path to permanent residence. By increasing the bargaining power of workers, their mobility, and their willingness to invest in U.S.-specific skills, legalization may have a significant impact on wages. Several studies (e.g., Barcellos 2010; Kossoudji and Cobb-Clark 2002; Rivera-Batiz 1999) have shown that, in the years after legalization, immigrants gain between 4 and 10 percent in their wages relative to the previous trajectory. These analyses consider the regularization program called the Immigration Reform and Control Act (IRCA) of 1986 and follow individuals after they participate.

If undocumented immigrants can circulate freely in the United States, they can consider more job opportunities and likely increase their productivity and the quality of their job matches, which will result in wage gains. Regularization will also allow those immigrants to leave the shadows and be more confident in participating in welfare programs for which their children qualify. For younger immigrants, it will give them a less uncertain outlook, encouraging them to acquire language skills and on-the-job skills. Even a very limited legalization reform granting undocumented immigrants the right to work legally, but restricting access to welfare or citizenship, would substantially improve their incomes and the prospects of their children. At the very minimum, protecting them from deportation unless they commit crimes (as the executive action of the president that in 2014 created the Deferred Action for Parents of Americans and expanded the Deferred Action for Childhood Arrivals) would provide some extra certainty and probably still improve their labor conditions. Less aggressive enforcement would also likely increase the participation of immigrant children in health care programs and in schools.

Reduce Barriers to Enroll in Welfare Programs

At least part of the limited participation in welfare programs—which would certainly improve health care and nutrition opportunities for immigrant children (Medicaid and SNAP)—may be due to difficulties in both applying for the programs and navigating the system. Support from more established Spanish-speaking communities, simplification of the process, and measures to ensure privacy and protection from deportation when enrolling may boost participation rates. There is clearly some opposition to policy proposals that aim to expand eligibility of social programs to be more inclusive of immigrants, as it may be perceived as adding to the cost of low-skilled immigrants. However, the idea that immigrants should be able to access and claim that for which they are already eligible should be rather uncontroversial, and helping them get such benefits and reducing the costs of doing so seems a reasonable and feasible policy.

Access to Education: Assistance to Highly Impacted Districts

The second most crucial policy that could benefit low-skilled immigrants and their communities is assisting school districts experiencing large inflows of non-English-speaking immigrants with more resources and better responding to their needs. If the inflow of immigrants is accompanied with investments in better, larger schools and more teachers, even the non-Hispanic flight to private schools can be stemmed and the effects of segregation reduced. One interesting idea is to put all the revenues from a regularization program—namely, the income from fines and back-taxes owed by undocumented immigrants in order to obtain regularization—toward the school districts where undocumented children reside, in proportion to their number. Similarly, the processing fees paid by employers for new visas for low-skilled immigrants (H1A) could be directed toward school districts in proportion of the presence of low-skilled immigrant workers.

Another proposal is to subsidize bilingual education in these communities for both immigrants and natives. This could turn the presence of immigrants into opportunities for natives. A bilingual education, which is regarded by many as a valuable asset for all children, could also substantially improve the level of integration of Hispanic immigrants into native communities.

Education and Opportunities: DREAM Act

A second important idea in promoting the assimilation and success of the second generation of immigrants is associating schooling achievements—and possibly a college degree—with the possibility of regularization. The DREAM Act, first proposed in the Senate in 2001 and reintroduced several times since, was such legislation. This proposal would first grant conditional residency to young individuals who arrived under the age of 16 and were enrolled in high school, and would have allowed a permanent residence permit if the individuals enrolled in an institution of higher learning (or in the military). A policy of this kind that associates the opportunity to regularize the immigration status (and eventually allows for permanent resident status) to a schooling career culminating with a college degree has two important benefits. First, it would provide strong incentives for attaining a college education to a group (children of low-skilled MCA immigrants) that may have otherwise opted for less education. Second, it would provide a less uncertain job outlook, significantly improving the labor market opportunities of undocumented young immigrants once they graduate and therefore strengthen their commitment to a U.S. education and learning economically valuable skills.

It is worth emphasizing that several states have already recognized the extreme importance of college education for the success of the young generation of children of undocumented immigrants. Thirteen states, including California, have passed state legislation that allows access to public universities for these undocumented students at the same conditions as citizens who are residents of the state. This is a great first step. However, without a legal option to work after graduation, the positive impact of college education would be greatly diminished.

Labor Market Policies: Minimum Wages

A policy that has been discussed recently, albeit in a much broader context, and would probably have an important impact on the poverty rate of immigrants, is the increase in the federal minimum wage. Some of the jobs performed by immigrants (in services and agriculture) are likely to be at or close to the minimum wage. Hence, an increase in the minimum wage will boost their income, provided employers do not respond by cutting hours or reducing employment. The existing empirical evidence on the employment effects of minimum wages does not seem to support the idea that its increase would reduce employment (e.g., Card and Krueger 1994; Krueger and Card 2000), hence, such a policy may help low-skilled immigrants by supporting their labor income.

The concerns over stagnation and declining wages at the low end of the distribution is driving the current support for an increase in the federal minimum wage, a measure already proposed by the Obama administration in 2014. As long as low-skilled immigrant workers constitute a large share of workers in the lower percentiles of the wage distribution, a measure that would push those up could affect immigrants' poverty in a significant way.

To summarize, a simple and overarching principle of effective policies to reduce poverty among low-skilled immigrants and help their children achieve economic success should focus on improving labor market access for the first generation and the quality of schools in immigrant-heavy districts for the second generation. Economically, it makes sense that the increased cost of public schools should be supported in part by the immigrants themselves, and in part by their employers, as those are the groups receiving the largest economic benefits from labor migration. Moreover, in doing so, part of the economic benefits generated by immigrants could benefit whole communities and help muster the political consensus to allow a larger inflow of low-skilled immigrants.

CONCLUSIONS

This chapter provides an overview of some important issues at the intersection of immigration and poverty in the United States. It emphasizes that a large part of the population at risk of poverty—because of low levels of education and thereby limited access to high paying jobs—is of immigrant origin, especially from Mexico and Central America. The chapter then shows that economically and socially low-skilled immigrants are quite different from similar natives. They are much more likely to be employed, they work more weeks, their incomes are in large part made of wage earnings, and they are strongly affected by the overall economic cycle. They do not rely on welfare programs and transfers as much as natives, and they have larger families, lower probability of incarceration, higher likelihood of moving across U.S. states in response to job availability, and are in better health than similar natives.

These features make immigrants particularly sensitive to policies that affect labor markets and to overall economic conditions. These immigrants, albeit poor, generally move to booming cities and contribute to local economic growth. They do not seem to worsen the labor market opportunities of natives. However, they may create some crowding of (and flight away from) local public schools. As schooling and education are key factors allowing their children—and the children of natives in the same communities—to succeed economically, directing policies and resources to reducing the crowding impact on schools should be a first-order concern.

Within this framework I see a path to legalization that requires payment of a fee and back taxes that generates local revenues for schools as a reasonable and profitable policy both for immigrants and native communities where they live. Other policies improving their labor market and schooling prospects, such as the DREAM act, are also win-win options for immigrants and the communities where they live. While also important, lowering barriers to their access to welfare—and increasing their eligibility—can come with advantages especially for their children, but at the cost of being perceived as a burden for natives and a disincentive to their employment.

Notes

1. The data we use are from the 2000–2014 March CPSs. Each figure note provides details on the variables shown.
2. The percentage of individuals with no high school diploma among MCA immigrants was about 60 percent in 2000 and declined to about 52 percent in 2014. The same percentage for natives decreased from 18 percent to 9 percent in the same period. Other immigrants' percentage of no diploma among 18 years and older was very close to that of natives'.
3. The Pew Research Center (2014) indicates that for the United States, 52 percent of illegal immigrants are from Mexico. Hence, the percentage of less-educated MCA likely to be undocumented is certainly very high.
4. "Hispanic Health," Centers for Disease Control, http://www.cdc.gov/vitalsigns/ hispanic-health/ (accessed on February 22, 2016).

References

Basso, Gaetano, and Giovanni Peri. 2015. "The Association between Immigration and Labor Market Outcomes in the United States." IZA Discussion Paper No. 9436. Bonn: Institute for the Study of Labor.

Barcellos, Silvia Helena. 2010. "Legalization and the Economic Status of Immigrants." RAND Working Paper No. WR-754. Santa Monica: RAND.

Bitler, Marianne, and Hilary W. Hoynes. 2011. "Immigrants, Welfare Reform, and the U.S. Safety Net." NBER Working Paper No. 17667. Cambridge, MA: National Bureau of Economic Research.

Bodvarson Örn B., Hendrik F. Van den Berg, and Joshua J. Lewer. 2008. "Measuring Immigration's Effect on Labor Demand: A Reexamination of the Mariel Boatlift." *Labor Economics* 15(4): 560–574.

Borjas, George J. 1999. "Immigration and Welfare Magnets." *Journal of Labor Economics* 17(4): 607–637.

———. 2003. "The Labor Demand Curve is Downward Sloping: Reexamining the Impact of Immigration on the Labor Market." *Quarterly Journal of Economics* 118(4): 1335–1374.

———. 2006. "Native Internal Migration and the Labor Market Impact of Immigration." *Journal of Human Resources* 41(2): 221–258.

———. 2015. "The Wage Impact of the Marielitos: A Reappraisal." NBER Working Paper No. 21588. Cambridge, MA: National Bureau of Economic Research.

Borjas George J., and Lawrence F. Katz. 2007. "The Evolution of the Mexican-Born Workforce in the United States." In *Mexican Immigration to the United States*, George J. Borjas, ed. Cambridge, MA: National Bureau of Economic Research, pp. 13–56.

Bollinger, Christopher R., and Paul Hagstrom. 2008. "Food Stamp Program Participation of Refugees and Immigrants." *Southern Economic Journal* 74(3): 665–692.

Bratsberg, Brent, James F. Ragan Jr., and Zafir M. Nasir. 2002. "The Effect of Naturalization on Wage Growth: A Panel Study of Young Male Immigrants." *Journal of Labor Economics* 20(3): 568–597.

Bratsberg, Bernt, Oddbjørn Raaum, and Knut Røed. 2010. "When Minority Labor Migrants Meet the Welfare State." *Journal of Labor Economics* 28(3): 633–676.

Brunello, Giorgio, and Lorenzo Rocco. 2013. "The Effect of Immigration on the School Performance of Natives: Cross Country Evidence Using PISA Test Scores." *Economics of Education Review* 32: 234–246.

Butcher, Kristin F., and Anne Morrison Piehl. 2007. "Why Are Immigrants' Incarceration Rates So Low? Evidence on Selective Immigration, Deterrence, and Deportation." NBER Working Paper No. 13229. Cambridge, MA: National Bureau of Economic Research.

Cadena, Brian C., and Brian K. Kovak. 2016. "Immigrants Equilibrate Local Labor Markets: Evidence from the Great Recession." *American Economic Journal: Applied Economics* 8(1): 257–290.

Card, David. 1990. "The Impact of the Mariel Boatlift on the Miami Labor Market." *Industrial and Labor Relations Review* 43(2): 245–257.

———. 2001. "Immigrant Inflows, Native Outflows, and the Local Labor Market Impacts of Higher Immigration." *Journal of Labor Economics* 19(1): 22–64.

———. 2009. "Immigration and Inequality." *American Economic Review* 99(2): 1–21

Card, David, and Alan B. Krueger. 1994. "Minimum Wages and Employment: A Case Study of the Fast-Food Industry in New Jersey and Pennsylvania." *American Economic Review* 84(4): 772–793.

Card, David, and Giovanni Peri. 2016. "Immigration Economics by George J. Borjas: A Review Essay." *Journal of Economic Literature* 54(4): 1333–1349.

Cortes, Patricia. 2008. "The Effect of Low-Skilled Immigration on U.S. Prices: Evidence from CPI Data." *Journal of Political Economy* 116(3): 381–422.

Cascio, Elizabeth U., and Ethan G. Lewis. 2012. "Cracks in the Melting Pot: Immigration, School Choice and Segregation." *American Economic Journal: Economic Policy* 4(3): 91–117.

Duncan, Brian, and Stephen J. Trejo. 2012. "The Employment of Low-Skilled Immigrant Men in the United States." *American Economic Review* 10(3): 549–554.

Dustmann, Christian, and Yoram Weiss. 2007. "Return Migration: Theory and Empirical Evidence from the UK." *British Journal of Industrial Relations* 45(2): 236–256.

Ellen, Ingrid Gould, Katherine O'Regan, Schwartz, Amy Ellen Schwartz, Leanna Stiefel, Derek Neal, and Thomas Nechyba. 2002. "Immigrant Children and New York City Schools: Segregation and Its Consequences [with Comments]." *Brookings-Wharton Papers on Urban Affairs* (2002): 183–214.

Furtado, Delia, and Nikolaos Theodoropoulos. 2013. "SSI for Disabled Immigrants: Why Do Ethnic Networks Matter?" *American Economic Review: Papers and Proceedings* 103(3): 462–466.

Gould, Eric D., Victor Lavy, and M. Daniele Paserman. 2009. "Does Immigration Affect the Long-Term Educational Outcomes of Natives? Quasi-Experimental Evidence." *Economic Journal* 119(540): 1243–1269.

Hansen, Jorgen, and Magnus Lofstrom. 2009. "The Dynamics of Immigrant Welfare and Labor Market Behavior." *Journal of Population Economics* 22(4): 941–970.

Hardoy, Inés, and Pål Schøne. 2013. "Does the Clustering of Immigrant Peers Affect the School Performance of Natives?" *Journal of Human Capital* 7(1): 1–25.

Hunt, Jennifer. 2012. "The Impact of Immigration on the Educational Attainment of Natives." NBER Working Paper No. 18047. Cambridge, MA: National Bureau of Economic Research.

Jensen, Peter, and Astrid Wurtz Rasmussen. 2011. "The Effect of Immigrant Concentration in Schools on Native and Immigrant Children's Reading and Math Skills." *Economics of Education Review* 30(6): 1503–1515.

Kaushal, Neeraj. 2005. "New Immigrants' Location Choices: Magnets without Welfare." *Journal of Labor Economics* 23(1): 59–80.

Koning, Edward A. 2011. "Ethnic and Civic Dealings with Newcomers: Naturalization Policies and Practices in Twenty-Six Immigration Countries." *Ethnic and Racial Studies* 43(11): 1974–1992.

Koning, Edward A., and Keith G. Banting. 2013. "Inequality below the Surface: Reviewing Immigrants' Access to and Utilization of Five Canadian Welfare Programs." *Canadian Public Policy/Analyse de Politiques* 39(4): 581–601.

Kossoudji, Sherrie A., and Deborah A. Cobb-Clark. 2002. "Coming out of the Shadows: Learning about Legal Status and Wages from the Legalized Population." *Journal of Labor Economics* 20(3): 598–628.

Krueger, Alan B., and David Card, 2000. "Minimum Wages and Employment: A Case Study of the Fast-Food Industry in New Jersey and Pennsylvania: Reply." *American Economic Review* 90(5): 1397–1420.

Lewis, Ethan. 2011. "Immigration, Skill Mix, and Capital Skill Complementarity." *Quarterly Journal of Economics* 126(2): 1029–1069.

Olney, William W. 2013. "Immigration and Firm Expansion." *Journal of Regional Science* 53(1): 142–157.

Orfield, Gary, Jongyeon Ee, Erica Frankenberg, and Genevieve Siegel-Hawley. 2016. *Brown at 60: Great Progress, a Long Retreat and an Uncertain Future*. Los Angeles: Civil Rights Project.

Orrenius, Pia, and Madeline Zavodny. 2010. "Immigrants' Employment Outcomes over the Business Cycle." IZA Discussion Paper No. 5354. Bonn: Institute for the Study of Labor.

Ottaviano, Gianmarco I.P., and Giovanni Peri. 2012. "Rethinking the Effect of Immigration on Wages." *Journal of the European Economic Association* 10(1): 152–197.

Peri, Giovanni. 2011. "The Impact of Immigration on Native Poverty through Labor Market Competition." NBER Working Paper No. 17570. Cambridge, MA: National Bureau of Economic Research.

Peri, Giovanni, and Chad Sparber. 2009. "Task Specialization, Immigration, and Wages." *American Economic Journal: Applied Economics* 1(3): 135–169.

———. 2011. "Assessing Inherent Model Bias: An Application to Native Displacement in Response to Immigration." *Journal of Urban Economics* 69(1): 82–91.

Peri, Giovanni, and Vasil Yasenov. 2015. "The Labor Market Effects of a Refugee Wave: Applying the Synthetic Control Method to the Mariel Boatlift." NBER Working Paper No. 21801. Cambridge, MA: National Bureau of Economic Research.

Pew Research Center, 2014. "Unauthorized Immigrants in the United States" available at http://www.pewhispanic.org/interactives/unauthorized -immigrants-2012/map/mexican-share/ (accessed 2/25/2016).

Rivkin Steven G., Eric A. Hanushek, and John F. Kain. 2005. "Teachers, Schools, and Academic Achievement." *Econometrica* 73(2): 417–458.

Rivera-Batiz, Francisco L. 1999. "Undocumented Workers in the Labor Market: An Analysis of the Earnings of Legal and Illegal Mexican Immigrants in the United States." *Journal of Population Economics* 12(1): 91–116.

Sacerdote, Bruce. 2001. "Peer Effects with Random Assignment: Results for Dartmouth Roommates." *Quarterly Journal of Economics* 116(2): 681–704.

Simpson, Nicole, and Chad Sparber. 2013. "The Short- and Long-Run Determinants of Less-Educated Immigrant Flows into U.S. States." *Southern Economic Journal* 80(2): 414–438.

Smith, Christopher L. 2012. "The Impact of Low-Skilled Immigration on the Youth Labor Market." *Journal of Labor Economics* 30(1): 55–89.

Watson, Tara. 2014. "Inside the Refrigerator: Immigration Enforcement and Chilling Effects in Medicaid Participation." *American Economic Journal: Economic Policy* 6(3): 313–338.

Wells, Ryan. 2009. "Segregation and Immigration: An Examination of School Composition for Children of Immigrants." *Equity & Excellence in Education* 42(2): 130–151.

Zavodny, Madeline. 1999. "Determinants of Recent Immigrants' Locational Choices." *International Migration Review* 33(4): 1014–1030.

5

Understanding the Consequences of Heightened Interior Immigration Enforcement

Catalina Amuedo-Dorantes
San Diego State University

Esther Arenas-Arroyo
University of Oxford

The unintended consequences of tougher immigration enforcement first emanated from tighter controls along the U.S.-Mexico border, with higher and multiple walls that separated us from our neighbors and led many desperate individuals seeking a better life in the United States to opt for riskier crossing methods. Drownings in the Rio Grande and deaths in the desert were just one manifestation of the harsher conditions migrants were willing to endure to make it to the other side. Yet, the consequences of intensified *interior* immigration enforcement have received lesser publicity, in part due to their more recent nature.

Interior immigration enforcement spending grew exponentially following the terrorist attacks of 9/11 (see Figure 5.1). Many local- and state-level measures that involved employers, as well as the local and state police, were enacted to identify, apprehend, and deport a population of undocumented immigrants that had been on the rise during the 1980s and 1990s, and that exceeded 10 million by the mid-2000s (see Figure 5.2). An array of interior immigration enforcement measures adopted over the first decade of the twenty-first century led to the deportation of more than 5 million undocumented immigrants during President Barack Obama's administration—a stand that ultimately earned him the title of "Deporter in Chief" (Department of Homeland Security 2016). It remains unclear what Americans gained from such actions; yet, the costs are becoming somewhat more palpable, especially as time goes by.

Figure 5.1 Immigration Enforcement Spending Adjusted to 2015 $, 1985–2018

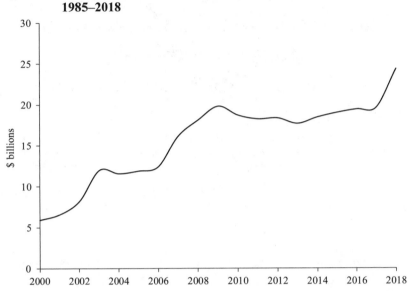

SOURCE: Department of Homeland Security, Budget in Brief.

Figure 5.2 Estimated Number of Unauthorized Resident Aliens, 1969–2015

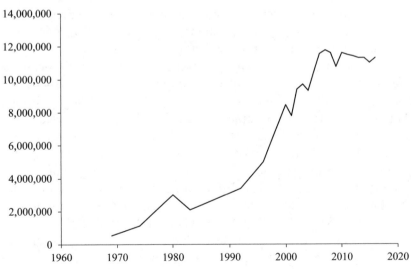

SOURCE: ProCon.org: http://immigration.procon.org/view.resource.php?resourceID=000844 (accessed November 17, 2017).

There are 11.4 million undocumented immigrants living in the United States, 66 percent of whom have been living in the country for more than a decade (Gonzalez-Barrrera and Krogstad 2017). As a result, it should come as no surprise that more than 4.5 million American children, including approximately 8 percent of all U.S.-born children, have an undocumented parent. To the extent that these are American children, it is still unclear what the consequences and costs of tougher interior immigration enforcement will be for the nation's political landscape as they come of age and head to the voting booth.

In this chapter, we provide an overview of some of the impacts of intensified interior immigration enforcement on families, ranging from living in broken households to enduring a life of poverty following restricted access to employment opportunities and the deportation of breadwinning household heads. Our hope is to inform about the development of interior immigration enforcement while raising awareness of its consequences.

BACKGROUND ON INTERIOR IMMIGRATION ENFORCEMENT

Spending on immigration enforcement has expanded greatly over recent decades. After 9/11 in particular, states and localities started to enact their own immigration policies, often justifying them on the inaction by the federal government concerning comprehensive immigration reform. Apprehensions and deportations from the interior quickly rose, especially after 2008, following the introduction of the Secure Communities program, as we shall discuss. Almost 2 million people were deported between 2009 and 2013 alone (Vaughan 2013). And although greater emphasis eventually would be placed on the deportation of serious criminals, the number of noncriminal removals continued to exceed that of removals for criminal offenses (see Figure 5.3).

To understand the evolution of interior immigration enforcement, we need to recall two main immigration acts that led to the growth of undocumented immigration to the United States. The first was the 1965 Immigration and Nationality Act, which established country-level numerical immigration quotas. Prior to its enactment, during the Bra-

Figure 5.3 Aliens Removed by the U.S. Department of Homeland Security, by Criminal Status

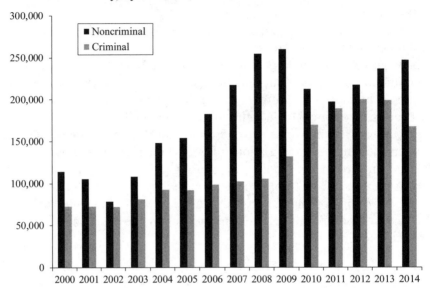

SOURCE: U.S. Department of Homeland Security: Yearbook of Immigration Statistics, 2004 and 2014.

cero program, nearly 450,000 guest worker visas were issued annually for Mexicans (Espino and Jimeno 2013). As a result, when the Mexican quota was set at 20,000 per year, the number of undocumented entries quickly rose and undocumented immigration grew from 540,000 in 1969 to roughly 3.2 million by 1986 (see Figure 5.2). To address the large number of undocumented immigrants in the country, Congress passed the Immigration Reform and Control Act (IRCA) in 1986, which allowed for the legalization of undocumented immigrants who satisfied certain conditions, made it illegal to knowingly hire undocumented immigrants, and paved the way for intensified border enforcement. However, employer sanctions were never seriously enforced, and crises in Latin America, along with economic growth in the United States, only contributed to the continued rise of undocumented immigration during the 1990s and well into the 2000s.

A second key piece of legislation came in 1996, when Congress passed the Illegal Immigration Reform and Immigrant Responsibility

Act (IIRIRA). This act further enhanced border control and, perhaps most importantly, set the guidelines for future employment verification and interior immigration enforcement. It is notable for setting the framework for future collaborations between the federal government and states/localities on immigration enforcement matters. Such collaborations, however, did not take place until after the terrorist attacks of 2001. In 2002, Florida became the first state to activate a 287(g) agreement of collaboration between the state police and Immigration Customs Enforcement (ICE) as contemplated in the 1996 IIRIRA. Soon after, in 2003, the Department of Homeland Security (DHS) was created to replace the old Immigration and Naturalization Service. By 2005, DHS had introduced a Consequence Delivery System, criminalizing illegal entry or reentry. Enforcement increased almost tenfold during 2004 and 2010 (see Figure 5.4), and removals, now often of newly classified criminals, rose as localities started to implement the 287(g) agreements contemplated in the 1996 IIRIRA. On average, they rose from 3 percent during the 1970–1996 period to 19 percent during 2003–2006, and to a record high of 65 percent in 2012 (Bergeron and Hipsman 2014).

In what follows, we describe the main *interior* immigration enforcement initiatives, distinguishing according to whether they were local (city or county) level or state level measures (see Table 5.1).

Local Policies

We focus our attention on two types of local initiatives that expanded rapidly after 9/11: 287(g) agreements and the Secure Communities program (currently, the Priorities Enforcement Program). We refer to them as police-based measures since they rely on local law enforcement resources to assist ICE in the implementation of federal immigration policy. In addition, both are responsible for much of the rapid growth in deportations from the interior of the United States.

The 287 (g)

These agreements evolved from the 1996 IIRIRA. Through a Memorandum of Agreement, state and local agencies could enforce federal immigration law. Designated officers who satisfied certain conditions and received four weeks training from DHS were deputized to act as

Figure 5.4 Expansion of the Total Enforcement between 2004 and 2010

2004

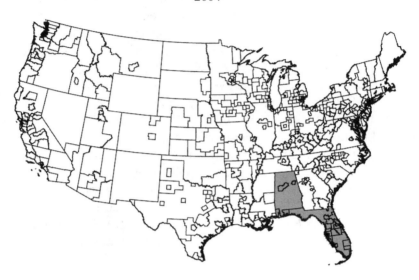

2007

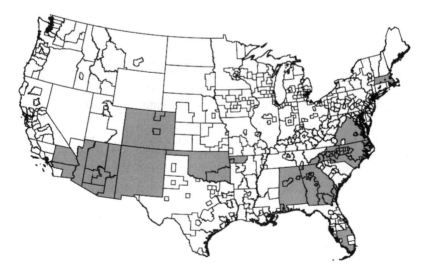

Figure 5.4 (continued)

2010

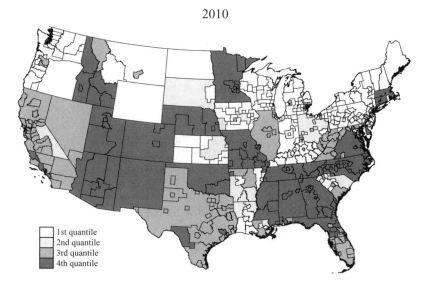

NOTE: Lighter shades correspond to lower levels of enforcement (captured by the interior immigration enforcement index) in CONSPUMA (Consistent Public Use) *c* in year *t*.
SOURCE: Authors' tabulation of their immigration enforcement index.

immigration enforcement agents in their corresponding jurisdictions.[1] The number of agreements increased from 8 in 2007 to 61 in 2008. Since the first agreement signed by the state of Florida in 2002, ICE has trained and certified more than 1,675 state and local officers to enforce immigration laws (U.S. Immigration and Customs Enforcement 2016).

There are three types of 287(g) agreements: task force, jail enforcement, and the hybrid kind. The task force model allows state and local law enforcement to interrogate and arrest noncitizens during their regular duties, whereas the jail enforcement model permits local and state law enforcement to question arrested immigrants about their immigration status. In 2012, the administration announced a decrease in funding for 287(g) agreements in order to expand the Secure Communities program. Several factors contributed to that decision, including accusations of racial profiling, high implementation costs, and minimal oversight and support from ICE, to name a few (Immigration Policy Center 2012).[2]

114

Table 5.1 Description of Enforcement Laws

Type	Measure	Year originated	Objective	Who implements it?	Geographic coverage	Signed by	Types
Police-based measures	287(g)	2002–	Make communities safer by the identification and removal of serious criminals.	State and local law enforcement	State and local	State and local law enforcement	**Task Force:** allows local and state officers to interrogate and arrest noncitizens during their regular duties on law enforcement operations. **Jail enforcement:** permits local officers to question immigrant who have been arrested on state and local charges about their immigration status. **Hybrid model:** allows participation in both types of programs.
	Secure Communities/Priority Enforcement Program	2008–	Make communities safer by the identification and removal of serious criminals using biometric information.	Police	Local	Local law enforcement	
	Omnibus immigration laws	2010–	Identification and removal of undocumented immigrants.	State and local law enforcement	State	State governor	
Employment-based measures	E-Verify	2006–	Prevent the hiring of undocumented immigrants.	Employer	State	State governor	

Secure communities

ICE announced the Secure Communities program in March 2008. Its purpose was to prioritize the use of enforcement resources to target noncitizens who had committed serious crimes. Under this program, ICE maintained an electronic presence in jails. Once arrested, criminal noncitizens were identified by checking their fingerprints against the Federal Bureau of Investigation data set on offenders and the DHS data set tracking their immigration history. Local agents were not deputized to implement immigration enforcement, however, as is the case with the 287(g) agreements.

Although it was established as a voluntary program, Secure Communities grew rapidly from its initial implementation in 7 jurisdictions in 2008 to all the nation's 3,181 jurisdictions by 2013. During the program's first years, the number of fingerprints submitted grew from 828,119 in 2009 to 6.9 million in 2011 (Meissner et al. 2013). The Priority Enforcement Program replaced Secure Communities in July 2015 (U.S. Immigration and Customs Enforcement 2017), although President Trump appears to have reinstated Secure Communities through a number of executive actions in February 2017.

As local law enforcement increased its cooperation with ICE, state and local governments became concerned about how the sharing of information and cooperation with ICE was potentially undermining community trust and the community cooperation with the police, both key for effective policing. The so-called sanctuary cities, as their opponents have labeled them, wanted to reassure immigrants that they could report to the police without fear of being deported. Through many city, county, or statewide ordinances, sometimes reflecting long-standing practices by the local/state police, they limited the cooperation with ICE, most notably by restricting the transfer of arrestees to ICE custody following a detainer. Nearly 6 million undocumented immigrants reside in these localities (Rosenblum 2015), and President Donald Trump has vowed to withhold funds from these jurisdictions.

State Level

Omnibus immigration laws

Several states further enacted legislation intended to intensify immigration enforcement. Arizona was the first state to do so in 2010 under the so-called Senate Bill 1070. After being challenged in court, the U.S. Supreme Court issued a ruling in the case *Arizona v. United States* in 2012. According to the ruling, the sections that made it a state misdemeanor for an immigrant not to be carrying documentation of lawful presence in the country allowed state police to arrest without a warrant in some situations, or made it unlawful under state law for an individual to apply for employment without federal work authorization were considered to be preempted by federal law. All justices agreed to uphold the portion of the law allowing Arizona state police to investigate the immigration status of anyone who is stopped, detained, or arrested if there is reasonable suspicion they might be in the country illegally. Five other states—Alabama, Georgia, Indiana, South Carolina, and Utah—followed Arizona's footsteps and enacted similar legislation in 2011, even though the lower courts have partially enjoined these statutes.

Employment verification systems

Another statewide immigration enforcement initiative, this one restricted to the labor market, has been mandated employment verification. While all employers are required to participate in paper-based employment eligibility verification by requesting that prospective hires complete an I-9 form and present two documents establishing identity (e.g., a driver's license) and work authorization (e.g., a Social Security card), in most states, employers can opt to use the online work authorization system, E-Verify. The program checks the individual's work authorization based on the information in the Social Security Administration and, if applicable, the DHS databases. The pilot program started back in 1997 with five states that had a greater immigrant concentration, and it has quickly grown over time as individual states enacted employment verification mandates. Arizona was the first state to require all public and private employers to enroll in the program in 2007. Afterward, Mississippi, Alabama, Louisiana, and South Carolina made E-Verify mandatory for all public and private employers. Many other states require work verification for some type of employers. Overall, enrollment in E-Verify increased by more than 400 between 2001 and 2015 (National Conference of State Legislatures 2017), despite some inherent problems with the system. DHS introduced several actions in order to improve the veracity of E-Verify screening, which led to a large number of false positive and false negative errors. One of these actions was the new "self-check" feature, which makes it possible for job applicants to check their own employment verification and resolve data discrepancies in advance.

DATA AND IDENTIFICATION CHALLENGES

Once some of the key interior immigration enforcement initiatives in place over the past two decades have been reviewed, it is worth discussing some of the various data and identification challenges studies have to confront when trying to gauge the impact of the aforementioned measures. This allows us, in turn, to understand the diverse approaches of the literature. We refer to them in what follows.

Measuring the Intensity of Interior Immigration Enforcement

Capturing the intensity of immigration enforcement to which an individual might be exposed is a difficult task because of the overlap of measures in place at any given point, as well as the distinct implementation of the measures by those responsible for doing so. Hence, one should start by emphasizing that any policy measure, whether it is a dummy or an index, is only a proxy for the intensity of immigration enforcement to which individuals are ultimately exposed to.

That said, how do most of the studies capture the *intensity* of immigration enforcement? The vast majority of the literature relies on dichotomous variables that take the value of 1 when a given policy is in place and 0 otherwise. This is traditionally the case in studies focusing on the impact of specific measures, including 287(g) agreements (Kostandini, Mykerezi, and Escalante 2013; Watson 2013), Secure Communities (Ciancio 2016; Miles and Cox 2014), omnibus immigration laws (Amuedo-Dorantes and Lozano 2017a; Good 2013), or employment verification mandates (Amuedo-Dorantes and Bansak 2012; Bohn, Lofstrom, and Raphael 2014; Orrenius, Zavodny, and Gutierrez 2016).

Several authors, however, have addressed the task of capturing the intensity of immigration enforcement by creating an index that incorporates the multiplicity of measures in place, while at the same time addresses a number of challenges that arise in empirical research. One such challenge emerges when the basic geographic unit in the study is larger than the geographic scope of the measure in question. For example, this is the case when the finest geographic detail in the data set is the metropolitan statistical area (MSA)—a geographic unit that can incorporate various counties. Some of those counties might have adopted tougher immigration enforcement policies, but others might have not. In those instances, it can be helpful to use population weights that take into account the share of the MSA population exposed to the measure in question along with the share that is not. A second challenge refers to the distinct period of times during which measures are in place in any given year. Some of them might have been in place for six months, whereas others might have been in place year-round. The index offers the opportunity to weight each measure by the number of months during any given year that the measure was in place. Finally, many of these measures are closely intertwined. They were, perhaps, enacted to substitute, replace, or add to a preceding or existing measure, as in the case of the Secure Communities program and the 287(g) agreements between ICE and the local/state police. They utilize the same local/state law enforcement resources. As such, their overlap might have a multiplicative impact easier to capture using a single index, such as

$$(5.1) \quad EI^k{}_{mt} = \frac{1}{N_{2000}} \sum_{a \in m}^{m} \frac{1}{12} \sum_{t=1}^{12} \mathbf{1}(E_{t,a}) P_{a,2000}$$

where $\mathbf{1}(E_{t,a})$ is an indicator function that informs about the implementation of a particular policy in city a at time (month) t. $P_{a,2000}$ refers to the population of city a according to the 2000 Census (prior to the rolling of any of the enforcement initiatives being considered), and N is the total population in MSA m. Hence, the overall enforcement to which an individual living in MSA m and year t are exposed to is computed as the sum of the indices for each enforcement initiative at the (MSA, year) level:[3]

$$(5.2) \quad Total\ Enforcement_{m,t} = \sum_{k \in K}^{K} EI^k_{m,t}$$

Identifying the Likely Unauthorized

If measuring the intensity of immigration enforcement in any given location is a challenging task, so is the ability to identify who is an undocumented immigrant. This is because representative data sets, such as the American Community Survey (ACS) or the Current Population Survey (CPS), lack information about the legal status of immigrants. Faced with that challenge, the literature has taken various approaches to identifying the population that we refer to as the "likely unauthorized" or "likely undocumented." Logical imputation methods are probably the most common in the literature. For example, most of the literature uses Hispanic noncitizens as a proxy for individuals who are likely to be undocumented (Bohn and Pugatch 2013; Orrenius and Zavodny 2016; Passel and Cohn 2009; Pope 2016). In recent work (Amuedo-Dorantes and Arenas-Arroyo 2017, 2018), we restrict our attention to Hispanic noncitizens who have not completed high school and who have lived in the United States five years or more in order to exclude low- and high-skill individuals with nonimmigrant visas. Using all these traits, along with the weights of the ACS, we obtain an estimated unauthorized immigrant population close to the estimated population of 11–12 million undocumented immigrants in the United States using the residual method.

The fact that the combination of these descriptors does a reasonable job when trying to proxy for the likely undocumented status of immigrants is understandable. First, the Census Bureau and DHS estimate that nearly 40 percent of noncitizens are authorized immigrants (Acosta et al. 2014; Hoefer, Baker, and Rytin 2013). That is, among noncitizens we have all unauthorized immigrants, as well as many authorized immigrants. Second, because of geographic proximity and poor economic and social conditions at home, as well as extensive migrant networks, more than two-thirds of unauthorized immigrants in the United States are Hispanics from Mexico and Central America. Third, as previous research has pointed out (see, for example, Bohn and Lofstrom [2013], and Orrenius and Zavodny [2016]), most unauthorized immigrants have relatively little education because they are from countries with low average levels of educational attainment. About three-quarters of adult unauthorized immigrants have no more education than a high school diploma (Passel and Cohn 2009). Finally, to address any concerns regarding the possibility that the sample might include low-skilled immigrants or college students with nonimmigrant visas, one can also restrict the designation of individuals as likely undocumented to Hispanic noncitizen individuals who have not completed high school and have lived in the United States for five years or longer. This last restriction further ensures that the low-skill migrant is not legally in the United States on a nonimmigrant visa, which is typically granted for a much shorter duration.

In some instances, when information on the immigration status and the dependent variable outcome of interest is jointly observed in a representative data set from the same sample universe, it is feasible to improve upon the aforementioned prediction of immigrant legal status using statistical imputation methods, as noted by Van Hook et al. (2015). Unfortunately, the ability of doing so is often constrained by various factors. First, one needs a "donor" data set that, in addition to containing information on the outcome of interest, is representative of the unauthorized migrant population, has information on their legal status, and is derived from the same sample universe. The donor sample is then used to predict migrants' legal status in the main data set (Rendall et al. 2013). Secondly, the donor data set needs to be representative for examining outcomes within the geographic unit of interest, often states, MSAs, or counties.

Identification Challenges

Anytime that we are interested in learning about the impact of intensified immigration enforcement on the well-being of unauthorized immigrants or their family members, we are faced with a number of identification challenges characteristic of most policy analyses. For instance, when using a quasi-experimental approach, such as a difference-in-differences methodology, it is crucial to ensure that any impacts attributed to the policy are not differences between unauthorized immigrants and their comparison group that predated the intensification of enforcement itself. In addition, while nonrandom, it is important to confirm that the outcome studied was not a determinant of tougher enforcement in the first place.

Still, one of the most prevalent challenges in immigration studies is the nonrandom residential location of likely undocumented immigrants.

To the extent that immigrants are a mobile population, more so in the case of unauthorized immigrants, addressing the selective exposure to tougher immigration enforcement is an essential, yet often missing, part of any analysis of enforcement impacts. One way to address this challenge is by instrumenting the location of these immigrants using historical data on the location of alike countrymen prior to the intensification of immigration enforcement. To address concerns of such locations potentially being correlated with economic conditions still dominant in those sites, researchers rely on data from 20-plus years ago, and control for trends in macroeconomic characteristics in those settlement areas.

THE WIDE SPECTRUM OF IMPACTS OF INTENSIFIED INTERIOR IMMIGRATION ENFORCEMENT

As we noted in the first section of this chapter, for quite some time now, the immigration literature has investigated the consequences of intensified border enforcement in the United States (see for example, Bean et al. [1990]; Espenshade [1990, 1994]). Recently, attention has shifted toward the impact of intensified interior immigration enforcement (see Table 5.2 for an overview of the literature). In what follows, we review some of the most recent research on the implications of intensified *interior* immigration enforcement on families with likely undocumented migrants to gain a better perspective about the impact that these policies appear to be having on the targeted population, as well as on their children, many of whom are U.S. citizens.

Residential Choices

Along with its impact on labor market outcomes, the most examined effect of intensified interior immigration enforcement is the one on the residential choices made by undocumented immigrants. These studies find mixed results likely due to their focus on distinct enforcement initiatives, time period, data, and methods. For example, Bohn, Lofstrom, and Raphael (2014) use the synthetic control method to document a decrease in the share of Hispanic noncitizens (a group more likely to include "likely undocumented immigrants") after Arizona

Table 5.2 Summary of Selected Literature Findings

	Policy	Sample	Residential choices		
			Specification	Group	Coefficient
Amuedo-Dorantes and Lozano (2017b)	SB 1070 and LAWA	ACS 2001–2012, and data on removals from Customs Border Patrol	Synthetic control method	Mexican noncitizens	Mexican noncitizens leaving the state of Arizona became 7 times more likely to relocate to New Mexico
Amuedo-Dorantes and Lozano (2017a)	SB 1070	Monthly CPS, 1998–2013	Synthetic control method	Hispanic noncitizens	Minimal to null (−0.0016)
Bohn, Lofstrom, and Raphael 2014	LAWA	Monthly CPS, 1998–2009	Synthetic control method	Hispanic noncitizens	Declines of 1.5 to 2.0 percentage points
Good (2013)	OILs	Monthly CPS, August 2005–September 2011	Differences-in-differences	Low-skilled, Hispanic noncitizens who arrived after 1982	Decline by 24%
Orrenius and Zavodny (2016)	E-Verify	ACS, 2005–2014	Ordinary least squares	Noncitizens from Mexico or Central America with at most high school and 20–54 years old	Decline by 40%
Watson (2013)	287(g)	ACS, 2005–2011	Ordinary least squares	*Aggregated analysis:* Population <65 years old *Individual analysis:* Population 18–49 years old	Probability of Leaving the U.S: Rises by 8.7 pp, Probability of Moving Elsewhere: Rises by 1.1 percentage point, No effect when Maricopa County is excluded

Employment and Wages

	Policy	Sample	Specification	Group	Coefficient
Amuedo-Dorantes and Bansak (2012)	E-Verify	CPS, 2004–2010	Ordinary least squares	Hispanic noncitizens 16–45-year-olds with a high school education or less	Employment: Decline 5.4%, Hourly wages: 9%
Amuedo-Dorantes and Bansak (2014)	E-Verify	CPS 2004–2011	Ordinary least squares	Hispanic noncitizens 16–45-year-olds with a high school education or less	Employment: Decline 4.8%, Female hourly wages: Increase 16.9%
Bohn and Lofstrom (2013)	LAWA	Monthly CPS, 1998–2009	Synthetic control method	Hispanic noncitizens	Wage: Decline 11.4 pp, Self-Employment: Increase 8.3 pp.
Bohn, Lofstrom, and Raphael 2015	LAWA	Annual Social and Economic Supplement to the Current Population Survey to the CPS, 1998–2010	Synthetic control method	Low-skilled, U.S.-born, non-Hispanic whites	Employment: Decline 4.43 pp., Weekly earnings: Increase by $124.73
Kostadini, Mykerezi, and Escalante (2013)	287(g)	ACS, 2005–2010	Differences-in-differences	Working population	Expense per worker: increase by $534.127, Farm income: Decrease by 51%, Worker per Acre: Decrease by 16%
Orrenius and Zavodny (2015)	E-Verify	CPS, 2002–2012	Ordinary least squares	Low-skilled Mexican immigrants	Real hourly earnings of non-citizen men: Decline by 8%, Employment of noncitizen women: Increase by 2.5%, Real hourly earnings Hispanic male citizens: Increase by 9%

Table 5.2 (continued)

	Policy	Sample	Specification	Group	Coefficient
			Families and Children Outcomes		
Amuedo-Dorantes et al. (2018)	287(g), SC, E-Verify, OILs	ACS, 2005–2011	Ordinary least squares and instrumental variables	Families with at least one U.S. citizen child and one noncitizen Hispanic parent	Household income: Decline by 18%, Poverty: Increase by 4%
Amuedo-Dorantes and Arenas-Arroyo (2016)	287(g), SC, E-Verify, OILs	ACS, 2005–2014	Ordinary least squares and instrumental variables	Low-skilled Hispanic non-citizen women	Probability of childbearing: Decline by 6%
Amuedo-Dorantes and Arenas-Arroyo (2017)	287(g), SC, E-Verify, OILs	ACS, 2005–2015	Ordinary least squares and instrumental variables	U.S.-citizen children	Probability of living in households singly headed by their moms with absent spouses: Increase by 20%, Probability of living without their parents: Increase by 19%
Amuedo-Dorantes and Lopez (2017)	287(g), SC, E-Verify, OILs	CPS, 2000–2013	Ordinary least squares	Hispanic children ages 6–17	Probability of repeating a grade: Increase by 14%; Probability of dropping out of school: Increase by 18%
			Crime		
Thomas J. Miles and Cox (2014)	SC	FBI's Uniform Crime Reports 2004–2012	Differences-in-differences	All U.S. counties	No effect

NOTE: SB 1070 = Senate Bill 1070; LAWA = Legal Arizona Workers Act; OILs = omnibus immigration laws; SC = Secure Communities; ACS = American Community Survey; CPS = Current Population Survey; pp = percentage points.

made it mandatory for all employers, public and private sector, to verify the employment eligibility of all new hires.

In the same line, looking at all states with employment restrictions policies and comparing the size of the immigrant population before and after the states enacted E-Verify mandates, Orrenius and Zavodny (2016) find that E-Verify reduced the number of Mexican noncitizens in some states as they relocate across other states or leave the country, many of them involuntarily through deportation. Amuedo-Dorantes and Lozano (2017b) examine the status in which Mexican noncitizens leaving Arizona were relocating following the adoption of tougher enforcement measures. They find that Mexican noncitizens who migrated from Arizona to other U.S. states went primarily to New Mexico and California. However, the trajectories of Mexican noncitizens leaving Arizona overlapped with those of non-Hispanic natives, hinting on the role that socioeconomic and political factors, in addition to potential complementarities between immigrants and natives, might have played in explaining the destinations of Mexican noncitizens leaving Arizona after 2007.

In that regard, Amuedo-Dorantes and Lozano (2017a) examine the effect of the Arizona's Senate Bill 1070, which includes the so-called "show me your papers" clause.[4] Following the same methodology as Bohn, Lofstrom, and Raphael (2014), the authors show that the impact of Arizona's 2010 omnibus immigration law was minimal to null. Like these authors, Watson (2013) studies the effect of the 287(g) agreements on location choice. While she finds some evidence of relocation of noncitizens with a college education, she notes that cross-border migration flows are not significantly affected by that particular immigration enforcement measure one Maricopa County in Arizona is excluded from the sample. Finally, using yet another enforcement measure, Good (2013) examines immigrant outflows from states with omnibus immigration laws. Using a difference-in-differences approach, he finds evidence of noncitizen immigrant outflows, but no evidence of significant impacts on native flows.

Employment and Wages

A vast literature has also explored the effect of employment verification mandates (E-Verify mandates) on the labor market outcomes of the likely unauthorized, as well as on those of natives. The studies find mixed effects on employment and wages, depending on the data sources, methodology, and gender of the respondents. However, they generally conclude that the mandates make it difficult to switch jobs for Hispanic immigrants who are likely to be unauthorized (see Amuedo-Dorantes and Bansak 2012, 2014; Bohn and Lofstrom 2013; Bohn, Lofstrom, and Raphael 2015; Orrenius and Zavodny 2009; Orrenius, Zavodny, and Gutierrez 2016).

In particular, Bohn and Lofstrom (2013) test whether the 2007 Legal Arizona Workers Act (LAWA) limited the employment and earnings of likely unauthorized immigrants. Using data from the CPS (1998–2009) and the synthetic control method, they find that LAWA lowered the wage and increased self-employment among noncitizen Hispanic men with at most a high school education. Using the same approach, Bohn, Lofstrom, and Raphael (2015) show that native non-Hispanic workers in Arizona are less likely to find a job but have higher earnings because of LAWA.

A common concern using the synthetic control method is coming up with a reasonable control group. In particular, it might be argued that it is not possible to find a suitable control for Arizona. Yet, studies using different estimation approaches sometimes conclude similarly. For instance, exploiting the geographic and temporal variation in the implementation of the employment verification mandates, Amuedo-Dorantes and Bansak (2012, 2014) document a decrease in the employment of those likely undocumented, mixed effects on their wages, and a redistribution of labor toward sectors where the implementation of the mandates is lax, such as agriculture or food services when using CPS data from 2004 through 2011. They also document that E-Verify mandates can increase employment and wages for non-Hispanics natives. Orrenius and Zavodny (2015) use CPS data from 2002 to 2012 and conclude that E-Verify mandates reduce the hourly earnings for undocumented Mexican men, increase the labor force participation among Mexican women, and raise the earnings of native Hispanics.

Employment verification mandates have even had some international consequences. At a micro level, the drop in earnings has curtailed remittances flows (Amuedo-Dorantes and Puttitanun 2014). At a macro level, they have curtailed foreign-direct investment in the United States, leading to employment cutbacks by U.S. affiliates of foreign companies

(Amuedo-Dorantes, Bansak, and Zebedee 2015). States have started to take immigration matters into their own hands. For example, many states have been mandating the use of E-Verify.

Focusing on the indirect employment impacts of other immigration enforcement measures, such as the 287(g), Kostandini, Mykerezi, and Escalante (2013) examine how intensified enforcement is impacting employment in the agriculture sector—a sector that depends heavily on immigrant labor. Using a difference-in-differences approach, and focusing on relative changes in immigrant labor and wages of farm workers by number of years elapsed since the adoption of each agreement, they document a decline in farm incomes, immigrant labor, and overall labor expenses in the affected counties.

Household Poverty

While much of the literature has focused on the impacts of intensified immigration enforcement on the size, residential choices, and labor market outcomes of likely undocumented immigrants, the effects of enforcement on families and children have started to receive increasingly more attention. This is imperative given the growing magnitude of this demographic. In 2009, 23 percent of youth under the age of 18 resided in an immigrant household, and 29 percent of those children had at least one undocumented parent (Passel and Cohn 2011). U.S.-born children with undocumented parents represented 8 percent of all U.S.-born children in 2012—twice as many as in 2002 (Passel, Cohn, and Rohal 2014). And, by 2016, second-generation Latinos made up about one-third (32 percent) of Latino eligible voters, up from 27 percent in 2008 and 26 percent in 2000 (Krogstad et al. 2016).

A first step in understanding the implications of tougher immigration enforcement on families is to look at how the latter is affecting their bottom line—namely, their household income and their exposure to life in poverty. The focus on household economic sources is critical, given their well-known role in children's health, education, and development outcomes later in life. To that end, Amuedo-Dorantes, Arenas-Arroyo, and Sevilla (2018) analyze how intensified interior immigration enforcement has impacted households, especially those headed by likely undocumented parents with U.S. citizen children. They discuss the various channels through which intensified immigration enforcement can impact household resources. First, employment verification mandates can adversely affect the labor market outcomes and overall employment opportunities of likely undocumented immigrants. Second, fear of apprehension might induce families to live in the shadows to evade encounters with law enforcement. For instance, they might decide not to drive their car to work to avoid police stops. Such behaviors can have negative consequences on labor market outcomes and household income. Third, the deportation of the main household earner, as has been the case in most instances, can lead to a drastic drop in household income and contribute to the drop of household income below the poverty threshold.

Using data from the 2005–2011 ACS, Amuedo-Dorantes, Arenas-Arroyo, and Sevilla (2018) show that the average yearly increase in interior immigration enforcement over that period lowered the household incomes of families with a likely undocumented parent and U.S. citizen children by 18 percent, raising their exposure to poverty by 4 percent. Furthermore, they provide evidence of local and police-based measures (the ones directly linked to deportations) being the most relevant ones in increasing the household's poverty exposure. The negative impacts of intensified immigration enforcement are present even among intact households—that is, households that have not suffered the deportation of one of their members. The fact that the negative effects are found even among these intact households suggests that deportation fears alone might be sufficient for the household to endure economic hardship. These findings are robust to alternative measures of our dependent variable, to whom is considered a likely unauthorized migrant, and to the exclusion of specific downturn years or of counties that are particularly harsher in their implementation of immigration enforcement measures, as in the case of Maricopa County in Arizona. Similarly, the effects prove robust to several identification tests accounting for the potential endogeneity of enforcement policies and the residential location of likely undocumented immigrants.

Immigrant Fertility

Household economic resources and a certain level of predictability regarding family unity are key determinants of fertility. Because immigrants and their offspring are key in guaranteeing the United States' ability to reach near replacement fertility rates and the sustainability of Social Security (Kotkin and Ozuna 2012), knowledge of how immigrant fertility responds to intensified enforcement is also important. This is particularly true following the decrease in Hispanic female fertility (see, for example, Livingston and Cohn [2012]).

Amuedo-Dorantes and Arenas-Arroyo (2016) explore whether the unexplained drop in the fertility rate of Hispanic women might be related to the intensification of interior immigration enforcement. Tougher enforcement can impact immigrant fertility through several channels. Inevitably, the deportation of the household's head or her/his partner is likely to either end fertility or place it on hold. And, even among families not afflicted by deportation, the uncertainty regarding the future of the family unit, its economic resources, and/or access to important health care services and benefits is likely to make the decision to conceive a risky and costly choice. These impacts are likely to curtail immigrant fertility. However, it is also foreseeable that, given the advantages of birthright citizenship, undocumented women might want to have their kids while still in the United States to provide them with better life opportunities.

Using data from the 2004–2013 ACS, we find that a one standard deviation increase in the intensity of interior immigration enforcement lowers the childbearing likelihood of likely undocumented women by 6.3 percent. This effect seems to be driven by police-based measures, as opposed to employment-based policies like E-Verify mandates. Furthermore, the fact that the effects are also present among intact families, families headed by a likely undocumented couple, as well as among the poorest families, suggests the importance of limited income resources, along with increased uncertainty emanating from an intensified fear of deportation, on likely unauthorized women's fertility.

Children's Living Arrangements

Ultimately, a main concern when examining the implications of intensified immigration enforcement on households headed by a likely undocumented immigrant is how it might be impacting other individuals in the household, especially more vulnerable populations, as would be the case with children. This concern becomes more salient when most of the children living in households headed by a likely undocu-

mented immigrant are U.S. citizens. The growing number of deportations accompanying the intensification of immigration enforcement at
the local and state levels since 9/11 have been breaking up families,
and it has changed the structure of many families headed by an unauthorized parent, typically through the deportation of fathers. Given the
emotional, cognitive, and long-run socioeconomic costs of being raised
in single-headed households or without parents, gaining a better understanding of the collateral damage of heightened enforcement on the
families to which these children belong is warranted.

To learn more about the consequences of intensified immigration
enforcement on these children, we explore how it may have contributed
to the incidence of two specific living arrangements: 1) the likelihood
of living in single-headed household with a mother whose spouse is
absent, and 2) the propensity to live without any of the parents. Using
2005–2015 ACS data, we find that the average yearly increase in interior immigration enforcement over that time span increases the likelihood by 20 percent that a Hispanic child might be living with her/his
likely undocumented mother in a female-headed household where the
other spouse is absent. It also elevates the child's propensity to live
without any parent by nearly 19 percent. The first result points to the
possibility that these children might have been impacted by the deportation of their fathers, given that undocumented migrants are more likely
to be married to other undocumented immigrants. The second finding
further points to the possibility that, through the deportation of one
or both parents, children might be left behind living with relatives or
friends who are not at risk of deportation. Both findings prove robust to
many identification and robustness checks, and reveal that the observed
impacts originate from immigration enforcement more directly linked
to deportations, as is the case with police-based enforcement—namely,
immigration enforcement involving local and state police.

As noted earlier in this chapter, in recent years, several localities
have enacted ordinances and legislation pieces (sometimes labeled
Trust Acts) with the purpose of increasing the community trust and
cooperation with the police after the chilling effect of prior immigration enforcement measures (Fagan and Meares 2008; Fagan and Tyler
2008; Skogan and Frydl 2004; Tyler 2010). To examine if the observed
impacts are indeed stemming from tougher immigration enforcement,
we reestimate our model excluding states with a statewide Trust Act

(so-called sanctuary city). Such estimates should be somewhat larger. Indeed, we find that the same increase in immigration enforcement raises these children's likelihood of residing in a household headed by their moms, whose spouses are absent, by 17 percent, and the probability of living without any parent by 22 percent.

Educational Attainment of Children

So far, this chapter has discussed how interior immigration enforcement has been particularly damaging to families headed by undocumented long-term residents of the United States (Rosenblum et al. 2014). Furthermore, even though most of the children are U.S. citizens from birth, and as such they are not the main target of intensified enforcement, they often face significant social and economic disadvantages because of a parent's unauthorized status (Debry 2012; Passel and Taylor 2010). These children endure the negative consequences of deportation fear, stress, and anxiety (Amuedo-Dorantes, Puttitanun, and Martinez-Donate 2013). Several authors have documented their changes in sleeping and eating patterns, anger, and physical ailment, along with difficulties accessing proper services as their families find it necessary to relocate or to start living in the shadows in order to evade apprehension (Bacon Immigration Law and Policy Program and the Southwest Institute for Research on Women 2011; Chaudry et al. 2010; Watson 2014). And, as shown earlier, it is not solely fear. The deportation of, typically, the household head leads to financial hardship, which translates to concentration difficulties, disruptive classroom behaviors, school absences, and parental disengagement, which can have detrimental impacts on schooling progression (Capps et al. 2007; Chaudry et al. 2010). This is particularly true for immigrant boys, given their lower educational attainment and overall outcomes compared to girls (Qin 2006; Suarez-Orozco and Qin-Hillard 2004).

Amuedo-Dorantes and Lopez (2015, 2017) examine how intensified interior immigration enforcement, through its link to deportation fear and financial constraints, impacts children's school performance. Using data on Hispanic children aged 6–17 from the 2000–2013 CPS October School Enrollment Supplement, they show that the intensification of interior immigration enforcement raises young children's (aged 6–13) probability of repeating a grade by 14 percent and the likelihood of dropping out of school of older children (aged 14–17) by 18 percent. While the effect on younger children aged 6–13 does not survive all identification and robustness checks, and is seemingly concentrated among Mexican children in particular, the impact of intensified immigration enforcement on the propensity of older youth aged 14–17 to drop out of school is robust. Additionally, the authors consider the policy channels through which these impacts are taking place and find that the increase in police-based enforcement from 2000 through 2013 raised the likelihood of grade repetition by 14 percent among kids aged 6–13 typically attending K–8. In addition, the spread of employment-verification mandates appears to have raised school dropout rates by 9 percent among older, often work-eligible, youth aged 14–17.

Overall, the findings from Amuedo-Dorantes and Lopez (2015, 2017) uncover some of the hidden costs of intensified enforcement on children who are, for the most part, U.S. citizens. This is an important area of research for various reasons. First, the fact that the number of U.S.-born children under the age of 18 living with at least one unauthorized parent more than doubled between 2000 and 2012 (Passel, Cohn, and Rohal 2014). Second, it is well known that that grade retention is one of the strongest predictors of dropping out of school. Finally, low educational attainment is the most important determinant of the earnings gap between Hispanics and non-Hispanic whites (Trejo 1997; Xia and Kirby 2009).

SUMMARY AND CONCLUSIONS

In this chapter, we have aimed to provide an overview of the growth and modalities of interior immigration enforcement, the data and econometric challenges encountered by researchers interested in examining its implications, and some of the consequences on undocumented immigrants and their families—many of them mixed-status households with U.S. citizen children. We show how, in addition to adversely impacting residential choices and the labor market outcomes of undocumented immigrants, the measures also break apart families, raise the poverty exposure of 4.5 million of U.S. citizen children, and negatively affect their schooling outcomes.

A better understanding of the collateral damage of intensified immigration enforcement on U.S. citizen children and immigrant families is crucial, given that some of the sought-after goals, such as reducing crime (e.g., Thomas and Cox 2014), do not seem to have materialized. The Trump administration is planning to recover the 287(g) mandates, together with the Secure Communities program. It has also expanded the priority list of ICE and raised deportations—actions that are leading to the broken families. Our hope is that the provided evidence will inform the public and guide us toward a joint effort to enact a comprehensive and more humane immigration reform.

Notes

1. The conditions included being U.S. citizens, having their backgrounds investigated, and having a minimum of one year of tenure in their current position (ICE 2016).
2. Various counties had the Department of Justice look into allegations of racial profiling. See, for example, the investigation by the Department of Justice in Maricopa County, which concluded that the sheriff's office regularly committed racial profiling of Latinos. https://www.justice.gov/sites/default/files/crt/legacy/2011/12/15/mcso_findletter_12-15-11.pdf% (accessed November 17, 2017).
3. Where k refers to each policy; that is, 287(g) local, 287(g) state, Secure Communities, omnibus immigration law, and E-Verify.
4. This clause established that police have to determine the immigration status of any person suspected of being an illegal during a lawful stop.

References

Acosta, Yesenia D., Luke J. Larse, and Elizabeth M. Grieco. 2014. "Noncitizens under Age 35: 2010–2012." *American Community Survey Briefs*. Washington, DC: U.S. Census Bureau.

Amuedo-Dorantes, Catalina, and Esther Arenas-Arroyo. 2016. "Immigrant Fertility in the Midst of Intensified Enforcement." GLO Discussion Paper No. 1. Global Labor Organization.

———. 2017. "The Changing Family Structure of American Children with Unauthorized Parents Catalina." Discussion Paper No. 11/17. London: Center for Reserach and Analysis of Migration.

———. 2018. "Immigrant Fertility in the Midst of Intensified Enforcement." WP-18-134. Oxford: Centre on Migration, Policy and Society, University of Oxford.

Amuedo-Dorantes, Catalina, Esther Arenas-Arroyo, and Almudena Sevilla. 2018. "Immigration Enforcement and Economic Resources of Children with Likely Unauthorized Parents." *Journal of Public Economics* 158(c): 63–78.
Amuedo-Dorantes, Catalina, and Cynthia Bansak. 2012. "The Labor Market Impact of Mandated Employment." *American Economic Review: Papers & Proceedings* 102(3): 543–548.
———. 2014. "Employment Verification Mandates and the Labor Market Outcomes of Likely Unauthorized and Native Workers." *Contemporary Economic Policy* 32(3): 671–680. doi:10.1111/coep.12043 (accessed November 30, 2017).
Amuedo-Dorantes, Catalina, Cynthia Bansak, and Allan A. Zebedee. 2015. "The Impact of Mandated Employment Verification Systems on State-Level Employment by Foreign Affiliates." *Southern Economic Journal* 81(4): 928–946. doi:10.1002/soej.12042 (accessed November 30, 2017).
Amuedo-Dorantes, Catalina, and Mary Lopez. 2015. "Falling through the Cracks? Grade Retention and School Dropout among Children of Likely Unauthorized Parents." *American Economic Review* 105(5): 598–603.
———. 2017. "The Hidden Educational Costs of Intensified Immigration Enforcement." *Southern Economic Journal* 84(1): 120–154.
Amuedo-Dorantes, Catalina, and Fernando Lozano. 2017a. "Interstate Mobility Patterns of Likely Unauthorized Immigrants: Evidence from Arizona." IZA DP No. 10685. Bonn: Institute for the Study of Labor.
———. 2017b. "Interstate Mobility Patterns of Likely Unauthorized Immigrants: Evidence from Arizona." Photocopy.
Amuedo-Dorantes, Catalina, and Thitima Puttitanun. 2014. "Remittances and Immigration Enforcement." *IZA Journal of Migration* 3(6). doi:10.1186/2193-9039-3-6.
Amuedo-Dorantes, Catalina, Thitima Puttitanun, and Ana P. Martinez-Donate. 2013. "How Do Tougher Immigration Measures Affect Unauthorized Immigrants?" *Demography* 50(3): 1067–1091. doi:10.1007/s13524-013-0200-x (accessed November 30, 2017).
Bacon Immigration Law and Policy Program and the Southwest Institute for Research on Women 2011. *Left Back: The Impact of SB1070 on Arizona's Youth*. Tucson: University of Arizona.
Bean, Frank D., Thomas J. Espenshade, Michael J. White, and Robert F. Dymowksi. 1990. "Post-IRCA Changes in the Volume and Composition of Undocumented Migration to the United States: An Assessment Based on Apprehensions Data." In *Undocumented Migration to the United States: IRCA and the Experience of the 1980s*, Frank D. Bean, Barry Edmonston, and Jeffrey S. Passel, eds. Washington, DC: Urban Institute, pp. 111–158.
Bergeron, Claire, and Faye Hipsman. 2014. "The Deportation Dilemma: Rec-

onciling Tough and Humane Enforcement." Washington, DC: Migration Policy Institute.

Bohn, Sarah, and Magnus Lofstrom. 2013. "Employment Effects of State Legislation against the Hiring of Unauthorized Immigrant Workers." In *Immigration, Poverty, and Socioeconomic Inequality*, David Card and Steven Raphael, eds. New York: Russell Sage Foundation, pp. 282–314.

Bohn, Sarah, Magnus Lofstrom, and Steven Raphael. 2014. "Did the 2007 Legal Arizona Workers Act Reduce the States Unauthorized Immigrants?" *Review of Economics and Statistics* 96(2): 258–269.

———. 2015. "Do E-Verify Mandates Improve Labor Market Outcomes of Low-Skilled Native and Legal Immigrant Workers?" *Southern Economic Journal* 81(4): 960–979.

Bohn, Sarah, and Todd Pugatch. 2013. "U.S. Border Enforcement and Mexican Immigrant Location Choice." *Demography* 52(5): 1543–1570.

Capps, Randy, Rosa Maria Castaneda, Ajay Chaudry, and Robert Santos. 2007. "Paying the Price: The Impact of Immigration Raids on America's Children." Washington, DC: Urban Institute. doi:10.1017/CBO9781107415324.004 (accessed November 30, 2017).

Chaudry, Ajay, Randy Capps, Juan Manuel Pedroza, Rosa Maria Castaneda, Robert Santos, Molly M Scott, and Urban Institute. 2010. "Facing Our Future: Children in the Aftermath of Immigration Enforcement." Washington, DC: Urban Institute. doi:10.1037/e726272011-001 (accessed November 30, 2017).

Ciancio, Alberto. 2016. "The Impact of Immigration Policies on Local Enforcement, Crime and Policing Efficiency." Working paper. Philadelphia: University of Pennsylvania.

Debry, Joanna. 2012. "How Today's Immigration Enforcement Policies Impact Children, Families, and Communities." Washington, DC: Center for American Progress. https://www.americanprogress.org/issues/immigration/reports/2012/08/20/27082/how-todays-immigration-enforcement-policies-impact-children-families-and-communities/ (accessed November 30, 2017).

Department of Homeland Security (DHS). 2016. "DHS Releases End of Year Fiscal Year 2016 Statistics." Washington, DC: DHS. https://www.dhs.gov/news/2016/12/30/dhs-releases-end-year-fiscal-year-2016-statistics (accessed November 30, 2017).

Espenshade, Thomas J. 1990. "Undocumented Migration to the United States: Evidence from a Repeated Trials Model." In *Undocumented Migration to the United States: IRCA and the Experience of the 1980s*. Frank D. Bean, Barry Edmonston, and Jeffrey S. Passel. Washington, DC: Urban Institute, pp. 159–182.

————. 1994. "Does the Threat of Border Apprehension Deter Undocumented U.S. Immigration?" *Population Council* 20(4): 871–892.

Espino, Rodolfo, and Rafael A. Jimeno. 2013. "Rhetoric and Realities: American Immigration Policy after September 11, 2001." In *Immigration and the Border*, David Leal and Jose E. Limon, eds. South Bend, IN: University of Notre Dame, Chapter 11.

Fagan, Jeffrey, and Tracey L. Meares. 2008. "Punishment, Deterrence and Social Control: The Paradox of Punishment in Minority Communities." *Ohio State Journal of Criminal Law* 6: 173–229.

Fagan, Jeffrey, and Tom R. Tyler. 2008. "Legitimacy, Compliance and Cooperation: Procedural Justice and Citizen Ties to the Law." *Ohio State Journal of Criminal Law* 6: 231–275.

Gonzalez-Barrera, Ana, and Jens Manuel Krogstad. 2017. "What We Know about Illegal Immigration from Mexico." *Fact Tank: News in the Numbers* (blog), Pew Research Center, March 2. http://www.pewresearch.org/fact-tank/2017/03/02/what-we-know-about-illegal-immigration-from-mexico/ (accessed March 22, 2018).

Good, Michael. 2013. "Do Immigrant Outflows Lead to Native Inflows? An Empirical Analysis of the Migratory Responses." *Applied Economics* 45(30): 4275–4397.

Hoefer, Michael, Bryan Baker, and Nancy Rytin. 2013. "Estimates of Unauthorized Immigrant Population Residing in the United States: January 2009." *Population Estimates*. Washington, DC: Office of Immigration Statistics.

Immigration Policy Center. 2012. "The 287 (G) Program : A Flawed and Obsolete Method of Immigration Enforcement." Washington, DC: Immigration Policy Center.

Kostandini, Genti, Elton Mykerezi, and Cesar Escalante. 2013. "The Impact of Immigration Enforcement on the U.S. Farming Sector." *American Journal of Agricultural Economics* 96(1): 172–192. doi:10.1093/ajae/aat081 (accessed December 1, 2017).

Kotkin, Joel, and Erika Ozuna. 2012. "America's Demographic Future." *Cato Journal* 32(1): 55–70.

Krogstad, Jens Manuel, Mark Hugo Lopez, Gustavo López, Jeffrey S. Passel, and Eileen Patten. 2016. "Millennials Make Up Almost Half of Latino Eligible Voters in 2016." Washington, DC: Pew Research Center. http://www.pewhispanic.org/2016/01/19/millennials-make-up-almost-half-of-latino-eligible-voters-in-2016/ (accessed November 30, 2016).

Livingston, Gretchen, and D'Vera Cohn. 2012. *U.S. Birth Rate Falls to a Record Low; Decline Is Greatest among Immigrants*. Technical report. Washington, DC: Pew Research Center. Washington.

Meissner, Doris, Donald M. Kerwin, Muzaffar Chishti, and Claire Bergeron. 2013. *Immigration Enforcement in the United States: The Rise of a Formidable Machinery*. Technical report. Washington, DC: Migration Policy Institute.

Miles, Thomas J., and Adam B. Cox. 2014. "Does Immigration Enforcement Reduce Crime? Evidence from Secure Communities." *Journal of Law and Economics* 57(4): 937–973.

National Conference of State Legislatures. 2017. "State E-Verify Laws." Washington, DC: National Conference of State Legislatures. http://www.ncsl .org/research/immigration/everify-faq.aspx#2012 State Action (accessed Decembe 1, 2017).

Orrenius, Pia M., and Madeline Zavodny. 2009. "The Effects of Tougher Enforcement on the Job Prospects of Recent Latin American Immigrants." *Journal of Policy Analysis and Management* 28(2): 239–57. doi:10.1002/ pam (accessed December 1, 2017).

———. 2015. "The Impact of E-Verify Mandates on Labor Market Outcomes." *Southern Economic Journal* 81(4): 947–59. doi:10.1002/soej.12023 (accessed December 1, 2017).

———. 2016. "Do State Work Eligibility Verification Laws Reduce Unauthorized Immigration?" *IZA Journal of Migration* 5(1). doi:10.1186/s40176-016 -0053-3 (accessed December 1, 2017).

Orrenius, Pia M., Madeline Zavodny, and Emily Gutierrez. 2016. "Do State Employment Eligibility Verification Laws Affect Job Turnover?" *Contemporary Economic Policy.* http://onlinelibrary.wiley.com/doi/10.1111/ coep.12251/full (accessed December 1, 2017).

Passel, Jeffrey S., and D'Vera Cohn. 2009. "A Portrait of Unauthorized Immigrants in the United States." Washington, DC: Pew Research Center. http:// www.pewhispanic.org/2009/04/14/a-portrait-of-unauthorized-immigrants -in-the-united-states/ (accessed December 1, 2017).

———. 2011. "Unauthorized Immigrant Population: National and State Trends, 2010." Washington, DC: Pew Research Center.

Passel, Jeffrey S., D'Vera Cohn, and Molly Rohal. 2014. "Unauthorized Immigrant Totals Rise in 7 States, Fall in 14: Decline in Those From Mexico Fuels Most State Decreases." Washington, DC: Pew Research Center.

Passel, Jeffrey S., and Paul Taylor. 2010. "Unauthorized Immigrants and Their U.S. Born Children." Washington, DC: Pew Research Center. http://www .pewhispanic.org/2010/08/11/unauthorized-immigrants-and-their-us-born -children/ (accessed December 1, 2017).

Pope, Nolan G. 2016. "The Effects of DACAmentation: The Impact of Deferred Action for Childhood Arrivals on Unauthorized Immigrants." *Journal of Public Economics* 143(c): 98–114. doi:10.1016/j.jpubeco .2016.08.014 (accessed December 1, 2017).

Qin, Desiree Baolian. 2006. "The Role of Gender in Immigrant Children's Educational Adaptation." East Lansing, MI: Michigan State University. https://files.eric.ed.gov/fulltext/EJ847390.pdf (accessed December 1, 2017).

Rendall, Michael S., Bonnie Ghosh-Dastidar, Margaret M. Weden, Elizabeth H. Baker, and Zafar Nazarov. 2013. "Multiple Imputation for Combined-Survey Estimation with Incomplete Regressors in One but Not Both Surveys." *Sociological Methods & Research* 42(4): 483–530.

Rosenblum, Marc R. 2015. "Federal-Local Cooperation on Immigration Enforcement Frayed; Chance for Improvement Exists." Washington, DC: Migration Policy Institute.

Rosenblum, Marc R., Doris Meissner, Claire Bergeron, and Faye Hipsman. 2014. "The Deportation Dilemma: Reconciling Tough and Humane Enforcement." Washington, DC: Migration Policy Institute.

Skogan, Wesley, and Kathleen Frydl, eds. 2004. *Fairness and Effectiveness in Policing: The Evidence*. Washington, DC: National Academies Press.

Suarez-Orozco, and Desiree Baolian Qin-Hillard. 2004. "Immigrant Boys' Experiences in U.S. Schools." In *Adolescent Boys: Exploring Diverse Cultures of Boyhood*, Niobe Way and Judy Chu, eds. New York: NYU Press.

Trejo, Stephen J. 1997. "Why Do Mexican Immigrants Earn Low Wages?" *Journal of Political Economy* 105(6): 1235–1268.

Tyler, T.R. 2010. "Legitimacy in Corrections: Policy Implications." *Criminology and Public Policy* 9: 127–134.

U.S. Immigration and Customs Enforcement (ICE). 2016. "Delegation of Immigration Authority Section 287(g) Immigration and Nationality Act." Washington, DC: ICE. https://www.ice.gov/factsheets/287g (accessed December 1, 2017).

———. 2017. "Secure Communities." Washington, DC: ICE. https://www.ice.gov/secure-communities#tab1 (accessed December 1, 2017).

Van Hook, Jennifer, James D. Bachmeier, Donna L. Coffman, and Ofer Harel. 2015. "Can We Spin Straw Into Gold? An Evaluation of Immigrant Legal Status Imputation Approaches." *Demography* 52(1): 329–354.

Vaughan, Jessica M. 2013. *Deportation Numbers Unwrapped: Raw Statistics Reveal the Real Story of ICE Enforcement in Decline*. Washington, DC: Center for Immigration Studies.

Watson, Tara. 2013. "Enforcement and Immigrant Location Choice." NBER Working Paper No. 19626. Cambridge, MA: National Bureau of Economic Research.

———. 2014. "Inside the Refrigerator: Immigration Enforcement and Chilling Effects in Medicaid Participation." *American Economic Journal: Economic Policy* 6(3): 313–338.

Xia, Nailing, and Sheila Nataraj Kirby. 2009. *Retaining Students in Grade:*

A Literature Review of the Effects of Retention on Students. Technical report prepared for the New York City Department of Education. Santa Monica, CA: RAND. http://www.rand.org/content/dam/rand/pubs/technical_reports/2009/RAND_TR678.pdf (accessed December 1, 2017).

6
Understanding Migration Policy

Insights from Models of International Trade

Alfonso Cebreros
Daniel Chiquiar
Monica Roa
Martín Tobal
Mexico Central Bank

Recent developments have placed immigration at the forefront of the policy debate, creating much controversy around the associated trade-offs for host economies. Indeed, immigration triggers opposing effects on the welfare of different groups within a country, and this opens the door for conflicting arguments and heated debates. The implication has been a proliferation of arguments both in favor of and against immigration. In turn, this creates a need for accomplishing theoretical and empirical work that can better inform the policy debate.

This chapter takes a step in this direction by showing how instruments traditionally included in the economists' tool kit can shed light on relevant but largely controversial issues. In particular, the chapter uses a standard model of international trade to show that immigrants with complementary skills may increase the productivity of scarce factors and, through this channel, enhance overall welfare in host nations.[1] However, the income levels of some groups within the host country may be negatively affected, and thus they may oppose migration.

There are several arguments that either have been or could in principle be used to support immigration. One of these arguments claims that immigrants play an active and indispensable role in promoting dynamism, innovation, and scientific progress in host economies. This argument is consistent, for instance, with the finding that 45 percent of high-tech firms from the Fortune 500 had either a first- or a second-generation immigrant among its founders (Partnership for a New American Economy 2011).[2] Moreover, the premise that immigrants largely contribute to scientific progress is consistent with Figures 6.1 and 6.2.[3] Figure 6.1 shows that the number of Nobel prizes obtained by a country is positively associated with the ratio of immigrants-to-natives that have won the prize, and Figure 6.2 shows that this ratio is positively correlated with the number of registered patents, even after controlling for real GDP per capita.

An additional argument in favor of migration could be that immigrants complement native workers in host labor markets. According to this argument, immigrants' skills are generally complementary to those possessed by native workers and, therefore, immigration reduces labor shortages in both low- and high-skilled occupations. By complementing native workers in production, immigration would create job opportunities and increase their wages. Consistent with this idea, Figure 6.3 shows that immigrants in the United States are relatively concentrated at the top and at the bottom of the skill distribution, while natives are relatively more concentrated in the middle.

Figure 6.1 Nobel Prizes Awarded, 1901–2014 (top 5 countries)

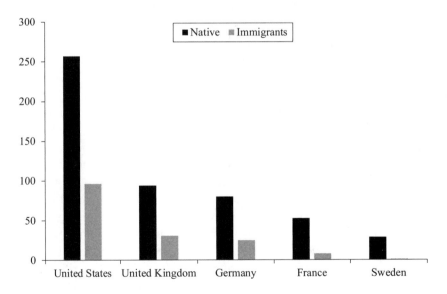

SOURCE: Authors' calculations based on data from Nobelprize.org and the World Atlas.

Figure 6.2 High-Skill Migration and Patents Registered (as a percentage of GDP per capita)

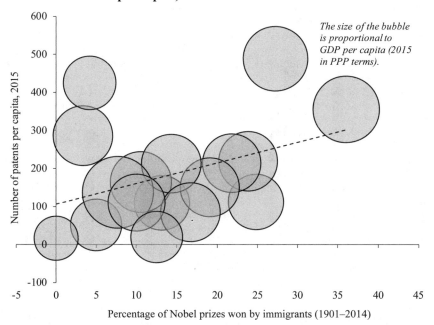

NOTE: Each observation in the figure is represented as proportion of real GDP per capita.

SOURCE: Authors' calculations based on data from Nobelprize.org, World Atlas, World Bank, and U.S. Patent and Trademark Office.

On the opposite side of the debate, several arguments have been or could be used to oppose immigration and favor restrictions to international labor mobility. One of these arguments emphasizes that, in those markets in which natives compete with foreigners, immigration triggers competition for the same types of jobs, depressing wages and raising unemployment (see De New and Zimmermann [1994] for evidence on the German labor market). Another argument relies on the fiscal costs that foreigners could impose on host countries. It has been argued that, due to their age, skill, fertility, and language characteristics, immigrants may consume large amounts of government-funded goods but, on the other hand, increase fiscal revenues only by a small amount (Nowrasteh 2015).

Figure 6.3 Native-Born Americans and Nonnatives (as a percentage of their total population, aged 25 and over, 2015)

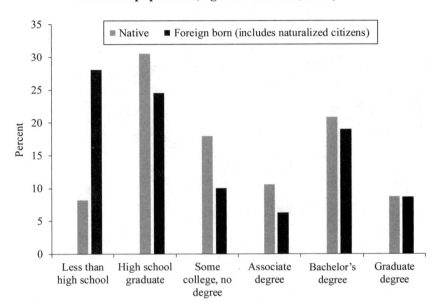

NOTE: The total population aged 25 and over is divided into native and foreign born, and then each category is divided according to educational attainment. Thus, the gray bars sum up to a 100% and the black bars sum up to 100%. The category "graduate degree" groups people with masters, doctoral, and professional degrees.
SOURCE: Authors' calculations based on data from the Current Population Survey, 2015.

The fact that immigration can in principle generate several and conflicting effects on welfare, as well as the existence of inconclusive answers to relevant questions, highlights the need for economists to take part of the policy debate that surrounds immigration. Indeed, economists need to steer this debate toward policy prescriptions and cost-benefit analysis, which is better informed by economic theory and empirical work. A proper cost-benefit framework and, more generally, a more proactive role by economists, could improve our understanding of relevant trade-offs and increase the number of good estimates about immigration impacts.

In this context, this chapter proposes a simple framework to formalize some of the trade-offs that have been associated with immigration.

Specifically, it sets a standard two-good, two-factor, two-country model of trade and explores a topic that has not yet been deeply investigated in the literature. To be more precise, the model explores the importance of assessing the skill composition of migration when performing welfare analysis and investigates how certain public policies affect migration.

The analysis is carried out by studying the impacts of international trade and migration under five different scenarios: (1) autarky; (2) free trade and no migration; (3) mutual trade restrictions and no migration; (4) free migration and no international trade; and (5) tax on migration and no international trade. This analysis generates several interesting and insightful conclusions.

First, when the welfare function of the recipient country is assumed to correspond to the well-being of local inhabitants—that is, either because immigration policy decisions are taken ex ante or because, just as in any theoretical model of political economy, decision makers care about voters—the free-trade and the free-migration scenarios generate isomorphic results in terms of welfare and redistribution. In other words, by complementing the abundant factor, immigrants increase overall welfare but reduce the returns to the scarce factor in the recipient country.

Although the aforementioned equivalence between trade and immigration is frequently evoked in academic circles, this chapter contributes to the literature by showing that the result holds precisely for the most relevant measure of welfare from a political point of view (migrants do not vote and, thus, electoral speeches frequently focus only on natives). Moreover, the use of this measure is an innovation relative to existing theories that investigate the effects of migration in factor proportion models (Dixit and Norman 1980).

Second, there is an additional and relevant contribution of the chapter that is also based on the equivalence between the free trade and the free migration scenarios, particularly on public policies associated with the associated equilibria. Specifically, we compare outcomes of the mutual trade restrictions environment analyzed in scenario (3) with those that arise from the immigration policy case considered in scenario (5). Through this comparison it is shown that, for each level of mutual trade restrictions, there is a migration tax that replicates the same results in terms of welfare and redistribution effects from the perspective of the host country.

Third, we can conclude that, given that migration enhances overall welfare but generates income redistribution, just as an import tariff does, migration policies may be strongly influenced by political economy concerns and not necessarily by efficiency considerations—that is, protectionist policies on trade and migration have the same redistribution effects and, therefore, may be based on the same kind of political economy considerations. Hence, we propose an extension of the model to illustrate one of the channels through which this influence may occur. That is, we combine a standard relative endowment framework with a political economy model for the determination of immigration policies. Consistent with the results of Galiani and Torrens (2015), we conclude that restrictions to international labor mobility may result from political economy motivations.

LITERATURE REVIEW

Economists have long been interested in understanding the effects and determinants of immigration, as well as the impacts of different immigration policy measures. This interest has given rise to both theoretical and empirical works, several of which keep a close relationship with this chapter. On the empirical front, economists' interest has produced a large body of literature performing evaluations in three domains: 1) the determinants of migration decisions, 2) the impacts of migration on host labor markets, and 3) the effects of migration policies.

As for the factors determining immigration decisions, Borjas (1991) and Chiquiar and Hanson (2005) are two relevant studies. Both coincide that educational attainment is a critical determinant of immigration, meaning that differences in the skill returns between source and host countries provide distinct incentives to migrate to workers located in different segments of the skill distribution. Along these lines, Chiquiar and Hanson show that Mexican immigrants to the United States are on average more educated than Mexican residents but less educated than U.S. natives. Continuing with this line of research, Mayda (2010), Beine, Docquier, and Özden (2011), and Ortega and Peri (2013) find that immigration decisions are also influenced by three additional determinants: 1) income per capita and unemployment in the source and destination countries, 2) the stock of people from the source nation residing in the destination country, and 3) the restrictiveness of immigration policies.

Regarding the strand of literature dealing with the impacts of migration on host labor markets, several of the arguments were proposed by Card and Borjas in the context of the "Mariel boatlift" episode—45,000 Cubans arrived in Miami, increasing its labor supply by 7 percent (mostly low-skill labor). On one hand, Card (1990) compared the labor market outcomes of workers from different ethnicities and workers at different segments of the wage distribution within Miami across time periods, and the outcomes for different workers in Miami with outcomes of similar workers in other American cities. This comparison led him to conclude that the surge of labor supply in 1980 had no discernible impact on labor market outcomes in Miami (i.e., the changes in employment and wages in Miami were comparable to those observed in other American cities over the same time period). On the other hand, Borjas (2016) later revisited the Mariel boatlift episode and argued that 60 percent of the influx of Cuban workers were high school dropouts and that, as one focused on this specific segment of the labor market, wages in Miami decreased between 10 and 30 percent.

The third strand of empirical literature explores the effectiveness of immigration policies mainly on the size and the composition of migration flows. It has been shown that tighter immigration restrictions significantly reduce the size of migration flows, except for the case of asylum migration (Czaika and de Hass 2014; Thielemann 2004).[4] In contrast, the impacts on the composition of migration flows are harder to assess, mostly because it is difficult to construct indexes that can capture the restrictiveness of policies on specific groups of immigrants. Along these lines, Thielemann (2004) and de Haas, Natter, and Vezzoli (2014) propose different indexes and using them show that immigration policies have affected the size of migration flows but not necessarily their composition. This suggests that more research is required to come up with appropriate restrictiveness measures when studying the composition of migration flows. An additional challenge is given by the lack of studies evaluating the long-term impact of immigration policies, because most existing studies focus on immediate impacts (Czaika and de Hass 2013, 2015).

As a final remark on the empirical literature it should be noted that, although much has been done in terms of assessing relevant impacts, there is further need for empirical work investigating the relationship between the skill profile of migrants and the skill profile of the host country's labor force. At the same time, it would be important to investigate whether the skill supply of migrants is generally complementary to or substitute of the skill supply of the native labor force.

On the theoretical front, two works relate closely to ours: Dixit and Norman (1980) and Galiani and Torrens (2015). Just as we do here, Dixit and Norman (1980) set a standard model of international trade to investigate the effects of immigration. In the benchmark case, they consider a neoclassical factor proportion framework with two countries, two factors, and two goods.

An interesting point of comparison between Dixit and Norman (1980) and our work refers to the measure of welfare used in each case. Unlike us, they take as a welfare measure the well-being of both native and migrant workers and, in this context, show that immigration entails two types of effects. First, there is a direct effect that results from changing the size of the host country's population while holding prices constant. Given our interest in using a more politically relevant measure, this is the effect that our model does not consider. Besides, there is an indirect effect that results from changes in the terms of trade. Dixit and Norman's conclusion (1980) is that there are no clear-cut answers for the net effects of migration.

The second theoretical paper related to ours is Galiani and Torrens (2015). In contrast with our factor proportion approach to international trade, they opt for a Ricardian framework featuring differences in technology across sectors and countries. However, just as our study does, their work extends a standard model of trade to account for political economy motivations. They combine their Ricardian economy with a simple international political economy model in which governments jointly decide on trade and immigration policies. In their framework, countries specialize in different goods and thus use different types of technologies. This implies that trade does not reduce real wages in any of the countries, but immigration diminishes them in the technologically advanced rich nation. Real wage differences induce workers to migrate there, increasing the labor supply and depressing real labor returns. Hence, while trade can be supported as a Nash equilibrium of the international political economy game, free international labor mobility cannot. In the same spirit of this chapter, they conclude that restrictions to migration are the result of political economy motivations.

MODEL SETUP

Consider a world with two countries, two factors, and two goods. The two countries, North and South, are indexed by N and S; the two factors, skilled and unskilled labor, are denoted by H and L; and the two goods are a skilled-intensive good and an unskilled-intensive good. The price of the former good is referred to as P, while the price of the latter good is chosen as the numeraire and will thus take the value of 1. North is assumed to be the skilled-labor abundant country; hence, $L_N/H_N < L_S/H_S$.

Technologies are identical across nations. In both countries, production is given by the following Cobb-Douglas constant-returns-to-scale functions:

$$(6.1) \quad Y_{js} = \varepsilon_s \left(H_{js}^{\beta} L_{js}^{1-\beta} \right),$$

$$(6.2) \quad Y_{ju} = \varepsilon_u \left(H_{ju}^{\alpha} L_{ju}^{1-\alpha} \right),$$

where Y_{js} and Y_{ju} refer to the production of the skilled- and unskilled-intensive goods in country j and our skill-intensity assumption implies $\beta > \alpha$, where $\beta < 1$ and $\alpha < 1$; H_{js} and L_{js} denote the amounts of skilled and unskilled workers used in the production of Y_{js}; and $\varepsilon_s = \beta^{-\beta}(1-\beta)^{-(1-\beta)}$ and $\varepsilon_u = \alpha^{-a}(1-\alpha)^{-(1-a)}$ are normalizations of the production functions.

Preferences, also identical across regions, are given by the following utility function:

$$(6.3) \quad U_j = c_{js}^{\gamma} c_{ju}^{1-\gamma},$$

where $\gamma < 1$ represents the relative preference for the skilled-intensive good and c_{js} denotes country j's consumption of this product. The indirect utility function associated with Equation (6.3) can be written as follows (see the online appendix for a full derivation):

$$(6.4) \quad V_j = \gamma^\gamma (1-\gamma)^{1-\gamma} I_j P_j^{-\gamma},$$

where I_j and P_j are the nominal income level and the price of the skilled-intensive good in country j. Equation (6.4) states that utility is increasing in real income; that is, given that the price of the unskilled-intensive good has been chosen as the numeraire, the price index faced by consumers in this region equals $(1)^{1-\gamma} P_j^\gamma = P_j^\gamma$.

Labor and product markets are perfectly competitive; therefore, in equilibrium, profits must equal zero. Finally, we assume that relative labor supplies are sufficiently similar across regions that there is always incomplete specialization in equilibrium.

PRELIMINARY CONSIDERATIONS

It is possible to illustrate common patterns among the five scenarios we consider in terms of welfare. For scenarios (1)–(3), we follow the literature and use the indirect utility function shown in Equation (6.4). In scenarios (4) and (5), the argument is subtler since these scenarios consider migration, which in turn may threaten the validity of the expression in Equation (6.4) as an appropriate indicator of welfare. To see this, note that when utility is measured as in (6.4), total income increases with factor endowments. The implication is that, when migration takes place, there is an almost mechanical increasing impact on utility through a rise in the country's population. In turn, the problem is that, by increasing the population size, immigration could also end up diminishing welfare in per capita terms.

Therefore, to prevent our measure from increasing mechanically in response to immigration, but also to concentrate on political economy aspects of migration policies, we focus on the welfare of native inhabitants. That is, in scenarios (6.4) and (6.5), the analysis abstracts from the direct impact of migration. Instead, this analysis focuses on the impact of migration on welfare through its effect on wages and on the relative price of the skilled-intensive good (see Equation [6.5] in the online appendix for a representation of the resulting measure of welfare). Hence, to evaluate welfare effects in scenarios (6.4) and (6.5), the chapter will concentrate on changes in real income and only on changes in this income arising from variations in relative prices, just as we will in scenarios (6.1)–(6.3). In this regard, it is important to note that this common pattern arises only from the fact that we have chosen the most relevant measure of welfare from a political economy point of view.

Indeed, in a perfect competition environment where profits are zero, real income equals the sum of real wage bills of skilled workers and unskilled employees. Thus, changes in a country's welfare—for instance, due to immigration—can be mapped to variations in its skilled wage, its unskilled wage, and its price index, which are in turn directly dependent on changes in the price for the skilled-intensive good (q_j, w_j and P_j).[5] Thus, consider for instance a rise in P_j. The direct impact of this rise is a profit increase for producers of the skilled-intensive good and a profit reduction for producers of the unskilled-intensive good. Hence, following the rise in P_j, the skilled wage must increase and the unskilled wage must fall so that the profits of both producer types return to zero. Moreover, the direction of these changes also holds for wages in real terms.

In summary, there are common patterns in terms of welfare among the five scenarios we consider. In all these scenarios, changes in a country's welfare depend on variations in its real income and, thus, on variations in its real skilled and unskilled wages, which in turn depend on movements on the price for the skilled-intensive good. That is, in the five scenarios we consider, changes in the welfare of country j can be expressed in terms of P_j. Equations (7) and (8) in the online appendix show that q_j and w_j can be written in terms of P_j and parameters of the production.

Taking this into account, Equations (6) and (9) in the online appendix derive an expression for real income and therefore for welfare that remains valid for each of the five scenarios we consider; thus, for instance, *to assess the welfare level obtained in a given scenario, it would suffice to plug in this common expression the relative price for the skilled-intensive good corresponding to the referred scenario.* Using this common expression, the online appendix shows that under certain conditions, real income in country j is well described by Figure 6.4. This figure shows that there is a value of P_j that we call P_j^* in which the effect of a price change on the skilled wage fully offsets its effects

Figure 6.4 Real Income (our measure of welfare) as a Function of P_j

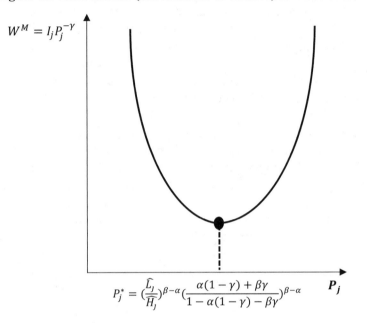

$$W^M = I_j P_j^{-\gamma}$$

$$P_j^* = (\frac{\widehat{L_j}}{\widehat{H_j}})^{\beta-\alpha}(\frac{\alpha(1-\gamma)+\beta\gamma}{1-\alpha(1-\gamma)-\beta\gamma})^{\beta-\alpha} \qquad P_j$$

SOURCE: Authors' calculations.

on the unskilled wage; that is, the effect of a marginal price change on real income is equal to zero.

AUTARKY

This section studies the equilibrium properties and welfare characteristics of two autarkic economies, North and South. The absence of international trade and migration implies that in the present section the two regions must be understood as fully separate economies, implying that their equilibria must be solved separately. In this scenario, North and South will have different prices for the skilled-intensive good and, thus, their real skilled and unskilled wages will differ in equilibrium.

Skilled and unskilled wages in each region are determined separately by the corresponding pair of zero-profit conditions—as noted above, profits equal zero for the producers of the two goods. Since this implies that goods prices equal unitary cost, which in turn depend on wages, the zero-profit conditions can be used to obtain skilled and unskilled wages in equilibrium. Precisely, these conditions allow writing skilled and unskilled wages in each region in terms of the price for the skilled-intensive good and, then, real wages also in terms of the same price. The online appendix uses the zero-profit conditions in Equations (10) and (11) to solve for skilled and unskilled wages in North under autarky in (12) and (13), i.e., q_N^{aut} and w_N^{aut}, in terms of the relevant price, P_N^{aut}; real wages are shown in (14) and (15); Equations (20) and (21) repeat the same procedure for South.

The results show that, as noted above for a more general case, a rise in the price of the skilled-intensive good increases the skilled wage while reducing the unskilled wage under autarky, and the intuition for this result goes as follows. In each region, the rise in this price increases profits for producers of the skilled-intensive good but reduces profits for producers of the unskilled-intensive good. Thus, the skilled wage must increase and the unskilled wage must fall so that the profits of both producer types return to zero. Moreover, given that real income depends directly on real skilled and unskilled wages, one can also write welfare in each region in terms of the price for the skilled-intensive good (see Equation [16] in the online appendix). In fact, this expression for welfare is symmetric to the expression that characterizes all scenarios mentioned in the previous section. Indeed, it is the same expression except for the fact that it contains the relative for the skilled-intensive good that corresponds to the autarky case, P_N^{aut}.

Having written wages in terms of this price, the ensuing expressions can be used to solve for the additional market-clearing condition—namely, equilibrium in the market of the skilled-intensive good—and, through this channel, find the equilibrium value of this price. Thus, using the expressions for wages obtained from the zero-profit conditions, we derive skill premia and use them to derive the supply of and demand for this good and, ultimately, the equilibrium. As stated in Equations (19) and (22) in the online appendix, the equilibrium price for the skilled-intensive good in a given region is increasing in the unskilled-to-skilled labor supply prevailing there.

This result is standard in the literature of factor-proportion models, and its intuition lies in the fact that regions with a relatively greater supply of skilled workers have, holding everything else constant, also a relatively greater supply of the skilled-intensive good. Thus, in these regions, the relative price for the skilled-intensive good must be smaller so that a larger amount of this is purchased in equilibrium. Moreover, given that in our model, North is the skilled-labor-abundant region, a direct implication of this standard result is that the price of the skilled-intensive good is greater in North than in South in equilibrium; that is, a $L_N/H_N < L_S/H_S$, as stated in the Model Setup section.

Regarding welfare, Figure 6.5 uses the expression in which welfare depends on the price for the skilled-intensive good that was mentioned earlier and that, as noted above, remains valid for all scenarios we consider. Specifically, this figure shows the two curves that result from plugging P_N^{aut} and P_S^{aut} separately in this expression. Note in this figure that the equilibrium price under autarky is the price at which the effect of a marginal price change on real income is equal to zero; using the notation from Figure 6.4, we write $P_N^{aut} = P_N^*$ and that $P_S^{aut} = P_S^*$. In this regard, it is important to note that, although Figure 6.5 would seem to suggest that the welfare function attains a minimum at P_j^* for given endowment levels, we are not minimizing welfare through resource allocation.

The autarky equilibria depicted in Figure 6.5 is the most efficient one among all feasible choices for the resources held in the economy. Any of the other allocations in this figure yield a higher welfare but, nonetheless, require relaxing the constraints defining this function—more resources or better technology. Indeed, as noted below, reaching greater welfare is possible through the separation of consumption and production decisions generated by international trade, which will lead the economies to different points of the curves by allowing them to consume a different bundle from the one they produce, just as if they had more resources.

FREE INTERNATIONAL TRADE

This section considers a scenario in which there is international trade but no migration flows. While international trade equalizes the price of the skilled-intensive good across regions, the absence of migra-

Figure 6.5 Real Income as a Function of P_j in Autarky

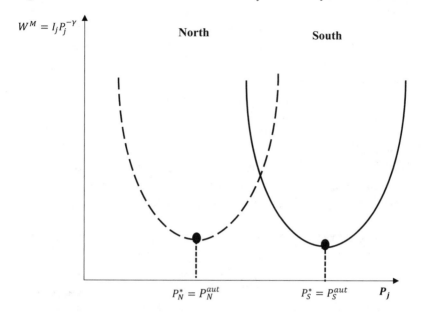

SOURCE: Authors' calculations.

tion implies that real wages in this section are only determined by this price and not by migration flows.

Just as in the previous section, the zero-profit conditions allow writing wages and real wages in terms of the price for the skilled-intensive good; although, as noted above, this equilibrium price and thus wages and real wages in this section are identical across regions. Equations (23)–(26) in the online appendix show their expressions. Also, as in the previous section, the price for the skilled-intensive good must be market clearing in equilibrium and thus can also be found by equating the demand for the skilled-intensive good to its supply. Yet, a difference with respect to the autarky case is that in the free trade scenario considered in this section, the relevant demand is the world demand while the relevant supply is the world supply. That is, unlike in the previous section, the market-clearing conditions for the skilled-intensive good with trade are defined at the global level.

Thus, we use the expressions for wages as a function of the price for the skilled-intensive good to derive skill-premia and the supply and demand of this good in each region, sum these supplies and demands, and then find the price that clears the world market (see Equations [27]–[30] in the online appendix). The result shows that the price for the skilled-intensive good is increasing in the unskilled-to-skilled labor supply of the world economy; Equation (31) in the online appendix shows this price, P^{FT}. Intuitively, this result is analogous to the one obtained in the previous section, implying that there is also a similar intuition behind in this case. Specifically, the greater the world supply of skilled workers, the greater the world supply of the skilled-intensive good becomes and therefore the smaller the price of the good must be in equilibrium. Indeed, the free trade equilibrium is analogous to the equilibrium of an autarkic economy in which the labor supplies result from summing the Northern and Southern supplies ($H_W = H_N + H_S$ and $L_W = L_N + L_S$).

Using these results, the effects of trade on welfare and income distribution in each region can be obtained by comparing the equilibrium price for the skilled-intensive good from this section to the one obtained for the autarky case. The results show that trade leads the equilibrium price of the skilled-intensive good to a point between the autarky price of the North and the autarky price of the South, i.e., $P_N^{aut} < P^{FT} < P_S^{aut}$. This is also a standard result in factor-proportion models and shows that the specialization induced by international trade obeys the patterns of relative labor supplies of each country. Compared to autarky, the relative price change generated by trade induces each country to increase production of the good for which it has a comparative advantage.

Furthermore, the change in the price for the skilled-intensive good has relevant implications for redistribution. In North, this price increases relative to the autarky case and this implies that, given that the zero-profits conditions must be fulfilled, the real skilled wage increases but the real unskilled wage falls in this region. In other words, as predicted by the traditional Stolper-Samuel Theorem and the so-called Jones Magnification effect (Jones 1965), while in "northern economies" skilled workers gain from international trade, unskilled workers lose. In contrast, the opposite movements are observed for South so that in this economy the unskilled workers are the winners from trade.

Beyond these redistribution effects, international trade in our model generates clear predictions for welfare in aggregate terms, and these predictions can be also assessed by comparing the price of the skilled-

Figure 6.6 Real Income as a Function of P_j under Free Trade

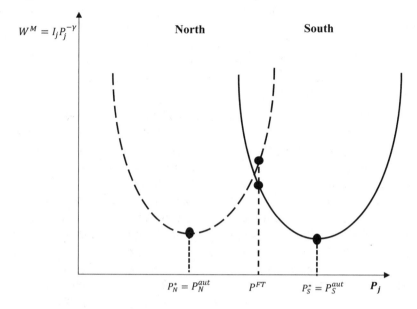

SOURCE: Authors' calculations.

intensive good in the free trade equilibrium and the autarky scenario. Figure 6.6 uses this result, and the expression for welfare that is valid for the five scenarios, to show the results. Note in this figure that in both North and South welfare increases relative to the autarky case. Indeed, trade allows countries to reach an allocation that would only be possible under autarky if each region had more resources and/or a better technology. The intuition for this result lies on the fact that, by allowing countries to separate consumption from production bundles, trade openness provides the opportunity to reach an otherwise unfeasible consumption basket.

MUTUAL TRADE RESTRICTIONS

Starting from a free trade environment, this section considers a scenario in which each region imposes an import tariff on the product of the other region, but immigration is still not allowed. The goal is to set a benchmark for comparison with the following section, in which immigration is permitted only to a certain extent, just as international trade is only partially permitted in the present section.[6]

The tariff is assumed to be identical across countries and to take the iceberg form so that, for one unit of a product to arrive in the other country, $\tau > 1$ must be shipped, i.e., the rest melts away in transit. This tariff increases the effective price of the imported product in each region, creating a wedge between domestic and international prices and, through this channel, preventing the effective relative price of the skilled-intensive good from being equal across regions—this price increases in South and diminishes in North. Considering these changes, and given that the zero-profit conditions must still hold, the skilled wage must fall and the unskilled wage must increase in North relative to free trade; by the same token, the skilled wage must increase and the unskilled wage must fall in South. Indeed, in the mutual restriction scenario, nominal wages lie within a region defined by their values of the free trade and autarky scenarios (see Equations [38]–[41] in the online appendix).

Regarding real wages, the import tariff generates an additional effect. By increasing the effective price of imported products, the tariff generates an increasing impact on the price index. This impact and the above-mentioned effect on nominal wages are shown in Equations (42)–(45) in the online appendix, in which real wages are written in terms of the price for the skilled-intensive good.

Given this result, and that real income depends directly on real wages, we obtain an expression for welfare that is asymmetric to those obtained for the remaining scenarios, if it were not for a single but relevant exception. That is, the expression for welfare we obtain in this section could be derived by plugging P^{MTR} in the common expression for welfare mentioned in the Preliminary Considerations section, if it was not for the fact that, in the present section, the import tariff creates a wedge between the relative price of the good and its effective relative price (see Equations [50] and [51] in the online appendix for the income and real income expressions in North and (52) for P^{MTR}). For the case of North, the implication is that the welfare expression contains the term P^{MTR}/τ rather than the term P^{MTR}.

With this result in mind, it is easy to see that a tax on immigration will be able to perfectly replicate the welfare implications of the import tariff in North as long as it is able to induce an equilibrium in which the relative price for the skilled-intensive good equals P^{MTR}/τ.

FREE MIGRATION AND NO INTERNATIONAL TRADE

This section explores the equilibrium characteristics and welfare implications of international labor migration. For this purpose, it considers a scenario in which there is no international trade but workers are allowed to migrate freely to a different region. To construct this scenario, the chapter takes as a point of departure the autarky regime presented earlier. Starting from this regime, it will find the incentives for migration and the equilibrium prices generated by these incentives.

Since workers' incomes are defined by the real wages they receive, their incentives for migration are fully determined by differences in real wages across regions. Workers will have incentives to migrate to a different region until real wages become equal between North and South. Real wage equalization across regions is the equilibrium condition introduced by free migration and, thus, the new condition considered in this section.

To understand what this new equilibrium condition requires in terms of international labor mobility, it will be useful to begin by looking at the determinants of real wages. In turn, since in this section trade does not take place, we can use the expressions for real wages obtained under autarky as a point of departure. As noted in the Autarky section, real wages under autarky depend on the price for the skilled-intensive good, and this price in turn depends on the unskilled-to-skilled labor ratio of each region. Precisely, the fact that the skilled-labor-abundant region (i.e., North) has a smaller equilibrium price for the skilled-intensive good implies that the real skilled wage in this region is also smaller under autarky, at the time that its real unskilled wage is greater. The intuition for this result can be obtained directly from noting that the supply of skilled labor is greater in North than in South, while the opposite holds true for the unskilled labor supply (see Equations [53]–[56] in the online appendix for real wages).

Most importantly, the implication of these real wage differences across regions is that they create incentives for unskilled workers to migrate North and for skilled workers to migrate South. The question then is, at which point do these real wages become equal so that the incentives for migration disappear? The answer lies in the fact that real wages depend on unskilled-to-skilled labor supplies: it is only when the ratio of unskilled-to-skilled labor is the same in the two regions that their real wages equalize, vanishing any incentive for immigration. Notably, the only case in which both unskilled-to-skilled labor supplies become equal is when they are in turn equal to the world unskilled-to-skilled labor supply. Hence, immigration will take place until this condition is fulfilled.

To assess the welfare implications of free migration, we must again return to thinking about the price for the skilled-intensive good. The fact that in the free migration equilibrium the ratio of unskilled-to-skilled labor supply is the same across the two regions implies that they also feature the same relative price for the skilled-intensive good. Thus, in this sense, it can be argued that in the same manner as international trade, free migration leads to price equalization across regions.

Furthermore, not only is it true that the two regions have the same price, but in equilibrium their unskilled-to-skilled labor supply is also equal to that of the world. The implication is that the equilibrium price in two regions equals the price of the free trade scenario (Equation [62] in the online appendix states this result). Interestingly, the fact that free migration yields the same price for the skilled-intensive good as free trade implies that we can easily derive the welfare implications of migration in our model. As largely known, free trade is welfare-improving relative to an autarky equilibrium. More generally, it is known that the prices under free trade reproduce any of the allocations within the continuum set of Pareto efficient allocations. This results from the First Fundamental Welfare Theorem and from noting that our framework does not exhibit market failures. Driven by these results, we know that, because free migration implements the same price vector as free trade, migration is not only welfare-improving but also optimal from a Pareto point of view.

Moreover, an important feature of the free migration equilibrium is that it does not determine the absolute number of workers of each type in each region—it only determines the unskilled-skilled labor ratio. The fact that the absolute number of workers in each region is not determined forces us to choose, so we proceed by focusing on migration going in a single direction, from South to North. Besides being consistent with one of the equilibria, a situation in which migrants only go North constitutes the most interesting case and, importantly, is also the only equilibrium configuration in a more realistic scenario in which this region has a technological advantage over South.[7]

Regarding the redistributive implications of free migration, it is worth emphasizing the consequences that immigrants have for income distribution in North, given that this region will be the focus of our analysis in the political economy analysis section. To the extent that real wages are determined by the price of the skilled-intensive good, and that this price is the same in free trade and the free migration equilibria, the redistributive implications of immigration are the same as those of international trade. Relative to autarky, migration reduces the real unskilled wage and increases the skilled wage, harming unskilled workers but benefiting skilled employees (Equations [63] and [64] in the online appendix show the comparison between the prices of the free trade and the free migration equilibria). Yet, unlike in the free trade scenario, in which unskilled workers are exposed to global competition through product markets, in the free migration scenario these workers are exposed to global competition through local labor markets.

GENERAL WELFARE IMPLICATIONS OF IMMIGRATION

Even though we have been able to show that fully removing migration barriers is optimal from a Pareto point of view, this section takes a more general approach and investigates the welfare consequences of migrants, regardless of whether moving across regions is fully or partially free. The goal is to simplify the welfare analysis that we will undertake in the next section.

Precisely, this section considers two types of migration effects on welfare. Given that, as noted below, we only consider the effect of migration on welfare through its impact on prices, these two types of effects are associated with changes in the price of the skilled-intensive good. The first effect raises interest only from an analytical point of view; it refers to migration flows that generate only marginal—that is, infinitesimally small—changes in this price. The results show that these types of migration flows have no impact on real income and thus welfare (see Equation [65] and Figure 7 in the online appendix for the expression). The intuition for this result goes as follows. In a situation where international trade is not allowed, such as the one considered as a point of departure in the free migration scenario, the increase in the real skilled wage benefiting Northern skilled workers is fully offset by the fall in the real unskilled wage harming Northern unskilled employees.

The second type of migration effect has a more relevant application; it refers to migration flows that induce discrete—non-infinitesimally small—changes in prices, such as those we observe in real life. The results show that this type of migration exerts a positive impact on welfare and the intuition goes as follows. Starting from any of the situation that lies between the free trade and the free migration scenarios, Southern migrants increase the real skilled wage. Thus, given that the zero-profit conditions must be fulfilled, the price for the skilled-intensive good rises in equilibrium. That is, migration takes the autarkic economy closer to the free trade equilibrium (as is well-known, trade openness always improves welfare in our model—see Equation [66] in the online appendix for the analytical expression showing this result and Figure 8 for a representation).

TAX ON MIGRATION

This section investigates the effects of a tax on migration. It departs from the autarky regime and focuses on migration flows of unskilled workers going from South to North, in the same manner as the Free Migration and No International Trade section does.

The tax on migration we consider is assumed to take the iceberg form. Thus, a worker migrating to North receives only a fraction $1 - \phi$ of her wage, and the rest melts away in "her transit." For the purpose of our analysis, this tax is a sufficient statistic of migration policy; that is, a sufficient indicator of policy-induced restrictions to international labor mobility.

We begin by considering differences in real unskilled wages between the two regions at our point of departure. In contrast with the free migration case, in a situation in which immigration is costly, the incentives for migration are exhausted even before real wages equalize across regions.

The tax diminishes the benefit from migration, inducing unskilled workers from South to migrate until the following indifference condition is satisfied:

$$\frac{w_N^{TM}}{P_N^{TM\ \gamma}}\,(1 - \phi) = \frac{w_S^{TM}}{P_S^{TM\ \gamma}}$$

(see Equations [67] and [68] in the online appendix for expressions of these wages). The tax on migration introduces a wedge between real wages across regions and, through this channel, diminishes immigration and imposes a wedge between unskilled-to-skilled labor ratios. Indeed, the migration incentives are exhausted as the real wage net of the migration costs in North is equal to the real wage in South. Thus, the equilibrium condition in this section is different from the condition considered in the free migration case.

This change has important implications for the price of the skilled-intensive good in equilibrium. A smaller number of unskilled migrants to North is associated with a smaller real skilled wage and, therefore, a smaller price for the skilled-intensive good. The implication is that, since income distribution and welfare in North depend crucially on this price, the tax on migration affects these variables in equilibrium.

Regarding welfare, it is important to note that because the tax diminishes the price of the skilled-intensive good in North, it triggers welfare-reducing effects. It is easy to see this by using the graphical tools shown above. Furthermore, the fall in the equilibrium price for the skilled-intensive good generates redistributive effects relative to the free international labor mobility equilibrium. The tax diminishes the number of unskilled immigrants and, thus the supply of unskilled labor increases to a lesser extent in North. This makes the real unskilled wages greater than in the free migration regime, implying that the real skilled wage must fall for the zero-profit conditions to be satisfied. Hence, the migration tax increases the real return to unskilled workers and reduces the real return to skilled workers with respect to a free migration regime, and therefore, in this sense, it can be argued that it has some effects as an imports tax in the context of international trade. This result is crucial to understand why special interest groups may want to constrain migration and therefore motivate the political economy analysis in the Political Economy Analysis section.

TAX EQUIVALENCE

The analyses in previous sections have shown that a migration tax harms the abundant factor, benefits the scarce factor, and triggers welfare-reducing effects relative to the free migration scenario. Interestingly, these impacts go in the same direction as those obtained in a situation in which each region imposes an import tariff on the products originating in the other region. Thus, the present section derives a migration policy that replicates the same equilibrium characteristics in North as the mutual trade restriction scenario considered above.

As noted above, for that purpose, it suffices to find for each value of τ a value of $1 - \phi$ that implements the same relative price in North as in the mutual trade restrictions scenario, P^{MTC}/τ. The implementation of the same relative price implies that the migration tax ϕ yields the same prices, real wages, and welfare as the mutual imposition of τ.

Equations (74) and (74') in the online appendix show the expressions for the migration tax replicating the mutual trade restriction equilibrium properties in North. An implication of these results is that a reduction in labor endowment differences across regions, which would imply diminished welfare gains from international trade, is associated with a smaller value of the migration tax.

POLITICAL ECONOMY ANALYSIS

The previous analysis has shown that immigration increases overall welfare but generates income redistribution effects. In this context, restricting migration may favor special interest groups. For the particular case analyzed in this chapter, a migration policy that restricts unskilled migration benefits unskilled workers in North at the cost of smaller aggregate welfare levels. More generally, this suggests that political economy concerns may influence the design and implementation of migration policies in advanced economies.

Indeed, the premise that public policies can be influenced by special interest groups has a long tradition in both economic theory and empirical work. For the case of regulatory measures, Djankov et al. (2002) suggest that entry regulation generates rents that accrue to bureaucrats and administrative employees. Yet bureaucrats, politicians, and administrative employees may be tempted to implement regulation not only to obtain profits directly, but also to collect bribes and contributions from the relevant interest groups (see De Soto [1990], McChesney [1987], Shleifer and Vishny [1993], and Tobal [2017] for the consequences on international trade).

In the domain of international trade policy, perhaps the most influential work is from Grossman and Helpman (1994). In their seminal paper, they show that lobbying groups have incentives for influencing the design of import tariffs. Along these lines, this chapter shows that there is some equivalence between international trade and migration policies in terms of welfare and redistribution effects. This again suggests that, just as with international trade policies, immigration policy may be influenced by interest groups.

In this section, we develop an extension of the factor proportion model presented previously with the goal of illustrating one among the several channels through which special interest groups may affect immigration policy. In contrast with several of the channels through which political economy concerns shape public policy in the literature, the extension we present does not rely on the existence of a government that attempts to extract private rents or to maximize political support. Instead, our extension shows that, even when a government is forward-looking and benevolent, it may have incentives to deviate from the migration policy associated with the first-best equilibrium.

As noted above, we consider the economy described by the factor proportion model presented in previous sections and set as our point of departure the autarky equilibrium. To simplify, it is assumed that there is a single interest group representing unskilled workers, such as unions. This group can affect Congress' decisions, possibly because their actions influence media coverage and, through this channel, have an impact on public opinion. When many unskilled workers go on a strike, large media coverage frequently exerts pressure on Congress.

For instance, if unskilled workers go on a strike, the pressure of the media forces Congress to reject the migratory reform proposed by the government, represented by the ϕ parameter.

More formally, assume that there is a probability that unskilled workers do not go on a strike $f(\phi)$ and that this probability fulfills the traditional Inada conditions: (1) $f(\phi = 0) = 0$: when free migration is proposed, unskilled workers always go on a strike; (2) $f(\phi)$ is continuously differentiable; (3) $f(\phi)$ is strictly increasing in ϕ: the probability of going on strike falls with the severity of the policy proposed (i.e., the higher the tax on migration, the lower the probability of going on strike); (4) the second derivative is negative; (5) the limit of the first derivative of $f(\phi)$ is infinite when ϕ tends to 0; (6) the limit of the first derivative of $f(\phi)$ is 0 when ϕ tends to infinite.

In this environment, the government is interested in maximizing expected welfare. In the context of our extension, this welfare can be written as follows:

$$EW(\phi) = f(\phi)\, W_N(\phi) + (1 - f(\phi))\, W_N^{aut}.$$

At the same time, it is known from the factor proportion model that

$$W_N(\phi) > W_N^{aut} \text{ and that } \quad \frac{\partial W_N(\phi)}{\partial \phi} < 0.$$

Under these conditions, it is easy to show that the benevolent and forward-looking government never chooses a migration tax equal to zero (the section titled General Welfare Implications of Immigration in the online appendix provides a formal proof). The intuition for this result goes as follows. Even though the government knows that choosing a zero tax would be optimal in the absence of political economy conflicts, it is also aware that doing so would lead the union to a strike and, consequently, the Congress to reject the proposal. Under these conditions, the economy would remain in the autarky regime and reach the lowest possible welfare level. Hence, to avoid this situation, the benevolent and forward-looking government opts for proposing a positive migration tax and improving the probability that the reform gets accepted.

CONCLUSIONS

We have provided some theoretical tools that illustrate useful and interesting insights into the economic effects of migration, as well as on political factors that may affect the design of migration policy. To illustrate these points, we set a standard factor proportion model of international trade and used it to investigate the impacts of free trade, free migration, an imports tariff, and a tax on migration.

The analysis generates several interesting conclusions. First, free-trade and free-migration generate isomorphic results, precisely when the most relevant measure of welfare from a political economy perspective is taken into account. Both trade and migration increase aggregate welfare but have redistributive effects. Second, along these lines, welfare outcomes arising from an imports tax can be replicated by implementing the proper migration policy. In light of these results, we then conclude that migration policies may be influenced by political economy concerns. Thus, we develop an extension of our standard model to illustrate one of the many possible channels through which these concerns may affect the determination of migration policies.

From a more general perspective, the takeaway from our analysis is that there is large room for using economists' tools to contribute to a now heated policy debate. Just as we already have a tool kit to analyze trade policy and its welfare, redistributive, and political economy dimensions, we can easily extend this literature to analyze migration policy in these same dimensions.

Notes

1. A longer, more technical draft of this chapter is available online at https://doi .org/10.17848/9780880999570.ch6A. Throughout this chapter it is referred to as the *online appendix*.
2. The report by the Partnership for a New American Economy (2011) also finds that by 2010 more than 40 percent of the Fortune 500 companies were founded by immigrants or their children, that 7 of the 10 most valuable brands in the world come from companies founded by first or second generations of immigrants, and that the revenue generated by Fortune 500 companies founded by immigrants or children of immigrants is greater than the GDP of every country in the world outside the United States, except China and Japan.

3. Although the figures provide information only on the correlation between the variables illustrated, they serve to suggest that high-skilled migration entails net benefits for host countries.
4. Even though both studies measure policy effectiveness in terms of volume, Thielemann (2004) specifically assesses the impact on noneconomic migrants—that is, those immigrants whose decisions are driven by political motivations.
5. Indeed, variations in the price depend exclusively on changes in the price of the unskilled-intensive good because that price has been chosen as the numeraire.
6. Along these lines, upcoming sections will show that the mutual trade restriction equilibrium can be replicated by an appropriate choice of a migration tax.
7. In this more realistic scenario, absolute wages for skilled and unskilled are greater in North.

References

Beine, Michel, Frédéric Docquier, and Çaglar Özden. 2011. "Diasporas." *Journal of Development Economics* 95(1): 30–41.

Borjas, George J. 1991. "The Wage Impact of the Marielitos: Additional Evidence." NBER Working Paper No. 21850. Cambridge, MA: National Bureau of Economic Research.

———. 2016. "Immigrants in the U.S. Labor Market: 1940–80." *American Economic Review* 81(2): 287–291.

Card, David. 1990. "The Impact of the Mariel Boatlift on the Miami Labor Market." *Industrial and Labor Relations Review* 43(2): 245–257.

Chiquiar, Daniel, and Gordon H. Hanson. 2005. "International Migration, Self-Selection, and the Distribution of Wages: Evidence from Mexico and the United States." *Journal of Political Economy* 113(2): 239–281.

Czaika, Mathias, and Hein de Haas. 2013. "The Effectiveness of Immigration Policies." *Population and Development Review* 39(3): 487–508.

———. 2014. "The Effect of Visa Policies on International Migration Dynamics." International Migration Institute Working Paper No. 89. Oxford: IMI.

———. 2015. "Evaluating Migration Policy Effectiveness." In *Routledge Handbook of Immigration and Refugee Studies*, Anna Triandafyllidou, ed. New York: Routledge. https://www.routledgehandbooks.com/doi/10.4324/9781315759302.ch2 (accessed December 8, 2017).

De Haas, Hein, Katharina Natter, and Simona Vezzoli. 2014. "Growing Restrictiveness or Changing Selection? The Nature and Evolution of Migration Policies." International Migration Institute Working Paper 96. Oxford: International Migration Institute.

De New, John P., and Klaus F. Zimmermann. 1994. "Native Wage Impacts of Foreign Labor: A Random Effects Panel Analysis." *Journal of Population Economics* 7(2): 177–192.

De Soto, Hernando. 1990. *The Other Path*. New York: Harper and Row.

Dixit, Avinash, and Victor Norman. 1980. *Theory of International Trade: A Dual, General Equilibrium Approach*. Cambridge, MA: Cambridge University Press.

Djankov, Simeon, Rafael La Porta, Florencio Lopez-de-Silanes, and Andrei Shleifer. 2002. "The Regulation of Entry." *Quarterly Journal of Economics* 117(1): 1–37.

Galiani, Sebastian, and Gustavo Torrens. 2015. "The Political Economy of Trade and Labor Mobility in a Ricardian World." NBER Working Paper No. 21274. Cambridge, MA: National Bureau of Economic Research.

Grossman, Gene, and Elhanan Helpman. 1994. "Protection for Sale." *American Economic Review* 84(4): 833–850.

Jones, Ronald W. 1965. "The Structure of Simple General Equilibrium Models." *Journal of Political Economy* 73(6): 557–572.

Mayda, Anna Maria. 2010. "International Migration: A Panel Data Analysis of the Determinants of Bilateral Flows." *Journal of Population Economics* 23(4): 1249–1274.

McChesney, Fred S. 1987. "Rent Extraction and Rent Creation in the Economic Theory of Regulation." *Journal of Legal Studies* 16: 101–118.

Nowrasteh, Alex. 2015. "The Fiscal Impact of Immigration." In *The Economics of Immigration: Market-Based Approaches, Social Science, and Public Policy*, Benjamin Powell, ed. Oxford: Oxford University Press, pp. 38–69.

Partnership for a New American Economy. 2011. *The "New American" Fortune 500*. New York: Partnership for a New American Economy. http://www.renewoureconomy.org/sites/all/themes/pnae/img/new-american-fortune-500-june-2011.pdf (accessed December 12, 2017).

Ortega, Francesc, and Giovanni Peri. 2013. "Migration, Trade and Income." IZA Discussion Paper No. 7325. Bonn: Institute for the Study of Labor.

Shleifer, Andrei, and Robert W. Vishny. 1993. "Corruption." *Quarterly Journal of Economics* 108(3): 599–617.

Thielemann, Eiko. 2004. "Does Policy Matter? On Governments' Attempts to Control Unwanted Migration." Working Paper No. 112. La Jolla, CA: Center of Comparative Immigration Studies.

Tobal, Martín. 2017. "Regulatory Entry Barriers, Rent Shifting and the Home Market Effect." *Review of International Economics* 25(1): 76–97.

7
Combining Physical and Financial Solidarity in Asylum Policy

Jesús Fernández-Huertas Moraga
Universidad Carlos III de Madrid

Hillel Rapoport
Paris School of Economics–Université Paris 1 Panthéon-Sorbonne

The drawbacks of the Common European Asylum System (CEAS) are so widely acknowledged that the European Commission itself launched the European Agenda on Migration in May 2015 with the objective of reforming it. One of the main issues of disagreement among the European member states was how to share the potential costs of receiving asylum seekers and hosting refugees, which is typically summarized as "burden sharing," although many practitioners and politicians prefer the terminology "responsibility sharing" as being less offensive to refugees. The initial proposal in the European Agenda on Migration (European Commission 2015a) contemplated a formula to relocate asylum seekers or resettle refugees according to GDP, population, unemployment, and past number of refugees hosted.

This chapter presents our own proposal for a system that can minimize the cost of allocating refugees at the European level, starting from the European Union (EU) distribution key. The distribution key would constitute the first stage of our three-stage proposal. The new elements would be the two following stages.

Stage two would be the creation of a compensation mechanism for the exchange of the refugee-admission quotas distributed in stage one. Allowing the member states to trade their initial quotas would let them choose whether they want to contribute to the European public good of providing refugee protection by accepting refugees (physical solidarity) or by paying other countries to accept them (financial solidarity).

Countries that perceive refugees as less of a burden would thus be compensated by other countries that perceive refugees as more of a burden.

Finally, stage three is needed to ensure that refugees' and asylum seekers' rights are respected. In particular, we introduce a matching mechanism that would assign refugees to their preferred destination and destinations to their preferred refugees. This has two objectives. First, we make sure that no refugee is forced to go to an undesired destination. Second, there are additional efficiency gains by letting countries choose their preferred types of refugees. The matching mechanism does not alter the cost minimization properties of the market, as long as we introduce a penalty mechanism for locations that refugees consider undesirable. If a country is paid to receive refugees by the market and refugees refuse to go there, we force this country to compensate the country where the refugees actually end up.

Our three-stage proposal was first developed and its efficiency properties were established by Fernández-Huertas Moraga and Rapoport (2014). In Fernández-Huertas Moraga and Rapoport (2015a), we sketch how the proposal could be adapted to the particular case of reforming the CEAS by considering refugees and asylum seekers jointly and by reviewing the problems and stated shortcomings of the European Relocation from Malta programme by which the EU relocated a number of refugees and asylum seekers arrived in Malta to other European Member States between 2011 and 2012. More recently, Fernández-Huertas Moraga and Rapoport (2015b) restate the proposal and apply some simulations of how it would work in the case of the refugees from the Syrian civil war.

This chapter focuses on a new set of simulations on how the system of tradable refugee-admission quotas (TRAQs), combined with a matching mechanism, would work. The new simulations incorporate the new elements of the European Agenda on Migration that the European Commission pushed during the second half of 2015, related to the relocation of 160,000 refugees coming from Italy and Greece and to the establishment of a permanent relocation mechanism. We also use the preferences of the European member states that have been revealed throughout the bargaining process, in particular, taking advantage of the differences between the quotas imposed by the European Commission and the voluntary relocation processes that the member states were willing to accept by July 2015.

These simulations will be done under different assumptions on cost functions. They are helpful to understand which countries would benefit more or less with and without the market for refugee admission quotas that forms the implicit basis of our compensation mechanism. They emphasize the flexibility of the market in adapting to the different circumstances of the member states and the suitability of the matching mechanism to make sure refugee rights are respected at all times. Finally, we show how the market can be instrumental in elucidating information about the preferences of countries.

THE MODEL

This section outlines the model that combines the physical and financial solidarity aspects of the proposed scheme. The model is simply sketched here, while its mathematical properties are relegated to Appendix 7A.

The theoretical problem that needs to be solved is the allocation of a total number of refugees and asylum seekers across a set of destination countries, which can be assimilated to the member states in the EU that will be participating in the mechanism. The model takes as given both the total number of refugees and asylum seekers to be allocated (such as the 160,000 in the EU proposal of September 2015) and the perceived costs and benefits that the refugees impose on the destination countries.

Setup

In the current absence of any coordination mechanism and abstracting from the rights of refugees and asylum seekers, each country will decide how many refugees and asylum seekers to accept by maximizing a welfare function with two elements.

The first one represents how countries benefit from the fact that other countries receive asylum seekers or refugees. There may be two fundamental reasons for this. On the one hand, there is the international public good aspect. We can consider that one country, either its government or its inhabitants, receive utility (welfare) from the fact that refugees are protected, regardless of where. On the other hand, even in the case in which this country does not directly care about refugees and perceives them as a simple cost, it benefits indirectly from the fact that other countries host them, since this may alleviate the pressure for it to host them itself. In other words, a country can expect its asylum claims to go down when the number of refugees hosted by other destinations increases. Both explanations imply that refugees and asylum seekers hosted by other countries exert a positive externality on the welfare of one particular country. This implies that the unilateral provision of protection to refugees and asylum seekers by individual countries leads to a globally inefficient solution. Fewer refugees are hosted overall than would be optimal from a global perspective. The second element of the welfare function is the net cost of hosting refugees and asylum seekers. This includes all the perceived costs and benefits associated with hosting refugees and asylum seekers, particularly the potential altruism of a country toward the reception of refugees—that is, the international public good element by which its welfare is increased whenever refugees and asylum seekers are protected. It also includes the physical and administrative costs of receiving refugees and asylum seekers and processing their paperwork, initial allowances, and initial accommodation for the period. The net cost also considers the potential long-run expected economic consequences of hosting these refugees and asylum seekers as assessed by the country, for example, the immigration surplus or the fact that these refugees may either benefit or harm domestic workers once they integrate into the labor market. Finally, the net cost also includes the social and political costs (or benefits) of hosting these refugees and asylum seekers.

Unilateral policies are not optimal because individual countries do not consider the fact that their reception of refugees and asylum seekers has a positive effect on other countries, and hence they perform this activity at a lower level than that implied by a full maximization problem.

As proved in Fernández-Huertas Moraga and Rapoport (2014, 2015a), the optimal solution involves equating the marginal costs of hosting refugees and asylum seekers among all the potential destination countries to a positive number that depends on the strength of the externality, while the noncoordinated solution equates these marginal costs to zero. Hence, the noncoordinated solution results in fewer refugees and asylum seekers receiving protection.

The Compensation Mechanism with Tradable Refugee-Admission Quotas

The optimal solution can be replicated by distributing responsibilities over the number of refugees and asylum seekers that each member state must host (quotas) and letting them trade these responsibilities.

We define the initial quotas as the total sum of refugees and asylum seekers that it becomes the responsibility of particular countries to host. If one country prefers to host a number lower than its quota, it should compensate another country a price per unfilled refugee admission quota so that the other country will host them.

This means that every country would simply equate the marginal cost of hosting an additional refugee or asylum seeker to the refugee-admission quota price. This is exactly the global optimal solution. Countries with a marginal cost over the price would prefer to pay other countries to comply with part of their quota. Conversely, countries with a marginal cost below the price would be willing to host more refugees or asylum seekers than their quota implies.

As long as the market is competitive and countries are unable to manipulate the quota price, every country will be better off under the compensation scheme than fulfilling their compulsory initial responsibilities. This does not imply that individual countries would be better off than under the noncooperative solution. However, the total welfare of all the member states would be higher under the compensation scheme than under the noncooperative solution or a mandatory distribution of quotas such as the one proposed by the European Commission.

It would be theoretically feasible to manipulate the initial quotas so that absolutely every country participating in the compensating scheme would prefer to do so. We will come back to this point later when we discuss our different simulations. The fact that this is theoretically possible does not mean that gathering the necessary information to implement it is feasible without generating perverse incentives for countries to manipulate their behavior.

The Matching Mechanism

Refugees' preferences

One crucial drawback with addressing the problem that countries face is the fact that refugees or asylum seekers are perceived as interchangeable and can be moved around at the will of the European member states. This is clearly not acceptable, since every movement for relocation or resettlement must be done with the full consent of the individuals involved.

A way to obtain this consent, while improving the final allocation of refugees, is to ask them directly to express whether they are willing to be relocated to any particular destination at all and also to rank the destinations to which they would be willing to be relocated, rather than remaining in their location at the time of questioning.

The matching literature (Roth 2002) provides many examples of how this information can be used to match refugees to their preferred destinations. The objective is to find a mechanism such that no pair of refugees can exchange their destinations and be made better off at the same time. One example is the top trading cycles mechanism (Abdulkadiroglu and Sonmez 1999), also known as the random serial dictatorship. It works in the following way:

- Each refugee ranks all potentially desired destinations (preferred to the current one).
- An ordering of refugees is randomly chosen.
- Assign the first refugee her first choice, the second refugee her first choice, and so on, until a refugee's first choice is a country whose quota is filled. Assign that refugee her second choice, or if that one is also filled, her third choice, and so on.

This type of mechanism does not present any problem for the quota allocation coming out of the market. In fact, there is only one situation in which the matching mechanism might interfere with the market. If one of the destinations is such an undesirable place that no refugee would consider going there, the quota of that country would not be filled, and some refugees, the last in the random ordering, would prefer to remain in their original location (say, a refugee camp) rather than move there. If this is the case, some countries could have an incentive to create a bad image (e.g., be lenient on violence against refugees) to discourage applications. They could even bid in the market to be paid for hosting refugees whom they hope would refuse to move there.

How can this possibility be avoided? Two solutions could prevent this from happening:

1) Since refugee preferences can be collected before opening the market, countries could be forbidden to bid beyond the actual number of individuals willing to relocate there. We would have trade restrictions, but this would ensure that all refugees are relocated through the market.

2) Alternatively, we can allow for a case in which the overall number of refugees and asylum seekers to be relocated or resettled is not realized and the "rejected" country pays the price for the unfilled part of its quota. This acts as a penalty and provides incentives for countries to become attractive destinations.

In equilibrium, the penalty would always be zero, but it is needed so that countries do not have incentives to become unattractive from the point of view of refugees and asylum seekers. In practice, the EU could oversee collecting this penalty in the case of some off-equilibrium behavior.

Still, equating the marginal costs of hosting refugees and asylum seekers across countries to the quota price is an optimal solution, even in the presence of the matching mechanism.

Host countries' preferences

Not only can refugee preferences be considered, there is also a scope for considering the preferences of host countries regarding the type of refugees that they would be more willing to host.

In the same way that refugees can establish a ranking of their preferred destinations, countries could establish a ranking of their preferred types of refugees or asylum seekers. For example, some countries might be more willing to host refugees than asylum seekers.

The only difference between the expressions of preferences on the side of host countries lies in the fact that they should not be allowed to refuse to take any refugee. Otherwise, they would have an incentive to misrepresent their preferences and declare that some types of refugees are unacceptable for them. Refugees, on the other hand, should retain the option to refuse to move to an undesired destination.

If countries' preferences are taken into account, we would need to change the algorithm governing the allocation of refugees to host countries. Both the country-proposing and the refugee-proposing deferred acceptance algorithm could be applied (Fernández-Huertas Moraga and Rapoport 2014, 2015a). According to Azevedo and Leshno (2016), both would attain the same result, given that the number of refugees and asylum seekers will be large.

In previous papers (Fernández-Huertas Moraga and Rapoport 2014, 2015a), we have argued that it could be best to adopt a country-proposing deferred acceptance algorithm on the grounds of its lower degree of manipulability according to Pathak and Sonmez (2013). Under this algorithm, countries would first propose their market-assigned quotas to their preferred refugees. Then, these refugees would have the option to accept or refuse among their offers. For the unfilled part of their quota, countries would then propose their second most preferred types of refugees, and so on, until all the quotas are filled, unless there is a destination that is so undesirable that no refugee is willing to go there. The introduction of the preferences of hosting countries would have the benefit of reducing their participating costs. As a result, either more refugees could be hosted at the same total cost or the same number of refugees could be hosted at a lower total cost.

In exchange for these advantages, the matching mechanism introduces some uncertainty about the types of refugees and asylum seekers that countries end up receiving. Again, this introduces a new bias favoring refugee-friendly countries, since it is more likely that the offers from these countries will be accepted earlier than the offers that are perceived as less refugee-friendly, and hence, are refugees' lowest preferences.

RELATED LITERATURE

There is a large body of literature on how to reform the EU Asylum Policy. Perhaps the best review of this literature corresponds to Hatton (2015), who explains how the harmonization of European policies alone is not enough for an efficient asylum policy. The reason for this is that the cost functions of the member states are too different, and harmonizing policies constrains the set of achievable outcomes. In this sense, the market we propose here could offer the flexibility countries need.

The idea of using a market to coordinate refugee-reception responsibilities across countries can be traced back to Schuck (1997), who offers the example of the Comprehensive Plan of Action for the resettlement of refugees from Vietnam in the 1980s. Bubb, Kremer, and Levine (2011) take Schuck's idea one step further and couple his bilateral exchange with a screening device aimed at separating "true" refugees from bogus asylum claims.

The main difference with the current proposal is the lack of a formal market in Schuck (1997) and Bubb, Kremer, and Levine (2011). We propose a centralized institution rather than a set of bilateral exchanges. The rationale for this is the need to design the market so that large players cannot manipulate the price. Furthermore, we argue for the consideration of refugee preferences over destinations and countries' preferences over refugees, both on humanitarian and efficiency grounds.

The first stage of our proposal—that is, the allocation of initial responsibilities among the member states—has often been considered in the literature. For example, Thielemann et al. (2010) and Wagner and Kraler (2014) calculate many different "burden-sharing" rules, comparable to the one finally adopted by the European Council (2015). In the case of Thielemann et al. (2010), the authors suggest that "fair burden sharing" implies that 33–40 percent of asylum seekers should be transferred to different European countries, many to new member states. In their view, this policy should be complemented with a harmonization of asylum seekers' costs across countries. They also advocate the use of larger financial compensation for receiving countries. Finally, they argue for the voluntary movement of asylum seekers from overburdened to less-affected states. The reason they gave for these voluntary movements is that forced movements end up being very costly. In fact, the two last elements are included in our proposal: the financial compensation operates through the market, while the matching mechanism makes sure that all movements are voluntary, and hence less costly.

Finally, Hatton (2015) also argues for the need to redistribute refugees across the European member states in order to achieve a social optimum. However, he also offers the option of providing asymmetric subsidies per refugee hosted to different countries—that is, the per capita compensation that the European Refugee Fund or the Asylum and Migration Fund has traditionally offered for the reception of refugees should have different levels for different countries. Countries for which it is more expensive to host refugees should receive higher subsidies, whereas countries for which it is less costly should receive lower subsidies. The problem with this scheme is the lack of information on the true costs and benefits of hosting refugees. Furthermore, such a system would create an incentive for countries to overreport how costly it is for them to host refugees.

THE EUROPEAN AGENDA ON MIGRATION

In May 2015, the EU launched the European Agenda on Migration to reform the European Asylum System. Before getting to that point, it is useful to summarize some of the main elements of the existing Common European Asylum System. Following Hatton (2015), we can situate the beginning of the policy with the signing of the Dublin Convention in 1990. The Dublin system, renewed in 2003 and 2013 (Dublin III), generally established that the country responsible for an asylum claim in the EU would be the country of first entry. We had to wait until 1999 for the formal launching of the CEAS in Tampere. The treaty of Amsterdam allowed the European Commission to legislate on asylum issues, and this prompted a whole series of directives aimed at harmonizing the asylum systems of the European member states in terms of reception conditions, recognition rates, and border surveillance. For example, the European Refugee Fund was created in 2000 with the objective of formally sharing the financial costs of hosting refugees among the member states. The fund continued after 2014 under the name of the Asylum and Migration Fund.

Other European programs and agencies were born out of the harmonization efforts, such as EURODAC in 2003, FRONTEX in 2005, and the European Asylum Support Office (EASO) in 2010.

It could be argued that the European Agenda on Migration emerged as a result of the concerns in European public opinion created by several shipwrecks involving asylum seekers on the Mediterranean shores. In fact, the main elements of the Agenda (European Commission 2015a) were:

- Emergency operations (Triton, Poseidon) to save lives at sea.
- Budget increases for existing policies and further harmonization.
- Relocation (40,000 from Italy and Greece) and resettlement (20,000 from outside the EU) of refugees and asylum seekers following a distribution key. This distribution key was the real new policy included in the European Agenda on Migration. It meant the creation of a new scheme for sharing the responsibility of hosting refugees that went beyond the Dublin regulations and the existence of financial compensation. The distribution key divided quotas according to a formula weighting:
  - 40 percent total GDP of the member states. The larger the GDP of the member states, the larger their responsibility in the relocation and resettlement of refugees and asylum seekers.
  - 40 percent population. The criterion works in the same way as the GDP. Larger countries (in terms of population) are supposed to have a larger capacity to absorb refugees.
  - 10 percent unemployment rate. This works in the opposite direction. Countries with a larger unemployment rate would have to host fewer refugees.
  - 10 percent number of asylum applications received and refugees resettled per 1 million inhabitants between 2010 and 2014. The rationale is that those countries that contributed the most to the international public good of the reception of refugees would be required to assume a lower responsibility.

The initial response of the member states to these proposals was not very favourable. In July 2015, the European Council refused to adopt mandatory quotas. The European countries preferred to stick to voluntary pledges that fell short of the European Commission's numbers: 32,256 for relocation (rather than 40,000) and 18,425 for resettlement (rather than 20,000). However, the commission insisted, and in September 2015 its president, Jean-Claude Juncker, extended the relocation mechanism to Hungary, while proposing to relocate 120,000 additional refugees and asylum seekers following the same distribution key. He also announced a permanent relocation mechanism that could only be avoided in exceptional cases by paying compensation equal to 0.002 percent of the GDP of the non-quota-complying state (European Commission 2015c).

Somewhat surprisingly, later in September 2015, the European Council approved the quotas for the relocation of 160,000 refugees and asylum seekers from Italy and Greece, although they still refused to approve the permanent mechanism.

The European Parliament also approved Juncker's plan, and it added that refugee preferences must be taken into account in the relocation and resettlement procedures (European Parliament 2014–2019).

In September 2017, the European Commission moved away from mandatory refugee relocations to a voluntary resettlement scheme, incentivized through financial subsidies of 10,000 Euros per resettled refugee. Half a billion euros have been set aside for EU members to take at least 50,000 refugees directly from Africa, the Middle East, and Turkey (with an "increased focus" on taking refugees from North Africa and the Horn of Africa, particularly Libya, Egypt, Niger, Sudan, Chad, and Ethiopia). For purposes of simplicity and considering that the recent propositions of the European Commission are in the process of development and consolidation with member states, in this analysis we will focus on the framework proposed in the 2015 European Agenda on Migration.

Moreover, the refugee allocation system proposed in this chapter is applicable to both resettlement and relocation schemes. Registering refugee characteristics and their preferences can take place in the countries of origin (resettlement) as well as in refugee camps in first entry countries (relocation). Therefore, at times this chapter uses *resettlement* and *relocation* interchangeably. In the following section, we base our simulation on the relocation scheme proposed by the European Commission in 2015, but as pointed out before, this simulation is transferrable to the European Commission's recent call for resettlement of 50,000 refugees directly from the source countries.

SIMULATIONS

This section presents a series of simulations of the outcomes that a compensation mechanism with tradable refugee-admission quotas might deliver if applied to the proposals of the European Agenda on Migration. The simulations will focus on the compensation aspect and disregard the matching component. In other words, we will assume that enough migrants want to move to each of the destinations so as to fill the quotas that come out of the market. Another implicit simplifying assumption is that the participating countries will be indifferent about the types of refugees and asylum seekers to be hosted. So, for simplicity, we now refer exclusively to refugees, although conceptually we are considering both refugees and asylum seekers.

The simulations must start from an initial distribution of responsibilities across the member states; that is, an initial distribution of quotas to be traded. We also take this initial distribution as given by the European Council decision of September 22, 2015 (European Council 2015).

We present two crucial inputs for the simulations below. The first is the cost function. The assumptions on the cost function determine what the equilibrium price will be and how much countries will gain or lose from the application of a particular mechanism. The second crucial input is the total number of refugees to be resettled or relocated. Obviously, the larger the number of refugees to be resettled, the higher the quota price and also the total cost of the mechanism will be.

We present one particular cost function in this section and present simulations of a different one in Appendix 7B. Both will have a key parameter governing the antirefugee sentiment in each destination country. We will obtain two different values of this parameter for each country. The first one, which we denote as revealed preferences, will be based on the voluntary quotas accepted by the European Member States in the Justice and Home Affairs Council on July 20, 2015. The second one, denoted by stated preferences, will be based, as in Fernández-Huertas Moraga and Rapoport (2015b), on the share of individuals in each EU country disagreeing with the statement that "the EU member states should offer protection and asylum to people in need" from the Special Eurobarometer 380 in 2011.

In terms of the total number of refugees to be resettled, we propose two different scenarios as well. The first one will be based on the first European Commission proposal from May 2015 for resettling 20,000 refugees from outside the EU and relocating 40,000 who arrived in Italy and Greece (European Commission 2015b), for a total of 60,000 refugees to be allocated among the European member states. The second one will correspond to the addition of 120,000 refugees in September 2015 (European Commission 2015c), thus totalling 180,000 refugees to be resettled across Europe. We present only the first one in this section and leave the simulations of the second one in Appendix 7B.

Overall, this adds up to eight different simulations: two cost functions times two preference parameterizations times two refugee totals. Two of them are presented in the main text, and we relegate the rest to Appendix 7B. Appendix 7B also introduces mathematically the two cost functions that we will use for the simulations.

Outcomes

Here we present the outcomes from two of the eight different simulation scenarios that we have run. We let every EU member state participate in the market, including those that did not choose to do so in the distribution key that we use (European Council 2015). These countries—namely, Denmark, Greece, Ireland, Italy, and the United Kingdom—are assigned a zero quota.

Simulation 1: Revealed Preferences, 60,000 Refugees, Quadratic Cost

Table 7.1 shows the results from the first simulation. We start from an overall quota of 60,000 refugees to be distributed across the 28 European member states. As stated above, the cost functions of the countries are assumed to be quadratic in the number of refugees hosted from the total quota, proportional to the revealed taste parameter, and inversely proportional to the population of the host country.

The "Voluntary quotas" column in Table 7.1 first shows the quotas agreed to by the European member states as of July 2015. They are shown for comparison purposes and because they were used to back out the refugee cost parameter shown in the third data column. The voluntary quotas from July 2015 fell short of the objective of 60,000 refugees to be resettled or relocated proposed by the European Commission, as they only totalled 50,671.

The column of "Initial quotas (EU proposal)" represents the distribution of 60,000 refugees that would be deduced from the key that the European Council approved in September 2015. We consider this the initial allocation of quotas in the market that can then be traded; that is, the first step of our market of tradable-refugee admission quotas with matching.

For most countries, the voluntary quotas are not far from the initial EU allocation. The reason is that the distribution key had already been made public in May 2015, so many countries had already made their voluntary contributions around the number they were supposed to get. In principle, this goes against the usefulness of the market in this simulation, since we are considering countries' "true" preferences to be close to the European Commission's proposal.

The results of the market are shown in the column "Market quota." We can see that even in this case, when, by construction, there is not a large difference between the voluntary and mandatory schemes, the market is able to reduce overall costs by 95 percent. This result is heavily influenced by the cost function for Hungary, whose refusal to participate in the voluntary mechanism implies that the calibrated revealed refugee cost parameter is extremely large. Hence, Hungary has a lot to gain from the market, which allows the country to host just 1 refugee rather than the 1,176 assigned by the EU proposal. Nevertheless, even if we disregard Hungary, the total cost reduction achieved by the market with respect to the initial EU quotas would be equal to 23 percent, which is not a negligible amount: 60 million euros, according to our simulation.

We must point out that we are able to assign monetary variables because we have assumed that the marginal cost of the voluntary quotas for each country equals 6,000 euros, the per refugee subsidy offered by the Asylum and Migration Fund. Using this metric, we can actually provide a monetary figure for the quota price in the market: It would be equal to 7,105 euros. This makes intuitive sense. The voluntary scheme managed to resettle just over 50,000 refugees, while the market deals with up to 60,000, an 18 percent increase. As a result, the price increases by 18 percent with respect to the subsidy, which is what we could expect from linear marginal costs.

Table 7.1 Revealed Preferences, 60,000 Refugees, Quadratic Cost

Countries	Voluntary quotas	Initial quotas (EU proposal)	Refugee cost parameter: deduced from voluntary quotas	Market quota	Cost reduction with respect to initial quota (%)	Cost reduction with respect to voluntary quotas (%)
Austria	1,900	1,775	26.9	2,250	7	19
Belgium	2,464	2,225	27.3	2,918	10	26
Bulgaria	500	775	86.9	592	6	-127
Croatia	550	516	46.3	651	7	18
Cyprus	242	134	21.3	287	131	109
Czech Republic	1,500	1,446	42.0	1,776	5	12
Denmark	1,000	0	33.8	1,184	inf	240
Estonia	150	181	52.6	178	0	-45
Finland	1,085	1,169	30.1	1,285	1	-15
France	9,127	11,784	43.3	10,807	1	-66
Germany	12,100	15,488	40.0	14,327	1	-63
Greece	354	0	186.3	419	inf	240
Hungary	0	1,176	59,264.2	1	100	-inf
Ireland	1,120	0	24.7	1,326	inf	240
Italy	1,989	0	183.4	2,355	inf	240
Latvia	250	255	48.0	296	3	-2
Lithuania	325	378	54.3	385	0	-35
Luxembourg	350	215	9.4	414	85	94
Malta	74	65	34.5	88	13	34

Netherlands	3,047	3,546	33.1	3,608	0	−35
Poland	2,000	4,620	114.1	2,368	24	−307
Portugal	1,500	1,493	41.7	1,776	4	5
Romania	1,785	2,250	67.0	2,114	0	−58
Slovakia	200	729	162.5	237	46	−623
Slovenia	250	306	49.5	296	0	−50
Spain	2,749	7,294	101.5	3,255	31	−388
Sweden	1,860	2,179	31.1	2,202	0	−37
United Kingdom	2,200	0	175.4	2,605	inf	240
Total	50,671	60,000		60,000	95	−40
Quotas traded				17%		

SOURCE: Authors' elaboration. Cost parameter divided by one million, with Hungary assumed to host one refugee voluntarily.

The result of the market is simple for individual countries. Each of them tries to revert from the initial quota allocation to their preferred (voluntary) quota from the first data column. However, they end up with higher numbers because the total number to be distributed is larger. The simulation shows that 17 percent of the initial quotas distributed would be traded.

The first cost reduction column (fifth data column) in Table 7.1 shows how the overall 95 percent (23 percent without Hungary) cost reduction of the market is distributed across the participating countries. Absolutely all of them see cost reductions; otherwise, they would not trade. The larger the difference between the EU's initial distribution of quotas and the voluntary quotas, the larger the cost reduction will be for participating countries. For some countries, the cost reduction is such that they can turn a profit out of the market. In this simulation, Cyprus, Denmark, Greece, Ireland, Italy, and the UK do so because most of them are assigned a zero responsibility in the initial quota distribution.

Finally, the last data column in Table 7.1 shows the comparison of costs with respect to the voluntary scheme. As can be expected, given that the voluntary scheme resettles 50,671 refugees, while the market would resettle 60,000, the market increases overall costs with respect to the voluntary scheme by 40 percent. The simulated total cost would increase from 152 million euros under the voluntary scheme to 213 million under the market. The total cost increases more than 18 percent (the increase in the number of refugees resettled) because we are assuming convex cost functions.

Again, the distribution of this increase in cost is shared very differently across countries. Cost increases are notably larger for countries whose initial quota is further from their voluntary scheme, notably Hungary, Slovakia, and Spain. On the other side, for countries with a large voluntary contribution with respect to the initial quotas, the market is an improvement even with respect to their voluntary contributions. This is the case for 13 out of the 28 countries, notably for the zero-quota countries mentioned above.

Simulation 2: Stated Preferences, 60,000 refugees, Quadratic Cost

In this simulation, the refugee cost parameter is not calibrated to match previous choices of countries, but it is assumed to come from stated preferences. More precisely, we use the share of people in each country who disagreed with the statement "The EU Member States should offer protection and asylum to people in need" in the Special Eurobarometer 380 in 2011.

Table 7.2 presents this information in the fourth column. According to this measure, Sweden appears as the country with a more favourable opinion toward refugees (only 4 percent of the respondents disagreed with the statement), followed by Denmark, Poland, and Romania with 7 percent. At the other side of the spectrum, 31 percent of Hungarian respondents disagreed with the statement, followed by Latvia (29 percent), Belgium, and Estonia (27 percent). The interpretation that we give to these shares is that they are related to the political cost of hosting refugees in each of the countries. Hence, hosting refugees would be comparatively more costly, relative to its population, for Hungary than for Sweden.

Other than the refugee cost parameter, the simulation in Table 7.2 is directly comparable to the simulation in Table 7.1. The total number of refugees to be relocated is 60,000, and the assumed functional form is the quadratic one. The resulting quotas from the market, though, are quite different in both cases.

First, it must be noted that more quotas are traded in the stated preferences simulation than in the revealed preferences: 32 percent vs. 17 percent. The reason is that the stated preferences are further away from the initial allocation of quotas proposed by the European Commission than the revealed preferences.

Second, the distribution of quotas is quite different in this case. Sweden takes relatively more refugees under the stated preferences—3,557 compared to 2,202—but this means that its cost is reduced more because of the market (40 percent vs. a cost reduction barely larger than 0 in the first simulation). Under the highest refugee cost assumption, Hungary ends up taking 470 refugees rather than 1. The reason is that the revealed preferences for Hungary implied an even larger refugee cost parameter than the stated preferences approach.

The countries that would be more involved in trade in this simulation are France on the paying side and Italy on the receiving side. In the case of France, this happens because they state a lower preference for refugees because of their relatively high cost: 26 percent. This results in France paying other countries to receive 8,048 of their initially assigned 11,784 refugees. For Italy, they are assigned a zero quota, so it is natural

190

Table 7.2 Stated Preferences, 60,000 Refugees, Quadratic Cost

Countries	Voluntary quotas	Initial quotas (EU proposal)	Refugee cost parameter: taken from Eurobarometer 2011	Market quota	Cost reduction with respect to initial quota (%)	Cost reduction with respect to voluntary quotas (%)
Austria	1,900	1,775	19	660	39	47
Belgium	2,464	2,225	27	612	53	61
Bulgaria	500	775	11	972	6	-124
Croatia	550	516	17	369	8	19
Cyprus	242	134	21	60	30	79
Czech Republic	1,500	1,446	22	705	26	31
Denmark	1,000	0	7	1,186	inf	241
Estonia	150	181	27	72	36	7
Finland	1,085	1,169	12	670	18	5
France	9,127	11,784	26	3,735	47	11
Germany	12,100	15,488	11	10,832	9	-49
Greece	354	0	12	1,351	inf	1,557
Hungary	0	1,176	31	470	36	-inf
Ireland	1,120	0	15	453	inf	116
Italy	1,989	0	17	5,274	inf	803
Latvia	250	255	29	102	36	33
Lithuania	325	378	15	289	6	-28
Luxembourg	350	215	14	58	53	82
Malta	74	65	12	52	4	27

Netherlands	3,047	3,546	8	3,103	2	−33
Poland	2,000	4,620	7	8,012	54	−146
Portugal	1,500	1,493	13	1,183	4	5
Romania	1,785	2,250	7	4,204	75	61
Slovakia	200	729	19	421	18	−991
Slovenia	250	306	17	179	17	−24
Spain	2,749	7,294	9	7,624	0	−603
Sweden	1,860	2,179	4	3,557	40	18
United Kingdom	2,200	0	25	3,795	inf	398
Total	50,671	60,000		60,000	42	21
Quotas traded				32%		

SOURCE: Authors' elaboration. Cost parameter from the share of individuals in each EU country disagreeing with the statement: "The EU member states should offer protection and asylum to people in need" from the Special Eurobarometer 380 in 2011. Croatia is assigned the Slovenian value.

that it can be advantageous for them to host some refugees. Thus, for this simulation they would end up hosting 5,274. Among the countries with a nonzero initial quota, Poland would be the one receiving more refugees and being paid for it: 3,392 more than their initially allocated 4,620. This comes from the fact that Poland states a relatively low cost of hosting refugees in this simulation: 7 percent. For comparison purposes, in the first simulation, the biggest traders were Spain on the paying side (4,039 refugees) and the UK on the receiving side (2,605 refugees).

The total cost reduction from adopting the market instead of the initial allocation is 42 percent with the assumed cost functions. Leaving Hungary out to make the comparison easier with respect to the previous simulations, the cost reduction is 43 percent, which is notably larger than the 23 percent coming out of the first simulation. In general, we can expect that more trade will be related to larger cost reductions, as in this case. The largest cost reduction (aside from zero-quota countries) accrues to Romania (75 percent), while the lowest corresponds to Spain, whose initial allocation turns out to be very close to the one resulting from the market, so that it trades very little. In this particular simulation, only the countries with an initial zero quota would actually turn a profit from the market.

One remarkable aspect about this simulation is that the total cost of the market is 21 percent lower than the total cost of the voluntary quotas described in the second column of Table 7.2. This is the case despite the fact that 60,000 refugees would be relocated, rather than 50,671. The reason is that the preferences stated by the citizens of the member states in 2011 may be far from the actual costs that government leaders had in mind when they agreed to host refugees in July 2015. However, this is useful to illustrate how the initial allocation of quotas could have been done in a way that would benefit every single member state, even without taking the externalities of refugee protection into account.

The fact that the total cost is lower under the market does not mean that there are not winners and losers from its creation because of the initial distribution of quotas. As the last column in Table 7.2 shows, 19 out of the 28 European member states would be better off with the market, notably the zero-quota countries, but also Luxembourg, Cyprus, Romania, and Belgium. On the negative side, the remaining nine countries would be worse off, notably Hungary, but also Slovakia, Spain, the Netherlands, and Bulgaria.

In principle, it would be theoretically possible to assign larger initial quotas to favored countries, such as Luxembourg, Cyprus, Romania, or the rest of the countries with positive cost reductions in Table 7.2, while reducing the initial quotas assigned to Hungary, Slovakia, Spain, the Netherlands, Bulgaria, and the rest of the countries in Table 7.2 with negative cost reductions (cost increases). For example, reducing the initial Hungarian quota by 1,000 (from 1,176 to 176) and increasing the French one by the same amount (from 11,784 to 12,784) would make Hungary turn a profit in the market, while France would still see its cost reduced by 2 percent rather than 11 percent.

The fact that this is theoretically possible does not imply that it is both feasible and desirable. From a feasibility point of view, the only way to achieve an allocation satisfying every member state would be to know their "true" cost functions. If that was the case, the market would not be needed to begin with, since the initial quotas would already be enough to share responsibilities. In terms of desirability, taking these "true" costs into account would introduce incentives for countries to try to manipulate them. For example, it would be beneficial for Hungary to show that refugees are particularly costly for them so as to be assigned a lower initial quota than France.

With the methodology spelled out in Appendix 7B, the quota price associated with the simulations in Table 7.2 is 6,600 euros, below the 7,105 euros obtained in the first simulation with revealed preferences. The total cost of the market is 198 million euros, which compares favorably with the 344 million euros associated with the initial allocation of quotas, and even with the 251 million euros that the voluntary quotas imply.

Discussion

The two simulations that we just presented (together with the six in Appendix 7B) are useful to illustrate several characteristics of the market for refugee-admission quotas. The first one is the relevance of the total number of refugees and asylum seekers to be relocated or resettled. Under the simple functional form assumptions for costs that we have described, the size of the total quota translates directly into both the final costs that countries bear and the equilibrium price in the market. Obviously, this is true both with and without a market. If refugees are assumed to represent a cost, it will be easier to relocate or resettle smaller numbers than larger numbers. In the case of the market, this is reflected in the equilibrium price.

With respect to the individual outcome of each of the countries from participating in the market, the key element is the initial attribution of responsibilities—that is, the distribution key for the initial quotas. Theoretically, we can set initial quotas in a way that encourages participation by absolutely every member state (Fernández-Huertas Moraga and Rapoport 2014). We discussed an example of how this could be done in our description of Table 7.2. As we mentioned there, it is not clear that this theoretical possibility is either feasible or desirable.

The feasibility argument lies in the lack of information about the actual cost functions of each of the countries. Generally, it is difficult to estimate the size of the externality in the welfare functions that governments maximize. As Fernández-Huertas Moraga and Rapoport (2014) show, we need this externality to make sure we can distribute initial quotas so that every participating country is better off under the market. Even in cases like simulations 2 and B4, where the savings from the market are so large it makes countries have lower costs overall than under a voluntary distribution of quotas, we still need to know the precise functional form of the cost function that each country attaches to refugees.

The market serves the role of revealing the actual marginal cost for each country in equilibrium. This equilibrium marginal cost of hosting an additional refugee runs from 6,600 euros in the first simulation to 266,985 in the last one in Appendix 7B. The price is larger when the total number of refugees to be hosted is larger and when the cost functions are assumed to be more sensitive to the number of refugees hosted (cubic vs. quadratic cost functions).

To reveal the marginal costs and to lead to an efficient (cost-minimizing) distribution, prices must be set up in a competitive market. We assumed that markets were competitive throughout our simulations, but empirically, there can be concerns that countries with a large initial allocation, such as Germany, or simply quite rich, such as the UK, could exercise some market power and distort the pricing mechanism. In this sense, there is scope for designing the market to prevent this from happening. Fernández-Huertas Moraga and Rapoport (2014) argue for a continuous computerized double auction mechanism, where buyers and sellers would submit ask and bid prices repeatedly, and an auctioneer—say, the European Commission—would choose the price clearing the market. Different experimental studies, starting with Friedman and Ostroy (1995), have shown that such a mechanism converges to the competitive equilibrium price, even in the presence of a reduced number of buyers and sellers. Intuitively, the mechanism promotes a Bertrand-type competition, even among large players.

IMPLEMENTATION ISSUES

This section clarifies some implementation issues related to our proposal. We do so by offering a direct comparison of how the system works according to the CEAS and the European Agenda on Migration and how it should work according to the proposal.

The Common European Asylum System implies that physical solidarity in the area of asylum provision is shared according to the country of arrival of the asylum seekers (Dublin Regulation). With the European Agenda on Migration, physical solidarity could also be achieved by relocating some refugees from overburdened countries to other member states according to a distribution key. At the same time, financial solidarity was exercised through contributions to the Asylum, Migration and Integration Fund out of the general EU budget. Hence, there were separate systems for physical and financial solidarity.

According to our proposal, physical and financial solidarity can be combined through the compensation mechanism, while the rights of refugees to choose their preferred destinations (and not be forced to go to undesired ones) would be guaranteed by the matching mechanism. We would still keep the distribution key as a way to attribute responsibilities, but this time, there would be a combined physical and financial system.

Does this mean countries could "buy their way out" of hosting refugees? Yes, but only if other countries and refugees themselves accept it. The other countries would have to accept it by obtaining a financial compensation large enough so that it is advantageous for them. The refugees would have to accept it by not objecting to moving to the final destination. In this sense, the deal between the EU and Turkey, so that Turkey accepts asylum seekers present in Greece in exchange for a financial compensation (European Council 2016) would only be acceptable in our proposal as long as asylum seekers accept being removed from Greece to Turkey. Otherwise, the financial compensation should correspond to Greece rather than to Turkey. This should incentivize Turkey to become attractive to refugees, otherwise Turkey would be unable to get any compensation.

It would not be feasible for every country to "buy its way out" of physical solidarity. Suppose every country in Europe refused to admit additional refugees: This implies that those with a large quota should increase the financial compensation they offer to get rid of it. If nobody accepted it, they should increase the amount until it would eventually become attractive for some country to take care of the refugees. Hence, not contributing physically could be very expensive financially. The expected outcome would be a mixture of the two contributions.

The compensation mechanism can be represented as a market in which more refugee-unfriendly countries sell the provision of protection to refugee-friendly countries. However, it does not need to be implemented as a market, and therefore we often use the more general term *compensation mechanism*. A tax and subsidy system could implement the market solution, or the European Commission could act as an auctioneer increasing the subsidy (currently 6,000 euros) until all refugees are protected.

Regarding the implementation of the matching mechanism, the fact that refugees can choose their preferred destinations does not mean that all of them would get into their first preference. In fact, they would only be allowed to go to destinations where some slots are available. The collection of preferences should and can, of course, consider the fact that families should move together. If there is a country to which no refugee wants to go, the optimal strategy for that country would be to contribute financially, rather than physically, in a voluntary way—through the compensation mechanism. Otherwise, the country risks being penalized because it would need to compensate the final destination of the refusing refugees (possibly, the original refugee camp) for those refugees who do not accept the move.

CONCLUSION

This chapter explores the ways in which tradable refugee-admission quotas (TRAQs), coupled with a matching mechanism taking into account refugees' preferences in terms of destination (as well as, possibly, countries' preferences about refugees' characteristics), may allow for an improved policy response.

The first part of the chapter shows, theoretically, that the combination of TRAQs and matching can go a long way toward addressing the shortcomings of the current system and provides a sound basis for asylum policies to try to jointly achieve efficiency and fairness in responsibility sharing at the European level. It also demonstrates that the usual concern with tradable quotas, namely social (or environmental or, in our context, humanitarian) "dumping," can largely be prevented owing to the role of the matching mechanism in determining the market (i.e., final) quota. Similarly, the existence of the market in which an implicit price is put on a visa allows for avoiding the risk of a race to the bottom in humanitarian standards that a matching mechanism alone would entail.

The second part of the chapter is dedicated to simulations of the possible workings of a market for refugee-admission quotas under different scenarios. In the absence of reliable information on countries' effective costs of admission (which include the full economic, social, and political costs of hosting refugees that a TRAQs system is precisely designed to reveal), it should be clear that these simulations are illustrative only. However, they constitute a useful exercise in that they demonstrate not only the overall gains, but also the distributive effects the proposed system would generate. As such, they have the potential to identify the participation constraints that impinge on the negotiations of the European member states, as well as the likely coalitions that can emerge in support of the quota system.

Note

We would like to thank Jonas Eriksson, Luc Bovens, and seminar participants at the Swedish Permanent Representation in Brussels and at the Ministry of Justice in Stockholm, as well as conference participants at Heidelberg University and the University of Western Michigan, for their helpful comments and suggestions. This chapter updates and extends our eponymous report to the SIEPS (Swedish Institute for European Policy Studies) of May 2016.

Appendix 7A

Mathematical Presentation of the Model

The theoretical problem that needs to be solved is the allocation of a total number of refugees and asylum seekers, denoted by $R + A$, across a set of destination countries, denoted by N, which can be assimilated to the member states in the European Union that will be participating in the mechanism. The model takes as given both the total number of refugees and asylum seekers to be allocated (such as the 160,000 in the EU proposal of September 2015) and the perceived costs and benefits that the refugees impose on the destination countries.

SETUP

In the current absence of any coordination mechanism and abstracting from the rights of refugees and asylum seekers, each country i will decide how many refugees (r_i) and asylum seekers (a_i) to accept by maximizing their welfare function

$$(7A.1) \quad \max_{r_i, a_i} g_i(R_{-i}, A_{-i}) - c_i(r_i, a_i)$$

This welfare function has two elements. The first one is $g_i(R_{-i}, A_{-i})$, where $\Sigma_{j \neq i} r_j$ and $A_i = \Sigma_{j \neq i} a_j$ denote the total number of refugees and asylum seekers that are received by other destination countries different from i. This function represents how country i benefits from the fact that other countries receive asylum seekers or refugees. There may be two fundamental reasons for this. On the one hand, there is the international public good aspect. We can consider that country i, either its government or its inhabitants, receives utility from the fact that refugees are protected, regardless of where. On the other hand, even in the case where country i does not directly care about refugees and perceives them as a simple cost, they benefit indirectly from the fact that other countries host them, since this may alleviate the pressure for it to host them itself. In other words, country i can expect its asylum claims to go down, the larger the number of refugees hosted by other destinations. Both explanations imply that refugees and asylum seekers hosted by other countries exert a positive externality on the welfare of country i. This would mean that

$$\frac{\partial g_i}{\partial R_{-i}} > 0 \text{ and } \frac{\partial g_i}{\partial A_{-i}} > 0.$$

The positive sign of these derivatives leads the individual maximization of Equation (7A.1) to a globally inefficient solution. Fewer refugees are hosted overall than would be optimal from a global perspective.

The second element of the welfare function of country i represented in Equation (7A.1) is the net cost function of hosting refugees and asylum seekers, denoted by $c_i(r_i, a_i)$. This function is a reduced form that includes all the perceived costs and benefits associated with hosting refugees and asylum seekers. In particular, it includes the potential altruism of country i toward the reception of refugees; that is, the international public good element by which the welfare in country i is increased whenever refugees and asylum seekers are protected in i. It also includes the physical and administrative costs of receiving refugees and asylum seekers and processing their paperwork, initial allowances, and initial accommodation for the period decided by country i. The function also considers the potential long-run expected economic consequences of hosting these refugees and asylum seekers as assessed by country i—for example, the immigration surplus or the fact that these refugees may either benefit or harm domestic workers once they integrate into the labour market. Finally, the function also includes the social and political costs (or benefits) of hosting these refugees and asylum seekers.

To ensure that the problem in Equation (7A.1) actually has a solution, we assume that the net cost function is convex in the number of refugees and asylum seekers; that is,

$$\frac{\partial^2 c_i}{\partial r_i^2} > 0 \text{ and}$$

$$\frac{\partial^2 c_i}{\partial a_i^2} > 0$$

Given the externality, the individual solutions for Equation (7A.1) will not be optimal from a global point of view. The reason is that individual countries do not take into account the fact that their reception of refugees and asylum seekers has a positive effect on other countries, and hence, they perform this activity at a lower level than that implied by a full maximization problem. This full maximization problem can be represented as

$$(7A.2) \quad \max_{\{r_i, a_i\}_{i=1}^N} \sum_{i=1}^{N} [g_i(R_{-i}, A_{-i}) - c_i(r_i, a_i)]$$

As proved in Fernández-Huertas Moraga and Rapoport (2014, 2015a), the optimal solution to (7A.2) involves equating the marginal costs of hosting refugees and asylum seekers among all the potential destination countries to a positive number that depends on the strength of the externality, while the optimal solution to Equation (7A.1), the noncoordinated solution, equates these marginal costs to zero.

THE COMPENSATION MECHANISM FOR TRADABLE REFUGEE-ADMISSION QUOTAS

The optimal solution can be replicated by distributing responsibilities over the number of refugees and asylum seekers that each member state must host (quotas) and letting them trade these responsibilities.

We define initial quotas q_{i0} as the total sum of refugees and asylum seekers whose hosting becomes the responsibility of country i. If country i prefers to host a number $r_i + a_i < q_{i0}$, then it should pay another country the market price p per unfilled refugee-admission quota, so that this other country will host them. That means country i should pay $p(q_{i0} - r_i - a_i)$.

More generally, country i would be solving the following maximization problem:

$$(7A.3) \quad \max_{\{r_i, a_i\}} g_i(R_{-i}, A_{-i}) - c_i(r_i, a_i) + p\,(r_i + a_i - q_{i0})$$

The optimal solution to such a problem is

$$(7A.4) \quad \frac{\partial c_i\,(r_i^M, a_i^M)}{\partial r_i} = p = \frac{\partial c_i(r_i^M, a_i^M)}{\partial a_i}$$

If we denote market outcomes by M, initial quotas by Q and noncooperative unilateral solutions by NC, it would be true that

$$(7A.5) \quad g_i\left(R_{-i}^M, A_{-i}^M\right) - c_i\left(r_i^M, a_i^M\right) + p\left(r_i^M + a_i^M - q_{i0}\right) > g_i\left(R_{-i}^Q, A_{-i}^Q\right)$$
$$- c_i\left(r_i^Q, a_i^Q\right)$$

Inequality (7A.5) implies that every participating country is better off under the market than under a system of mandatory quotas, such as the one proposed by the European Commission.

$$(7A.6) \quad \sum_{i=1}^{N} \left[g_i \left(R_{-i}^{M}, A_{-i}^{M} \right) - c_i \left(r_i^{M}, a_i^{M} \right) + p \left(r_i^{M} + a_i^{M} - q_{i0} \right) \right]$$

$$> \sum_{i=1}^{N} \left[g_i \left(R_{-i}^{NC}, A_{-i}^{NC} \right) - c_i \left(r_i^{NC}, a_i^{NC} \right) \right]$$

It follows from Inequality (7A.6) that it would be theoretically feasible to manipulate q_{i0} so that absolutely every country participating in the market would actually prefer to do so.

THE MATCHING MECHANISM

Refugees' Preferences

We can allow for the case where the overall number $R + A$ is not realized and the "rejected" country pays the price p for the unfilled part of its quota. This acts as a penalty and provides incentives for countries to become attractive destinations. The problem that the countries solve becomes:

$$(7A.7) \quad \max_{\{r_i, a_i\}} g_i \left(R_{-i}, A_{-i} \right) - c_i \left(r_i^{MM}, a_i^{MM} \right) + p \left(r_i + a_i - q_{i0} \right)$$

$$- p \left(r_i + a_i - r_i^{MM} - a_i^{MM} \right)$$

$$s.t. \quad r_i^{MM} = F_i \left(r_1, r_2, ..., r_N; a_1, a_2, ..., a_N \right)$$

$$a_i^{MM} = G_i \left(r_1, r_2, ..., r_N; a_1, a_2, ..., a_N \right)$$

The term $p \left(r_i + a_i - r_i^{MM} - a_i^{MM} \right)$ is a penalty that unattractive countries would have to pay for not being able to attract as many refugees and asylum seekers through the matching mechanism as they would bid for in the market. We denote by MM the allocations coming out of the matching mechanism, which is mathematically represented by the functions $F_i(.)$ and $G_i(.)$. Countries would bid quotas $\{r_i, a_i\}$, but finally only $r_i^{MM} + a_i^{MM}$ individuals would end up going to country i through the matching mechanism. If some individuals refuse to move to country i, we would have $r_i^{MM} + a_i^{MM} < r_i + a_i$.

In equilibrium, the penalty would always be zero, but it is needed so that countries do not have incentives to become unattractive from the point of view of refugees and asylum seekers. In practice, the EU could be in charge of collecting this penalty in case of some off-equilibrium behavior.

The first order conditions of the problem are:

$$(7A.8) \quad \frac{\partial F_i}{\partial r_i} \left(\frac{\partial c_i}{\partial r_i} \left(r_i^{MM}, a_i^{MM} \right) - p \right) + \frac{\partial G_i}{\partial r_i} \left(\frac{\partial c_i}{\partial a_i} \left(r_i^{MM}, a_i^{MM} \right) - p \right) = 0$$

$$(7A.9) \quad \frac{\partial F_i}{\partial a_i} \left(\frac{\partial c_i}{\partial r_i} \left(r_i^{MM}, a_i^{MM} \right) - p \right) + \frac{\partial G_i}{\partial a_i} \left(\frac{\partial c_i}{\partial a_i} \left(r_i^{MM}, a_i^{MM} \right) - p \right) = 0$$

Still, equating the marginal costs of hosting refugees and asylum seekers across countries to the quota price would be an optimal solution, even in the presence of the matching mechanism.

Host Countries' Preferences

The formulation of Problem (7A.7) is general enough that not only can refugee preferences be taken into account, there is also scope for considering the preferences of host countries regarding the type of refugees that they would be more willing to host.

Appendix 7B

Mathematical Presentation of the Cost Functions and Additional Simulations

COST FUNCTIONS

The first cost function that we employ comes from the original paper by Fernández-Huertas Moraga and Rapoport (2014), but it was also used in Fernández-Huertas Moraga and Rapoport (2015b). It is assumed to take this shape:

$$(7\text{B}.1) \quad c_i^{quad}(r_i) = \frac{\gamma_i}{2} \frac{r_i^2}{pop_i}$$

The cost perceived by each country i increases convexly on the total number of refugees resettled (r_i). The two other elements in the function are the population of the country (pop_i) and a parameter that expresses the "dislike" for refugees (γ_i). The function is decreasing in the population, with the rationale being that more populated countries can have a comparative advantage in hosting larger numbers of refugees. The population numbers are those corresponding to 2014 according to Eurostat. We will refer to the cost function in (7B.1) as the quadratic one.

In order to understand the role of functional form assumptions, we introduce a second cost function that multiplies the costs of hosting refugees that we will term the cubic cost function. The exact expression is the following:

$$(7\text{B}.2) \quad c_i^{cub}(r_i) = \frac{\gamma_i}{3} \frac{r_i^3}{pop_i}$$

The marginal cost associated with the cubic cost function simply multiplies the marginal cost of the quadratic one times the total number of resettled refugees.

The parameter γ_i is the one for which we offer two different simulations. In the case of revealed preferences, we will back it up as:

$$(7\text{B}.3) \quad c_i^{quad'}\left(r_i^{voluntary}\right) = \gamma_i^{revealed} \frac{r_i^{voluntary}}{pop_i} = s$$

$$(7\text{B}.4) \quad c_i^{cub'}\left(r_i^{voluntary}\right) = \gamma_i^{revealed} \frac{(r_i^{voluntary})^2}{pop_i} = s$$

The value of s can be used to pin down a monetary valuation for the cost functions. We will be using the reference of 6,000 euros, since this is what the Asylum and Migration Fund from the Common European Asylum System offered the Member States for each particular refugee that they committed to resettle (European Commission 2015c).

In the case of stated preferences, the value of the parameter γ_i will just be equated to the share of individuals in each EU country disagreeing with the statement "The EU Member States should offer protection and asylum to people in need" from the Special Eurobarometer 380 in 2011. In this case, we do not have a direct monetary equivalence, which is a disadvantage. For stated preferences, Equation (7B.3) no longer holds; that is,

$$\text{(7B.5)} \quad c_i^{quad'}\left(r_i^{voluntary}\right) = \gamma_i^{stated}\frac{r_i^{voluntary}}{pop_i} \neq s$$

To pin down a monetary value for comparison purposes, we can scale the marginal cost in Expression (7B.5) by a factor f, so that the marginal cost for each country approximates the subsidy of 6,000 euros established by the Asylum and Migration Fund ($s = 6,000$):

$$\text{(7B.6)} \quad f\gamma_i^{stated}\frac{r_i^{voluntary}}{pop_i} \neq s$$

We can transform the inequality in Expression (7B.6) into a proper equality by introducing an error term (ϵ_i):

$$\text{(7B.7)} \quad \log f + \log \gamma_i^{stated} + \log r_i^{voluntary} - \log pop_i - \log s = \epsilon_i$$

Finally, we can estimate the value of f that minimizes the sum of errors: $\Sigma_i \epsilon_i$.

OUTCOMES

Simulation B1: Revealed Preferences, 60,000 Refugees, Cubic Cost

Table 7B.1 simulates the same market as Table 7.1 in the main text, but under a more convex cost function, cubic on the number of refugees hosted, rather than quadratic. Given the way we back out the refugee cost parameter, the cubic cost function leads to exactly the same market quota as the quadratic cost function. The only difference between the two markets lies in the difference in total costs, which is obviously more pronounced for the case of the cubic cost function.

Under the assumed cubic costs of hosting refugees, the quota price increases from 7,105 euros to 8,412 euros. However, larger costs also imply larger cost reductions resulting from the market. In this case, the total cost reduction increases from 96 percent (23 percent excluding Hungary) to 100 percent (48 percent excluding Hungary). As before, every country stands to benefit from participating in the market rather than keeping the initial EU allocation.

The relative winners and losers from Table 7.1 are still the same, although their relative earnings and losses are accentuated by the larger assumed costs.

Simulation B2: Revealed Preferences, 180,000 Refugees, Quadratic Cost

This simulation goes back to the cost function assumed in the first one (Table 7.1). This time, the difference comes from the total number of refugees to be relocated, three times as many: 180,000 rather than 60,000.

The effect from having to allocate a larger number of refugees can be observed in Table 7B.2. Given the assumed linear marginal cost, Table 7B.2 simply multiplies by 3 the columns of the initial allocation of quotas and the market quotas from Table 7.1.

The market price also multiplies by 3 and goes up to 21,314 euros. In the case of the total cost, it multiplies times 9 rather than 3 because of its quadratic structure, but in relative terms, the savings are the same. Excluding Hungary, the euro savings from the market would still be 23 percent, but this would mean 540 million rather than 60 million.

Simulation B3: Revealed Preferences, 180,000 refugees, Cubic Cost

This simulation presents the last combination for the case of revealed preferences. In this case, the cubic cost functions are assumed to guide countries in allocating the 180,000 refugees.

Table 7B.3 is also a scaled version of Tables 7.1 and 7B.1, where the initial quotas and the quotas resulting from the market are tripled.

The difference between Table 7B.2 (quadratic cost) and Table 7B.3 (cubic cost) lies in the equilibrium market price. The latter is nine times the former: 75,711 euros, rather than 8,412. The difference is compounded for the total costs, which multiply in this case by 27 with respect to the second simulation. Again, we must remind the reader that larger costs also imply larger savings coming from the market in absolute terms.

Table 7B.1 Revealed Preferences, 60,000 Refugees, Cubic Cost

Countries	Voluntary quotas	Initial quotas (EU proposal)	Refugee cost parameter: deduced from voluntary quotas	Market quota	Cost reduction with respect to initial quota (%)	Cost reduction with respect to voluntary quotas (%)
Austria	1,900	1,775	14.1	2,250	25	39
Belgium	2,464	2,225	11.1	2,918	35	52
Bulgaria	500	775	173.9	592	14	−220
Croatia	550	516	84.2	651	24	37
Cyprus	242	134	87.9	287	692	200
Czech Rep.	1,500	1,446	28.0	1,776	18	26
Denmark	1,000	0	33.8	1,184	inf	432
Estonia	150	181	350.9	178	0	−75
Finland	1,085	1,169	27.8	1,285	3	−21
France	9,127	11,784	4.7	10,807	2	−111
Germany	12,100	15,488	3.3	14,327	2	−106
Greece	354	0	526.3	419	inf	432
Hungary	0	1,176	59,264,190.0	1	100	−inf
Ireland	1,120	0	22.0	1,326	inf	432
Italy	1,989	0	92.2	2,355	inf	432
Latvia	250	255	192.1	296	8	2
Lithuania	325	378	167.2	385	0	−57
Luxembourg	350	215	26.9	414	413	173
Malta	74	65	466.1	88	47	65
Netherlands	3,047	3,546	10.9	3,608	0	−57
Poland	2,000	4,620	57.0	2,368	48	−540
Portugal	1,500	1,493	27.8	1,776	12	13
Romania	1,785	2,250	37.6	2,114	1	−98
Slovakia	200	729	812.4	237	75	−1,101
Slovenia	250	306	197.9	296	0	−83
Spain	2,749	7,294	36.9	3,255	58	−684
Sweden	1,860	2,179	16.7	2,202	0	−61
U.K.	2,200	0	79.7	2,605	inf	432
Total	50,671	60,000		60,000	100	−66
Quotas traded				17%		

SOURCE: Authors' elaboration. Cost parameter divided by 1,000 with Hungary assumed to host one refugee voluntarily.

Simulation B4: Stated Preferences, 60,000 Refugees, Cubic Cost

In this sixth simulation, stated preferences are assumed again to allocate 60,000 refugees. The difference compared to the one in Table 7.2 is the cost function, which becomes cubic, rather than quadratic.

Table 7B.4 presents the results. The larger total and marginal costs lead both to more trading (36 percent vs. 32 percent in the previous simulation) and to larger cost reductions: 78 percent vs. 42 percent in the previous simulation. This also means that the savings from the market with respect to the voluntary quotas are larger: 55 percent rather than 21 percent. In fact, under this sixth simulation, only four countries would be worse off under the market than under the voluntary quotas: Hungary, Spain, Poland, and the Netherlands.

If we follow the methodology described in the previous section to scale the marginal costs into monetary values, the equilibrium price would be calculated at 29,665 euros, more than a four-fold increase over the second simulation. The increase is also notable with respect to Table 7B.1, which also featured cubic cost functions, where the price was just 8,412 euros. Such a high price would lead many countries on the receiving side of the market to actually obtain a profit. In addition to the five zero-quota countries, 12 out of 23 remaining countries would be in that situation. This simulated market would only have six countries on the paying side: Germany, France, Spain, Belgium, the Netherlands, and Austria.

This simulation in Table 7B.4 is quite different in terms of the final distribution of market quotas from the one in Table 7.2. The difference stemming from the comparison between the quadratic and the cubic cost functions is particularly striking if we remember that the first simulation in the text and the first in the appendix led to exactly the same distribution of market quotas (see Tables 7.1 and 7B.1). This comes from the fact that the refugee cost parameter (γ_i) took different values in the first simulation in the text and the first in the appendix, while we are keeping the same value for the second simulation in the text and this one. Hence, the equivalent results in Tables 7.1 and 7B.1 were due to the way we defined revealed preferences, while the differences between Table 7.2 and Table 7B.4 can be completely traced back to the distinction in the functional forms.

Simulation B5: Stated Preferences, 180,000 refugees, Quadratic Cost

The seventh simulation goes back to the quadratic cost function assumption under stated preferences. This means that the simulation corresponds to the same cost function that was underlying the second simulation in the text.

The only difference is that the number of refugees to be allocated triples from 60,000 to 180,000.

In that case, the market leads to the final distribution of quotas that can be observed in Table 7B.5. As we could already see in the comparison between simulations 1 and B2 (Tables 7.1 and 7B.2), the linear marginal cost associated with the quadratic cost function implies that tripling the total number of refugees to be allocated just triples the market quota of each of the participating countries. Of course, the market price is also tripled: from 6,600 euros to 19,799 euros, while the total costs are multiplied by 9.

The multiplication of the total costs means that the market for allocating 180,000 refugees is no longer cheaper than the voluntary contributions to allocate 50,671. Only the zero-quota countries are better off and can actually make a profit, although we must remind the reader that our definition of "worse" or "better off" only contemplates cost functions, since we did not make any assumption on the positive effect of the externality that the market addresses.

Simulation B6: Stated Preferences, 180,000 Refugees, Cubic Cost

Our last simulation replicates the previous one under stated preferences for a cubic cost function. Hence, it is directly comparable to the sixth simulation in terms of its cost function, with the only difference being that 180,000 refugees are distributed, rather than 60,000.

The results are presented in Table 7B.6. Since the relative differences in marginal costs are the same as in the sixth simulation, the final distribution of market quotas is exactly the same that can be observed in Table 7B.4, but multiplying every number by 3. For example, Germany would host 5,945 refugees in Table 7B.4, while it would host 17,836 in Table 7B.6. However, the quota price does not triple, as in simulation B4, it multiplies by 9, due to the quadratic marginal costs implied by the cubic total cost functions. The total price is hence 266,985 euros, the largest in all the simulations we ran.

Other than in magnitudes, this simulation is completely analogous to the sixth one. The total costs are exacerbated (they multiply by 27), but the sellers and the buyers in the market are still the same. They are just willing to trade at higher prices and three times as much, as the total size of the quota market is three times larger.

Table 7B.2 Revealed Preferences, 180,000 Refugees, Quadratic Cost

Countries	Voluntary quotas	Initial quotas (EU proposal)	Refugee cost parameter: deduced from voluntary quotas	Market quota	Cost reduction with respect to initial quota (%)	Cost reduction with respect to voluntary quotas (%)
Austria	1,900	5,326	26.9	6,749	7	−630
Belgium	2,464	6,676	27.3	8,753	10	−563
Bulgaria	500	2,324	86.9	1,776	6	−1,940
Croatia	550	1,549	46.3	1,954	7	−639
Cyprus	242	401	21.3	860	131	185
Czech Rep.	1,500	4,339	42.0	5,328	5	−693
Denmark	1,000	0	33.8	3,552	inf	1,362
Estonia	150	543	52.6	533	0	−1,209
Finland	1,085	3,507	30.1	3,854	1	−935
France	9,127	35,351	43.3	32,421	1	−1,390
Germany	12,100	46,463	40.0	42,982	1	−1,366
Greece	354	0	186.3	1,257	inf	1,362
Hungary	0	3,529	59,264.2	4	100	−inf
Ireland	1,120	0	24.7	3,979	inf	1,362
Italy	1,989	0	183.4	7,065	inf	1,362
Latvia	250	766	48.0	888	3	−816
Lithuania	325	1,135	54.3	1,154	0	−1,118
Luxembourg	350	646	9.4	1,243	85	50
Malta	74	194	34.5	263	13	−497
Netherlands	3,047	10,637	33.1	10,824	0	−1,118
Poland	2,000	13,860	114.1	7,105	24	−3,562
Portugal	1,500	4,478	41.7	5,328	4	−759
Romania	1,785	6,750	67.0	6,341	0	−1,325
Slovakia	200	2,187	162.5	710	46	−6,408
Slovenia	250	919	49.5	888	0	−1,250
Spain	2,749	21,881	101.5	9,765	31	−4,293
Sweden	1,860	6,537	31.1	6,607	0	−1,135
U.K.	2,200	0	175.4	7,815	inf	1,362
Total	50,671	180,000		180,000	95	−1,162
Quotas traded				17%		

SOURCE: Authors' elaboration. Cost parameter divided by 1,000,000 with Hungary assumed to host one refugee voluntarily.

Table 7B.3 Revealed Preferences, 180,000 Refugees, Cubic Cost

Countries	Voluntary quotas	Initial quotas (EU proposal)	Refugee cost parameter: deduced from voluntary quotas	Market quota	Cost reduction with respect to initial quota (%)	Cost reduction with respect to voluntary quotas (%)
Austria	1,900	5,326	14.1	6,749	25	−1,548
Belgium	2,464	6,676	11.1	8,753	35	−1,193
Bulgaria	500	2,324	173.9	1,776	14	−8,528
Croatia	550	1,549	84.2	1,954	24	−1,597
Cyprus	242	401	87.9	860	692	2,793
Czech Rep.	1,500	4,339	28.0	5,328	18	−1,886
Denmark	1,000	0	33.8	3,552	inf	9,065
Estonia	150	543	350.9	533	0	−4,632
Finland	1,085	3,507	27.8	3,854	3	−3,172
France	9,127	35,351	4.7	32,421	2	−5,598
Germany	12,100	46,463	3.3	42,982	2	−5,471
Greece	354	0	526.3	1,257	inf	9,065
Hungary	0	3,529	59,264,190.0	4	100	−inf
Ireland	1,120	0	22.0	3,979	inf	9,065
Italy	1,989	0	92.2	7,065	inf	9,065
Latvia	250	766	192.1	888	8	−2,540
Lithuania	325	1,135	167.2	1,154	0	−4,150
Luxembourg	350	646	26.9	1,243	413	2,074
Malta	74	194	466.1	263	47	−841
Netherlands	3,047	10,637	10.9	10,824	0	−4,150
Poland	2,000	13,860	57.0	7,105	48	−17,169
Portugal	1,500	4,478	27.8	5,328	12	−2,237
Romania	1,785	6,750	37.6	6,341	1	−5,251
Slovakia	200	2,187	812.4	710	75	−32,336
Slovenia	250	919	197.9	888	0	−4,852
Spain	2,749	21,881	36.9	9,765	58	−21,067
Sweden	1,860	6,537	16.7	6,607	0	−4,240
U.K.	2,200	0	79.7	7,815	inf	9,065
Total	50,671	180,000		180,000	100	−4,383
Quotas traded				17%		

SOURCE: Authors' elaboration. Cost parameter divided by 1,000 with Hungary assumed to host one refugee voluntarily.

Table 7B.4 Stated Preferences, 60,000 Refugees, Cubic Cost

Countries	Voluntary quotas	Initial quotas (EU proposal)	Refugee cost parameter: taken from Eurobarometer 2011	Market quota	Cost reduction with respect to initial quota (%)	Cost reduction with respect to voluntary quotas (%)
Austria	1,900	1,775	19	1,468	8	25
Belgium	2,464	2,225	27	1,413	30	49
Bulgaria	500	775	11	1,781	945	3,240
Croatia	550	516	17	1,097	663	566
Cyprus	242	134	21	444	4,106	775
Czech Rep.	1,500	1,446	22	1,517	1	11
Denmark	1,000	0	7	1,967	inf	1,623
Estonia	150	181	27	484	1,788	3,061
Finland	1,085	1,169	12	1,479	25	6
France	9,127	11,784	26	3,491	79	55
Germany	12,100	15,488	11	5,945	67	31
Greece	354	0	12	2,100	inf	41,852
Hungary	0	1,176	31	1,239	1	−inf
Ireland	1,120	0	15	1,216	inf	356
Italy	1,989	0	17	4,149	inf	1,915
Latvia	250	255	29	576	870	922
Lithuania	325	378	15	972	1,514	2,327
Luxembourg	350	215	14	435	522	198
Malta	74	65	12	413	40,244	26,740
Netherlands	3,047	3,546	8	3,182	3	−53
Poland	2,000	4,620	7	5,113	4	−1,088
Portugal	1,500	1,493	13	1,965	36	37
Romania	1,785	2,250	7	3,704	179	259
Slovakia	200	729	19	1,171	155	2,769
Slovenia	250	306	17	764	1,336	2,374
Spain	2,749	7,294	9	4,988	24	−1,326
Sweden	1,860	2,179	4	3,407	131	150
U.K.	2,200	0	25	3,519	inf	919
Total	50,671	60,000		60,000	78	55
Quotas traded				36%		

SOURCE: Authors' elaboration. Cost parameter from the share of individuals in each EU country disagreeing with the statement "The EU member states should offer protection and asylum to people in need" from the Special Eurobarometer 380 in 2011. Croatia is assigned the Slovenian value.

Table 7B.5 Stated Preferences, 180,000 Refugees, Quadratic Cost

Countries	Voluntary quotas	Initial quotas (EU proposal)	Refugee cost parameter: taken from Eurobaro- meter 2011	Market quota	Cost reduc- tion with respect to initial quota (%)	Cost reduc- tion with respect to voluntary quotas (%)
Austria	1,900	5,326	19	1,981	39	−376
Belgium	2,464	6,676	27	1,836	53	−248
Bulgaria	500	2,324	11	2,915	6	−1,920
Croatia	550	1,549	17	1,106	8	−628
Cyprus	242	401	21	181	30	−92
Czech Rep.	1,500	4,339	22	2,115	26	−517
Denmark	1,000	0	7	3,558	inf	1,366
Estonia	150	543	27	216	36	−734
Finland	1,085	3,507	12	2,010	18	−755
France	9,127	35,351	26	11,206	47	−700
Germany	12,100	46,463	11	32,495	9	−1,241
Greece	354	0	12	4,054	inf	13,215
Hungary	0	3,529	31	1,410	36	−inf
Ireland	1,120	0	15	1,359	inf	247
Italy	1,989	0	17	15,823	inf	6,429
Latvia	250	766	29	305	36	−500
Lithuania	325	1,135	15	868	6	−1,052
Luxembourg	350	646	14	174	53	−59
Malta	74	194	12	157	4	−560
Netherlands	3,047	10,637	8	9,310	2	−1,100
Poland	2,000	13,860	7	24,036	54	−2,114
Portugal	1,500	4,478	13	3,550	4	−753
Romania	1,785	6,750	7	12,611	75	−252
Slovakia	200	2,187	19	1,262	18	−9,718
Slovenia	250	919	17	537	17	−1,017
Spain	2,749	21,881	9	22,871	0	−6,223
Sweden	1,860	6,537	4	10,671	40	−641
U.K.	2,200	0	25	11,384	inf	2,778
Total	50,671	180,000		180,000	42	−611
Quotas traded				32%		

SOURCE: Authors' elaboration. Cost parameter from the share of individuals in each EU country disagreeing with the statement "The EU member states should offer protection and asylum to people in need" from the Special Eurobarometer 380 in 2011. Croatia is assigned the Slovenian value.

Table 7B.6 Stated Preferences, 180,000 Refugees, Cubic Cost

Countries	Voluntary quotas	Initial quotas (EU proposal)	Refugee cost parameter: taken from Eurobaro-meter 2011	Market quota	Cost reduction with respect to initial quota (%)	Cost reduction with respect to voluntary quotas (%)
Austria	1,900	5,326	19	4,404	8	−1,928
Belgium	2,464	6,676	27	4,240	30	−1,288
Bulgaria	500	2,324	11	5,342	945	84,887
Croatia	550	1,549	17	3,290	663	12,673
Cyprus	242	401	21	1,331	4,106	18,315
Czech Rep.	1,500	4,339	22	4,550	1	−2,303
Denmark	1,000	0	7	5,902	inf	41,212
Estonia	150	543	27	1,453	1,788	80,058
Finland	1,085	3,507	12	4,437	25	−2,441
France	9,127	35,351	26	10,474	79	−1,128
Germany	12,100	46,463	11	17,836	67	−1,762
Greece	354	0	12	6,300	inf	1,127,417
Hungary	0	3,529	31	3,716	1	−inf
Ireland	1,120	0	15	3,647	inf	7,007
Italy	1,989	0	17	12,447	inf	49,108
Latvia	250	766	29	1,729	870	22,288
Lithuania	325	1,135	15	2,916	1,514	60,237
Luxembourg	350	646	14	1,304	522	2,756
Malta	74	194	12	1,239	40,244	719,385
Netherlands	3,047	10,637	8	9,547	3	−4,029
Poland	2,000	13,860	7	15,340	4	−31,963
Portugal	1,500	4,478	13	5,895	36	−1,593
Romania	1,785	6,750	7	11,112	179	4,383
Slovakia	200	2,187	19	3,514	155	72,158
Slovenia	250	919	17	2,292	1,336	61,509
Spain	2,749	21,881	9	14,964	24	−38,397
Sweden	1,860	6,537	4	10,221	131	1,448
U.K.	2,200	0	25	10,557	inf	22,200
Total	50,671	180,000		180,000	78	−1,108
Quotas traded				36%		

SOURCE: Authors' elaboration. Cost parameter from the share of individuals in each EU country disagreeing with the statement "The EU Member States should offer protection and asylum to people in need" from the Special Eurobarometer 380 in 2011. Croatia is assigned the Slovenian value.

References

Abdulkadiroglu, Atila, and Tayfun Sonmez. 1999. "House Allocation with Existing Tenants." *Journal of Economic Theory* 88: 233–260.

Azevedo, Eduardo M., and Jacob D. Leshno. 2016. "A Supply and Demand Framework for Two Sided Matching Markets." *Journal of Political Economy* 124(5): 1235–1268.

Bubb, Ryan, Michael Kremer, and David I. Levine. 2011. "The Economics of International Refugee Law." *Journal of Legal Studies* 40(2): 367–404.

European Commission. 2015a. *A European Agenda on Migration. Communication from the Commission to the European Parliament, the Council, the European Economic and Social Committee and the Committee of the Regions.* COM (2015) 240 final, March 13. Brussels: European Commission.

———. 2015b. *Proposal for a Council Decision Establishing Provisional Measures in the Area of International Protection for the Benefit of Italy and Greece.* COM (2015) 286 final, March 27. Brussels: European Commission.

———. 2015c. *Proposal for a Regulation of the European Parliament and of the Council Establishing a Crisis Relocation Mechanism and Amending Regulation (EU) No 604/2013 of the European Parliament and of the Council of 26 June 2013 Establishing the Criteria and Mechanisms for Determining the Member State Responsible for Examining an Application for International Refugee Protection Lodged in one of the Member States by a Third Country National or a Stateless Person.* COM (2015) 450 final, 2015/0208 (COD). September 9. Brussels: European Commission.

———. 2016. *Communication from the Commission to the European Parliament, the European Council and the Council: First Report on Relocation and Resettlement.* COM (2016) 165 final, March 16. Brussels: European Commission.

European Council. 2015. "Council Decision (EU) 2015/1601 of 22 September 2015 Establishing Provisional Measures in the Area of International Protection for the Benefit of Italy and Greece." L 248/80. Brussels: European Council.

———. 2016. "EU-Turkey Statement, 18 March 2016." Press Release 144/16. Brussels: European Council. http://www.consilium.europa.eu/en/press/press-releases/2016/03/18/eu-turkey-statement/ (accessed January 24, 2018).

European Parliament. 2014–2019. *Provisional Measures in the Area of International Protection for the Benefit of Italy and Greece. European Parlia-

ment Legislative Resolution of 9 September 2015 on the Proposal for a Council Decision Establishing Provisional Measures in the Area of International Protection for the Benefit of Italy and Greece. COM (2015) - 0286: C8-0156/2015-2015/0125 (NLE) (Consultation). P8 TAPROV(2015) 0306. Brussels: European Parliament.

Fernández-Huertas Moraga, Jesús, and Hillel Rapoport. 2014. "Tradable Immigration Quotas." *Journal of Public Economics* 115: 94–108.

———. 2015a. "Tradable Refugee-Admission Quotas and EU Asylum Policy." *CESifo Economic Studies* 61(3-4): 638–672.

———. 2015b. "Tradable Refugee-Admission Quotas (TRAQs), the Syrian Crisis and the New European Agenda on Migration." *IZA Journal of European Labor Studies* 4(1): 23.

Friedman, Daniel, and Joseph Ostroy. 1995. "Competitivity in Auction Markets: An Experimental and Theoretical Investigation." *Economic Journal* 105(428): 22–53.

Hatton, Timothy J. 2015. "Asylum Policy in the EU: The Case for Deeper Integration." *CESifo Economic Studies* 61(3-4): 605–637.

Pathak, Parag A., and Tayfun Sonmez. 2013. "School Admissions Reform in Chicago and England: Comparing Mechanisms by Their Vulnerability to Manipulation." *American Economic Review* 103(1): 80–106.

Roth, A. E. 2002. "The Economist as an Engineer: Game Theory, Experimental Economics and Computation as Tools of Design Economics." *Econometrica* 70(4): 1341–1378.

Schuck, Peter H. 1997. "Refugee Burden-Sharing: A Modest Proposal." *Yale Journal of International Law* 22: 243–297.

Thielemann, Eiko, Richard Williams, Christina Boswell, and Matrix Insight Ltd. 2010. "What System of Burden-Sharing between Member States for the Reception of Asylum Seekers?" Directorate General for Internal Policies, Policy Department C: Citizens' Rights and Constitutional Affairs, Civil Liberties, Justice and Home Affairs. Brussels: European Parliament.

Wagner, Martin, and Albert Kraler. 2014. "An Effective Asylum Responsibility-Sharing Mechanism." ICMPD Asylum Programme for Member States: Thematic Paper. Vienna: International Centre for Migration Policy Development.

Authors

Catalina Amuedo-Dorantes is a professor and chair of the San Diego State University Department of Economics.

Esther Arenas-Arroyo is a postdoctorate at the University of Oxford's Centre on Migration, Policy and Society.

Alfonso Cebreros is a researcher at the Mexico Central Bank.

Brian Duncan is a professor of economics at the University of Colorado Denver.

Daniel Chiquiar is director of the Economic Measurement Division in the research department of the Mexico Central Bank.

Jesús Fernández-Huertas Moraga is an associate professor at the Charles III University of Madrid.

Stephanie Gullo is a research analyst at the Federal Reserve Bank of Dallas.

Pia M. Orrenius is vice president and senior economist at the Federal Reserve Bank of Dallas.

Giovanni Peri is a professor and chair of the University of California, Davis, Department of Economics.

Susan Pozo is a professor of economics at Western Michigan University.

Hillel Rapoport is a professor of economics at the Paris School of Economics, University Paris 1 Panthéon-Sorbonne.

Monica Roa is a researcher at the Mexico Central Bank.

Martín Tobal is a director of research and development at the Mexico Central Bank.

Stephen Trejo is a professor of economics at the University of Texas at Austin.

Index

Note: The italic letters *f, n,* or *t* following a page number indicate a figure, note, or table, respectively, on that page. Double letters mean more than one such consecutive item on a single page.

About the Institute

The W.E. Upjohn Institute for Employment Research is a nonprofit research organization devoted to finding and promoting solutions to employment-related problems at the national, state, and local levels. It is an activity of the W.E. Upjohn Unemployment Trustee Corporation, which was established in 1932 to administer a fund set aside by Dr. W.E. Upjohn, founder of The Upjohn Company, to seek ways to counteract the loss of employment income during economic downturns.

The Institute is funded largely by income from the W.E. Upjohn Unemployment Trust, supplemented by outside grants, contracts, and sales of publications. Activities of the Institute comprise the following elements: 1) a research program conducted by a resident staff of professional social scientists; 2) a competitive grant program, which expands and complements the internal research program by providing financial support to researchers outside the Institute; 3) a publications program, which provides the major vehicle for disseminating the research of staff and grantees, as well as other selected works in the field; and 4) an Employment Management Services division, which manages most of the publicly funded employment and training programs in the local area.

The broad objectives of the Institute's research, grant, and publication programs are to 1) promote scholarship and experimentation on issues of public and private employment and unemployment policy, and 2) make knowledge and scholarship relevant and useful to policymakers in their pursuit of solutions to employment and unemployment problems.

Current areas of concentration for these programs include causes, consequences, and measures to alleviate unemployment; social insurance and income maintenance programs; compensation; workforce quality; work arrangements; family labor issues; labor-management relations; and regional economic development and local labor markets.